COWBRIDGE AND LLANBLETHIAN

'Llanblethian hangs pleasantly, with its white cottages, and orchard and other trees, on the western slope of a green hill; looking far and wide over green meadows and little or bigger hills, in the pleasant plain of Glamorgan; a short mile to the south of Cowbridge, to which smart little town it is properly a kind of suburb.'

Extract from *The Life of John Sterling* (Thomas Carlyle, 1851)

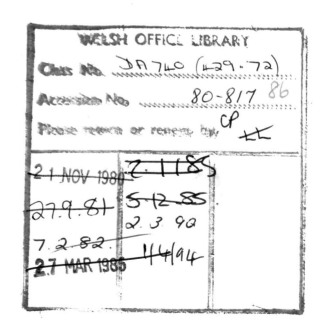

High Street, Cowbridge in the early part of this century

COWBRIDGE
and
LLANBLETHIAN
Past and Present

BRIAN LL. JAMES AND DAVID J. FRANCIS

STEWART WILLIAMS, PUBLISHERS, BARRY

AND

D. BROWN & SONS LTD., EASTGATE, COWBRIDGE

1979

© Joint Publishers 1979

ISBN 0 900807 36 9

*Printed in Wales
by D. Brown & Sons Ltd., Eastgate Press,
Cowbridge*

Contents

(Parts I, II and III are written by Brian Ll. James
and Part IV by David T. Francis.)

Illustrations

Introduction

Our subject in this book is the story of the two communities of Llanblethian and Cowbridge which lie together in the centre of the Vale of Glamorgan, since 1974 situated in the county of South Glamorgan and borough of the Vale of Glamorgan. Our theme is the development of these two communities from the earliest times to the present day. The origins of Llanblethian as a community are back in the shadowy centuries of the Dark Ages, or even further back in the Roman period or the Iron Age; it had a church, possibly as early as the sixth century, which became the centre of a large parish extending far beyond its present boundaries. The village also became the centre of a typical Anglo-Norman manor with castle, mills, demesne lands and open fields farmed communally by the lord's tenants. Cowbridge (perhaps under the name of Bomium) enjoyed a few brief centuries of prosperity under Roman rule and then ceased to exist (as far as we can tell) until more than eight hundred years later the lord Richard de Clare decided that here on the main road through Glamorgan where it crossed the valley of the river Thaw was a good site for a borough. He decided wisely and the markets, fairs and townspeople of Cowbridge flourished exceedingly in the first hundred years of their existence. A small borough of no more than 85 acres taken out of the manor of Llanblethian and enjoying the usual privileges conferred by successive charters — culminating in the charter of incorporation obtained for the town in the reign of Charles II by one of its most eminent sons, Sir Leoline Jenkins, the Secretary of State — continued to exist until local government reform in 1974.

Written examples of the name of Llanblethian are found, with growing frequency, from the twelfth century onwards. The name probably commemorates the founder of the church; it has not changed significantly during eight hundred years. The name of Cowbridge — in the form of 'Coubruge' — is first recorded in a document probably to be dated to the year 1262. (Although the first charter is known to have been granted in 1254 the original document has long been lost.) The Welsh version, y Bont-faen, is not known to have been in use earlier than the second half of the fifteenth century when it occurs in a Welsh poem written in praise of one of the town's leading merchants. Curiously the town is also mentioned in the same poem as 'Cwbris'. There has been much discussion about these two names for the town, both referring to bridges but the English calling it 'Cow Bridge' and the Welsh 'Stone Bridge'. Authorities differ about which name came first (though we suggest here that the English name is the older), but they seem to agree that two different bridges are being commemorated, the Cow Bridge being the one over the Thaw and the Stone Bridge (no longer in existence) that which crossed a brook near Llwynhelyg in the West Village.

Having passed through many centuries of quiet growth and prosperity (interspersed with periods of decline and depression) the two closely inter-connected communities of Llanblethian and Cowbridge have at the present time about 4,000 inhabitants. In recent years there have been many pro-found changes. New houses and estates have been built, especially in the valley and on the ridge which separate the town from the village of Llanblethian, and old properties have changed hands and been renovated. The social structure and pattern of economic activity are both now very different from what they were only a quarter of a century ago. But the cen-turies of history and tradition—perhaps symbolised by the continuing suc-cess of Cowbridge as a market town—cannot be eradicated in so short a time, and the present still owes a great deal more than it realises to the past. Our belief is that we should attempt to give equal attention to describing the life of the communities at the present as to writing the story of the past.

Naturally we owe a great deal to previous writers and we would especially mention the work of the Rev. L. J. Hopkin-James and the Rev. E. O. T. Lewis, two former vicars of Llanblethian with Cowbridge, Miss Maud Gunter, Mr John Richards and Mr Iolo Davies. And if we have aimed to write an essentially new version of the history which differs from theirs in im-portant particulars, this does not deny or diminish our indebtedness to them. We would even express the hope that in the not too distant future someone else will interpret the story in yet another way which may show ours to have been wide of the truth. Although the present book is not intended for the specialist or scholarly reader, we hope nevertheless that our history, in terms of today's knowledge and understanding of the local past, will not be found too amateurish.

Many other persons deserve the most sincere thanks for assistance of many kinds. David Francis wishes particularly to acknowledge the help which he has received from the staffs of the South Glamorgan and Mid Glamorgan County Libraries. Many people in Cowbridge and Llanblethian have pro-vided information, help and encouragement. Councillor Selwyn Davies, Mrs Muriel Phillips, Mr. J. L. S. Miles, Mr Colin Adams, Mr J. M. Roberts, Mr. D. Lewis, Mr Alfred Charles, Mr Reg Sanders, Mrs Lyn Mander and many others too numerous to mention individually have all kindly assisted David Francis's researches into the present and recent history of the two com-munities.

A special mention must be accorded to two friends, namely Mr M. B. Edwards of Maendy whose reminiscences of the Grammar School where he taught for so many years have been incorporated into David Francis's chapter, and Mr Haydn Baynham who took a vast number of superb photographs, a selection of which is included in the book.

B.Ll.J.
D.J.F.

PART I

From the Earliest Times to the Norman Conquest

Stone Age Axes

There is ample evidence that there were men living in the neighbourhood of what is now the town of Cowbridge in prehistoric times. The oldest relics of primitive man which have yet come to light here are two stone axes, one fashioned from a piece of dolerite and found on the site of the railway station, the other, of felsite, found near Pant Wilkin. Both are now in the National Museum of Wales. The experts describe them as Neolithic, which is to say that they were fashioned in the New Stone Age — probably between 3,000 and 2,000 years before Christ. The people who made and used the axes had brought with them into these parts the knowledge of agriculture and pottery. Since they were the first people to begin to cultivate the soil of the Vale of Glamorgan their stone axes were probably mainly used in the clearing of the natural forest. Although they were probably few in number and although their technology was extremely primitive, these were probably the people who were the builders of the immense communal tombs at Tinkinswood and Maesyfelin near St Nicholas, the monuments we call cromlechs.

Bronze Implements and Round Barrows

There have been numerous finds around Cowbridge indicating a greater intensity of occupation of the district by people in the Bronze Age, the earliest phase of human history in which men had the knowledge and use of metal for their weapons and tools. The Bronze Age in the Vale of Glamorgan extended from about 1600 B.C. to about 500 B.C. A socketed axe made of bronze was found somewhere near Cowbridge in 1929, and a dagger was found together with a skeleton in the grounds of the High School in 1894. It also seems probable that the two stones — once a single stone, now broken in two—standing in the garden of Rhoscelyn, Eastgate, were first erected in the Bronze Age. The original stone is an example of what archaeologists vaguely call a 'standing stone'. They do not seem to be generally agreed on the purpose of standing stones; some certainly mark a grave and others probably mark routeways. There is no reason to suppose that the stones at Rhoscelyn are in their original position. In a deed of 1629 there is a reference to 'A house and garden, being one half burgage, near a stone called y Carreg Gwynn, without the east gate of Cowbridge'. And in a manuscript of Iolo Morganwg's (about 1800) 'Carreg Gwynn y Bontfaen' (the white stone of Cowbridge) is listed. The stone was evidently still whole in Iolo's time. We depend upon Iolo Morganwg entirely for our knowledge of the former existence of some kind of stone circle at Beggar's Bush, near the road to St Athan. In a list which he compiled of ancient remains in Glamorgan is the entry: 'Gorsedd gylch y Beggar's Bush, a symmudwyd gan Dr Walton' (Gorsedd circle at Beggar's Bush, which was removed by Dr Walton[1]). Of course, Iolo Morganwg's interpretation of these stones was 'druidical' and the local tradition is recorded that the white stone was an altar at which druids conducted marriage ceremonies; the couples linked arms through a hole cut in the stone.

Far more important than any of these relics of the Bronze Age are the seven barrows or round cairns near Breach Farm and Marlborough Grange, towards the western extremity of the parish of Llanblethian. The seven cairns are part of a large group of such monuments concentrated in the area between Llanblethian and Nash Point. One of the barrows, still visible as a slight mound in a field near Crossways, was excavated by W. F. Grimes in 1937. The turf and clay mound was found to cover a circular stone wall nearly eighty feet in diameter. There was a central pit containing the cremated remains of three persons, together with two bronze axes, a dagger, a pigmy cup, thirteen flint arrowheads, and two stone arrowshaft straighteners. All are exquisite examples of their kind. Archaeologists think that the builders of this grave may have originated in Brittany, at some date in the Early or Middle Bronze Age, perhaps about 1350 B.C. A somewhat similar, but smaller, barrow nearer Marlborough Grange was excavated by H. N. Savory in 1967 and was dated by him to between 1450 and 1250 B.C. The grave goods consisted of a poor pigmy cup only, but a particularly interesting feature was that the mound had been reused long afterwards for two cremated burials which are to be dated, in all probability, to the Early Iron Age, about 500-200 B.C.

---

[1] John Walton was bailiff of the town on several occasions in the late 18th century. He died in 1790.

Iron Age Hill-Forts

There is an important local monument of the later Iron Age and Romano-British period, namely the hill-fort at Llanblethian which archaeologists call Caer Dynnaf[2]. A contemporary site is the small defended settlement of Mynydd Bychan, between Pentre Meyrick and Colwinston. This is well known from Dr Savory's excavation in 1949-50. Within the ditch and earth bank at Mynydd Bychan there were three (possibly five) timber-framed round huts. These date from about 50 B.C. to 50 A.D. A second phase in the occupation of the site followed from about 50 A.D. to 120 A.D., but the elaborate defences of the previous hundred years were allowed to fall into ruin and the ditch silted up and was used for burials. At this time there were at least three round dry-stone huts, each standing in a walled enclosure. Judging by the bones found at Mynydd Bychan cattle, sheep, pigs and horses were domesticated there and, along with shellfish, were eaten by the inhabitants. A quern-stone proved that corn had been grown and bread made. The people who lived at Mynydd Bychan were probably a prosperous family group with a few servants.

This information from Mynydd Bychan, although from a site outside the district with which this book is concerned, is useful because it supplements the meagre information which we have relating to the Llanblethian hill-fort, which has not been fully excavated. This is a large fort, having an area within the ramparts of about twelve acres. Although the earth banks are not especially clear to the observer on the ground, the fort is impressive seen from an aerial view. On the north is a short but steep descent to the Cowbridge-Llantwit road, and on the east is the precipitous drop to the river Thaw. To the south and west the land descends more gently to the road from Llanblethian Church to Cross Inn. Aerial photographs show up slight traces of settlement, low bank, terraces and hollows within the earthen ramparts. It is possible that these represent a group of small farmsteads. A small-scale excavation of part of the site in 1965-67 revealed much Romano-British pottery and broken quern-stones thought to range in date from the late first century A.D. to the fourth century. A pit on the site contained a few sherds of pre-Roman Iron Age pottery.

The importance of this site in our story will become clearer when we realise that the Romano-British farmsteads on Llanblethian Hill are the earliest dwellings known to have existed within what eventually became the parish of Llanblethian. Although we have talked of much earlier inhabitants we have in fact used the term 'inhabitants' rather imprecisely;

[2] This name is not used by the local inhabitants today. It seems to have been invented by the Ordnance Survey, and is based on an obsolete name which may probably be rendered Dinny or Caer Dinny (possibly Cae'r Dinny), the meaning of which is obscure. An alternative name, used by Dr Hopkin-James, was Angel Hill; this may strictly have applied to the common on the eastern slope of the hill, alternatively known as Tyle Llanblethian in the 17th century. Nowadays it is just Llanblethian Hill, while the steep slope down to the Thaw is jocularly known as Mount Ida. For reference to a medieval building within the hill-fort see page 25.

there is no evidence of their having actually lived here—they may have simply passed by on a hunting expedition; the dwelling places of those who were so grandly buried within the graves at Breach and Marlborough Grange have never been identified. Presumably they lived somewhere nearby; but it is with the tiny cluster of farmsteads within the stronghold of Caer Dynnaf that we can identify the first village. The interesting, but at present unanswerable, question is whether the later village of Llanblethian itself can really be thought of as the descendant or successor of this primitive Romano-British hamlet. Was there a gap in time between the abandonment of Caer Dynnaf as a place of habitation and the founding of Llanblethian? We may never know.

There is another Iron Age hill-fort, at Llanquian, a little to the east of the Stalling Down. This is a roughly circular construction with two widely spaced banks and ditches, one within the other; the outer defences enclose about five acres. There appear to be no remains of structures inside the fort, but in the absence of excavation there is little more that can be said about it. The name of this monument a hundred years ago was Erw Gron, round acre.

Roman Cowbridge

Mynydd Bychan (small mountain), Caer Dynnaf and Erw Gron were fortresses and settlements of the local inhabitants who belonged to the tribe of the Silures. They were speakers of a Celtic language—the ancestor of modern Welsh—and they lived here slightly before and during the period of the Roman occupation. The Romans first entered Britain in force in 43 A.D. and quickly overran the territories of the tribes of southern and eastern England. But resistance to their advance into the land of the Silures, in south east Wales, was fierce—this we know from the historian Tacitus who relates the exploits of the famous chieftain Caratacus, the Welsh hero Caradog. It was not until about 75 A.D. that Roman authority was fully established in South Wales and roads and forts were built. One such road, the southern route from the legionary headquarters of Isca (Caerleon) to the westerly outpost of Moridunum (Carmarthen), crossed the Vale of Glamorgan and linked the forts at Cardiff, *Bomium*, Neath and Loughor. For much of the way the road is still more or less followed by the modern main road, A.48, and the proverbial straightness can clearly be seen from the summit of the Stalling Down looking west over Cowbridge, or from a point south of Penllyn Castle looking east. The important thing for this present history is that the main street of Cowbridge (west of the bridge, anyway) follows the line of the Roman road. There was a community of people living on either side of this road in Cowbridge in Roman times, as we shall see, but where was *Bomium?*.

2. The Roman Site at 75 High Street, Cowbridge. A view of the excavation showing the circular pedestal thought to have been the base for an altar

Scholars have long known of a document called the *Antonine Itinerary*, which was written in its final form about 300 A.D. The twelfth itinerary, which lists places and distances from Carmarthen to Wroxeter, include (in the ablative case) the name *Bomio*, 15 Roman miles from Neath and 27 Roman miles from Caerleon. There is no other evidence for the existence of *Bomium*, but it fits so well into the pattern of the occupation of South Wales by the Romans that it can almost certainly be accepted as a fort founded, among so many others, late in the first century A.D. But where was it? The distance given from Neath to Caerleon in the *Itinerary* is only 42 Roman miles, whereas the actual distance would have been about 57 Roman miles. Recent writers have attempted to account for the discrepancy in two ways: either they alter the number of miles assuming that the man who copied the information down got it wrong (xv and xxvii could be scribal errors for xx and xxxvii) or they suggest that the copyist accidentally omitted a stage in the journey. Several modern authorities agree in placing *Bomium* near the crossing point of the River Ewenny, a little to the south of Bridgend, though there is at present no archaeological evidence to locate the precise site. There is, however, plenty of evidence for Roman occupation in Cowbridge, but whether or not the site will prove to include a Roman fort is something that only excavation could tell us. Meanwhile it can be tentatively suggested that the *Antonine Itinerary* might be amended so that an omitted fort is located somewhere near Kenfig or on Stormy Down (12 Roman miles from Neath); it would then follow that *Bomium* was at Cowbridge (15 Roman miles from Kenfig/Stormy Down). Assuming that the road eastwards did not deviate to the fort at Cardiff but went on a more northerly and direct course through Llandaff, the distance from Cowbridge to Caerleon would be about 27 Roman miles[3].

Generations of antiquarians have been confused by an apparent relationship between the place-name *Cowbridge* and the place-name *Bovium*. The latter suggests the Latin word for cow, *bos, bovis*. William Camden, in his famous topographical work *Britannia*, first published in 1586, thought that modern Cowbridge was Roman *Bovium*:

> Now, whereas Antoninus placed BOVIUM, which also is corruptly expressed as BOMIUM, in this district, and whereas the name of Cowbridge agrees with the meaning of Bovium, truth is so dear to me that I dare not seek Bovium elsewhere.

Camden himself seems to be responsible for the assertion that the Latin name was *Bovium* rather than *Bomium*, though the manuscripts and printed texts all agree on the latter reading, and do indeed place *Bovium* upon another itinerary, near Chester — probably the Roman fort at Holt. It became an article of faith at Cowbridge, especially among the Latinists of the Grammar School — 'Schola Boviensis' — that *Bovium* was the ancient Latin name of the town. Yet the belief was based on nothing more than an error of Camden's, a belief quite unshaken by the great Camden's change of mind! His book went through many editions and in the first English edition which came out in 1610 he argues as follows:

> Now, whereas *Antonine* the Emperor in this very coast, at the same distance from ISCA, placed BOVIVM, which also is corruptly red BOMIVM, my conjecture liked me so well, that I have beene of opinion, this towne was the said BOVIVM: but seeing that three miles from hence there standeth *Bouerton*, which fitly accordeth in sound with *Bovium*, so love me truth, I dare not seeke for BOVIVM elsewhere.

After 1610 the argument amongst antiquarians swung from Boverton to Cowbridge and back again, and occasionally embraced Llantwit Major. Richard Fenton, the historian of Pembrokeshire, visited Cowbridge in 1812 and thought that it was Bovium; he suggested that the medieval town walls followed the ramparts of the Roman fort. The formidable antiquary, G. T. Clark, also thought that the claim of Cowbridge to be Bovium was

---

[3] This is one of the possibilities discussed by B. Trott in a note in *Archaeologia Cambrensis*, vol. CXXIV (1975), pp. 113-4.

strengthened by the fact that its plan resembled that of a Roman fort. This is not acceptable to modern scholars, however, because the fourteenth-century town walls enclose an area of more than thirty acres while a Roman fort would have been unlikely to exceed five or six acres. It is possible, though, that the medieval walls of Cowbridge were founded upon the fortifications of a Roman town; the fort itself might then be supposed to have occupied a small area within the defences of the town. But this is conjecture until the archaeologists can come up with more evidence.

The existing archaeological evidence of a settlement at Cowbridge in the Roman period can now be summarised. The quantity of the evidence is already not inconsiderable, though it does little more than whet the appetite for more. Dr Hopkin-James recorded that from time to time coins of the Emperors Domitian, Trajan, Antoninus, Claudius and Constantine (whose reigns dated between 81 and 337 A.D.) and a well-preserved fibula (a clasped brooch) had been found at Cowbridge. He also mentioned that remains of stonework cemented with Roman concrete were discovered in excavations on the site of the town hall, and that Roman bricks were brought to light also.

Since 1962 there have been several discoveries and one significant archaeological dig in the town. Roman material has been found at five sites, four within the medieval walls and a fifth just outside, between the east gate and the bridge. The spacing of the sites seems to indicate the existence in Roman times of a linear or ribbon settlement stretching for at least 350 yards on either side of the High Street from the river as far as Old Hall and the Old Brewery (75 High Street) opposite. At one site on the north side of High Street Roman occupation levels were traced as far back as the former line of the medieval town wall, but on the south side of the street, in the garden of Old Hall, evidence of Roman occupation gradually petered out away from the house towards the town wall.

Before the excavation at 75 High Street in 1977-78 the archaeological evidence consisted of casual finds and a few hastily dug trenches which had revealed at varying depths below the present ground level layers of black soil or grey clay containing fragments of pottery (including Samian ware), roofing tiles and charcoal. There was sufficient material, taken together with the earlier discoveries of coins, to date the Roman occupation at Cowbridge to the period from the late first to the fourth century, virtually the whole chronological span of Roman rule in this part of the country. The recent excavation, carried out by Mr David Allen of the Glamorgan-Gwent Archaeological Trust, has added considerable detail to the shadowy picture of Roman Cowbridge which had been emerging. The dig revealed a V-shaped ditch, five feet wide, which ran parallel with the Roman road but at least ten feet away from it. The ditch had been deliberately filled in with soil and rubbish among which were found quantities of coarse pottery, oyster shells and charcoal. Built over the ditch were two buildings, one founded on sleeper beams, the other on stone wall-footings, both having probably had half-timbered superstructures. The buildings were probably houses and shops. Numerous objects of pottery, glass, bronze, iron, bone, ceramic tile and stone were found in association with the buildings, but until these have been intensively studied only very rough dates can be given — three coins of the reigns of Domitian (81-96 A.D.) and Trajan (98-117 A.D.) are the only immediately datable finds. The most curious discovery was a circular pedestal composed of small limestones and a block of sandstone surmounted by bricks or tiles. Mr Allen suggests that it might have been the base for an altar. It stood near the corner of a large room whose length was some 58 feet.

At some date, probably in the third century, both buildings were destroyed by fire, resulting in a thick layer of red clay being deposited across much of the site. The scores of nails and clamps embedded in this layer are clear evidence of the quantity of timber in the structure of the building. It is interesting to speculate on the coincidence of particles of burnt clay or daub which were observed throughout a layer of black soil discovered on the site of Fine Fare (57 High Street) in 1972; it would appear that a building there too had been destroyed by fire in the Roman period. Conceivably there was a conflagration which destroyed a large part of this sector of Roman Cowbridge. After the fire the houses on the Old Brewery site were not rebuilt, but there was an abrupt change in the use of the area with the construction of a minor road running northwards at right angles to the main street. It was well-constructed but its purpose cannot be determined because of the limited extent of the recent excavation. Possibly it gave access to a small industrial site the existence of which is hinted at by some of the finds. Several coins called 'minimi' and a radiate coin of the Gallic Emperor Tetricus (270-274 A.D.) were found near the surface of this by-road.

What can now be deduced about the general character of the Roman settlement at Cowbridge? The first thing to note is that no direct evidence of military occupation — no fort, in other words — has yet been brought to light, but the existence of one at Cowbridge can now be suggested or inferred. The founding of a fort here about 75-80 A.D. would have provided the initial stimulus for the growth of a civilian community of native traders, the evidence for which is now overwhelming. Such a market town set upon a main road might have been sufficiently prosperous to have survived even if the fort were later dismantled and its garrison moved elsewhere. The discovery at 75 High Street of a roof tile stamped LEG II AUG — the name of the Second Augustan Legion whose headquarters were at Caerleon — is visible proof of a military presence in the immediate vicinity. It seems possible that the small town here in Roman times — whether one is to call it *Bomium* or not still needs to be made clear — was technically a 'vicus', such being the smallest unit of urban administration within a Roman province.

The Dark Ages

During the fourth century A.D. Roman control over Britain weakened. The province was seriously shaken by the 'Barbarian Conspiracy' of 367 and in 383 Magnus Maximus (the Macsen Wledig of Welsh romance) withdrew a considerable part of the British garrison into Gaul in an attempt to set himself up as emperor. By 410, after another usurper, Constantine III, had taken troops from Britain into Gaul, the province became virtually independent and was made responsible for its own defence against increasingly insistent barbarian invasions. There is ample archaeological evidence dating from the fourth century to show the decline of Roman power and the decline of the Roman way of life in this part of Glamorgan. The comfortable villas and the forts seem mostly to have been abandoned by the middle of the century, or at least to have become far less prosperous. The evidence for Roman or Romano-British settlement at Cowbridge also ceases in the fourth century; it is not possible at present to be more precise about the date. The place would seem to have been deserted. Three centuries of settled living under Roman rule thus came to an end, and very little indeed is now known about what followed in the next six or seven hundred years.

At some unknown date, and in circumstances which could only be guessed at, a kingdom was founded upon the ruins of the Roman administration of south east Wales, the territory of the native tribe of the Silures. Its founder was apparently named Glywys and from him the kingdom was called Glywysing. His dynasty retained power until the seventh century when it was replaced by Meurig ap Tewdrig, under whose grandson, Morgan ab Athrwys, the name Glywysing was displaced by that of Morgannwg. The kingdom was a remarkably elastic affair, at times stretching from the Wye to the Tywi, at other times contracting between the Usk and the Tawe. The Vale of Glamorgan was the very centre and heart of the territory. There were seven cantrefs in Morgannwg, one of which was the cantref of Penychen; its boundaries must be to some extent conjectural, nevertheless there is certainty that it lay roughly between the Thaw and the Taff, and that it extended from the coast of the Bristol Channel to the borders of modern Breconshire. Clearly, what became the manor and parish of Llanblethian was within Penychen. It can even be suggested that the cantref of Penychen was itself divided into commotes, and that one of these commotes was Tal-y-fan. Its boundaries can only be reconstructed from evidence of a much later date which will be reviewed when the manorial history is discussed in the next chapter.

Though it is thus possible to reconstruct something of the administrative areas of Dark-Age Glamorgan, there is very little information about the people who lived there. It is true that Dinas Powys, where Professor Leslie Alcock has uncovered a princely court of the fifth to the seventh centuries, was also within Penychen and so may conceivably have been the residence of the ruler of the Cowbridge area, may indeed have been the residence of the early kings of Glywysing. The archaeological record for the Cowbridge-Llanblethian district itself in the Dark Ages is however quite blank. What happened to the fairly sizeable community which had lived in Roman Cowbridge? (With the end of Roman rule there probably ceased to be much traffic or much trade and so the community at Cowbridge ceased to have any economic base. The same would have been true if the civil inhabitants had depended upon supplying the needs of a garrison in the fort.) What happened to the small group of farmers living within the ramparts of Caer Dynnaf? That there were inhabitants within the commote of Tal-y-fan between 400 and 1100 A.D. we must assume, but the faint glimpses of their townships are only to be seen in the pages of that highly problematical manuscript, the *Book of Llandaff*. There is some reason for supposing that a community existed at Aberthin before the Norman conquest of Glamorgan. The *Book of Llandaff* contains a copy of a grant by King Meurig ap Hywel to the Church of Llandaff of a place called 'Villa Fratrus super Nadauan'; the date would be about 1040. At the end of the document the boundaries of the 'villa' are described in Welsh, and among them are streams called Nadauan (i.e. the Thaw) and Ebirthun (i.e. the Berthin brook). What exactly is to be understood by the words 'Villa Fratrus' is not readily apparent, but 'villa' is probably used as the Latin equivalent of the Welsh 'tref' and English 'township'. Some writers have found proof here of the existence of some monastic or religious community, but the Latin word cannot really be mistaken for 'fratris' or 'fratrum', friar(s) or brother(s).

The existence of Llanblethian itself before the Norman conquest is something which can only be presumed; there is no proof. Our evidence is solely the place-name. The name is first found in documents written in the twelfth century, in the abbreviated forms of Lanbleth' and Landbleth'; and from the spellings of the name which can be collected in fairly considerable numbers from that time onwards it is clear that the name has changed very little—at least in the way it is spelt by those writing in Latin or English.

The correct modern Welsh spelling is Llanfleiddan, but the Welsh-speaking inhabitants of the parish used to call it 'Llanddiddan'. This is quite a considerable variation from the original, but the sequence of changes which produced it can be confidently listed as: Llanfleiddan > Llanleiddan > Llanliddan > Llanddiddan. Although the experts in place-names are confident about how the name developed and changed, they are by no means certain about what it really means. About 'llan' there is no doubt; this is one of the commonest words met with in Welsh place-names and for practical purposes we can take it to mean 'church', though its original meaning was 'clearing' or 'enclosure'. As is well known, place-names beginning with 'llan' generally incorporate the name of a holy man who may be thought of either as the founder of the church there or as the head of the monastery or mother church from which the church in question was established. Thus Llanilltud, Llanddewi, Llanbadarn—the examples are legion. It would appear that here we have a church founded by one

Bleiddan or Bleiddian. Nothing is known of a holy man of this name, though various attempts have been made to provide him with some history. Iolo Morganwg, whose mind was a fertile source of information of this kind, suggested that Bleiddan was the Welsh version of the Latin name Lupus, since both evidently mean 'wolf'. (Actually the Welsh means 'wolf cub'.) Lupus was a prominent bishop in fifth-century Gaul, and is known to have accompanied St Germanus of Auxerre on his first visit to Britain in 429 A.D. Baring-Gould and Fisher, in their monumental but now largely discredited *Lives of the British saints*, suggested two things, the first, that Bleiddan might have been a monk of the community of St Illtud at Llantwit Major, and the second, on the basis of some place-name evidence, that his could be the same name as that commemorated at St Lythan's. The only possibility out of all this guesswork that scholars today might entertain is that Bleiddan was a monk of Llantwit; there is no proof, of course, but neither is there any disproof.

One other writer, the learned Dr A. W. Wade-Evans, has noticed a curious fact and made an intriguing suggestion. What he noticed was the isolated church of Llanfrynach, only half a mile in a straight line from Llanblethian church. Now Brynach was a very important Celtic saint who lived around the year 500 and whose chief church was at Nevern in Pembrokeshire. In the life of Brynach, written in the twelfth century, the saint is associated with a cow and a wolf—the picturesque details of the legend need not concern us. The association of the saint, the cow and the wolf is also to be found in place-names in Pembrokeshire and Carmarthenshire; Wade-Evans makes the observation that the same association is repeated at Llanfrynach (Brynach's church), Llanfleiddan (wolf cub's church) and *Cow*bridge. This is a piece of purest speculation which is unfortunately seriously weakened by the late date of the name of Cowbridge (after 1260). Its only real value is in pointing out the possibility of a connection between Bleiddan (surely a man, not a wolf) and Brynach, the West Wales saint. It also tends to support a possible dating of the building of the first Christian church at Llanblethian to about 500 A.D.

PART II

The Middle Ages—
from the Norman Conquest
to the Act of Union

Introduction: The Norman Conquest of Glamorgan

The Middle Ages, as far as Glamorgan is concerned, begin with the conquest of the native Welsh kingdom of Morgannwg by the Norman baron
Robert Fitzhamon and his followers. The date of the conquest is not recorded, but modern scholarly opinion favours the year 1093. The process of the
conquest can only be reconstructed in a very tentative way from later
evidence of administrative arrangements within Glamorgan, and from the
political geography of the county. It may well be that Fitzhamon's invasion
was seaborne, launched from his port of Bristol and landing at the mouth of
the Taff, or possibly at the mouth of the Usk. It seems possible that the first
district of the old kingdom to be taken by Fitzhamon was the lowland of the
cantref of Gwynllwg (modern Wentloog, between Cardiff and Newport),
and that from there the Normans moved westward into the territory called
Cibwr or Kibbor, which was probably one of the commotes of Senghennydd.
In Cibwr a motte, forty feet high and surmounted by a wooden stockade,
was constructed within the remains of the Roman fort at what came to be
called Cardiff, the fortress on the Taff; this castle became the *caput*, the
centre of government, of Fitzhamon and his descendants, the new lords of
Glamorgan. Next to be subdued were the lowlands of the Vale of
Glamorgan, the fertile southern commotes of the cantrefs of Penychen and
Gwrinydd. This was the area of Glamorgan—between the Rhymni and
Ogmore rivers, and roughly south of the Roman road—which became most
thoroughly reorganised and settled by the Norman knights and their English
tenantry. Corn-growing manors were established and farmed communally
by free and unfree tenants living in clustered dwellings under the shadow of
castle or fortified manor house. This small, but important and prosperous,
area of Anglo-Norman settlement in the Vale of Glamorgan became the

medieval 'county' of Glamorgan, often referred to as the 'shire-fee', and the lords of manors within this county held their land as vassals of the lord of Cardiff Castle, and owed him military service.

The Manor of Llanblethian

The district which we are particularly concerned with was however just out-side the shire-fee. It is likely that the commote of Tal-y-fan was not overrun by Fitzhamon at the time of his initial conquest of the Vale. The annexation of Tal-y-fan was very probably achieved by the private enterprise of a family whose presence in Glamorgan cannot (because so few documents have sur-vived from this early date) be detected before 1126, but who are known to have been in neighbouring Gwynllwg as early as 1102. The family was, of course, that of St Quentin. In the traditional story of the conquest of Glamorgan by Fitzhamon and his twelve knights the lordship of Llanblethian is assigned to Robert St Quentin. The earliest members of the family to be found in local records are actually named Herbert and Richard, but this matters little; the point is clear enough that the St Quentins were on the scene at a very early date, much earlier in fact than several other individuals, such as St John, Stradling and Siward, who are also mentioned as being among the twelve knights. The one vital piece of documentary evidence often quoted to show that Robert St Quentin was among the original conquerors of Glamorgan is, alas, quite bogus. A version of the Welsh Chronicle known as *Brut Aberpergwm* has the following entry:

> Oed Crist 1091, gwalgylched y Bont Faen, gan Robert Sancwintin. a gwedi hynny y gwnaeth ef Gastell Llanfleiddan[4].

Brut Aberpergwm has been proved to be the work of Iolo Morganwg and any fact which appears in it but in no other version of the *Brut* must be re-jected as one of Iolo's inventions. He was not, however, the author of the story of Fitzhamon and his twelve knights, for this was current at least as early as the sixteenth century when it was written down by Sir Edward Stradling.

The most likely course of events is that the St Quentins managed to take over the territory of Tal-y-fan from the rightful Welsh ruler and to set themselves up as lords, acknowledging only a nominal allegiance to the lord of Cardiff Castle. Their first stronghold was probably at Ystradowen where a large mound may be seen on the west side of the church. The suggestion has been made that this castle at Ystradowen was never completed; whether this was or was not so, the site was soon abandoned in favour of the more easily defended site of Castell Tal-y-fan on a low ridge half a mile away. This was,

---

[4] A.D. 1091 Cowbridge was walled around by Robert St Quentin, and after that he built the castle of Llanblethian.

and remained, the military centre of the lordship of Tal-y-fan, while civil administration focussed on the nearby hamlet of Trerhingyll, the name of which means 'township of the beadle' the beadle being the official who collected the lord's rents. The boundaries of Tal-y-fan encompassed a very considerable area of land, probably including the modern parishes of Llanblethian, St Hilary, Welsh St Donat's, Pendoylan, Ystradowen, Llansannor and Llanhari.

Much of the land of Tal-y-fan was comparatively poor. In medieval times, and indeed much later, there were patches of cultivated land separated by forest, marsh and heath; where there was arable land there would be small hamlets. Little attempt was made to introduce the manorial system over much of the lordship; the land remained probably in the hands of native, Welsh-speaking farmers. In the southern part of the lordship, however, where the land was of the better quality found in the lower part of the Vale, the St Quentins established three manors: Llanblethian, Llanquian and St Hilary. These manors were settled by English immigrants who farmed the land according to the Anglo-Norman notion of how this should be done, while the northern part, Tal-y-fan itself, remained a 'Welshry'. St Hilary is not part of our brief, but Llanquian, which remained ecclesiastically attached to Llanblethian, is. But first the manor of Llanblethian must be considered.

Lords of the Manor

The first lords of Llanblethian that we know of are, of course, the St Quentins. Their name is found in various Glamorgan documents until the early thirteenth century. There is then a gap in the records until the 1240s by which time Richard Siward, the most powerful man in Glamorgan at that time, had become lord of Llanblethian, Tal-y-fan and Ruthin. Initially high in the favour of the de Clares, Siward became involved in a dispute between his neighbours, Gilbert de Turberville, lord of Coity and Hywel ap Maredudd, lord of Miskin, which resulted in Siward's being forced to surrender his lordships to Richard de Clare. He was eventually outlawed. Hywel ap Maredudd was defeated in battle by de Clare. By this one incident the Lord of Glamorgan took into his own hands a very large tract of country in the Border Vale as well as the lordships of Miskin and Glynrhondda which extended northwards as far as Aberdare and Rhigos. Thus the manor of Llanblethian came into the possession of the lords of Glamorgan. It passed through the families of the de Clares, the Despensers, Beauchamps and Nevills—some of the greatest magnates of medieval England—until the Battle of Bosworth in 1485. Henry VII defeated Richard III and seized the crown of England; Richard was also lord of Glamorgan on account of his marriage to Lady Anne Nevill, co-heiress of the Nevills and descendant of Robert Fitzhamon. Henry VII thus became lord of Glamorgan by conquest, and the lordship remained in his family until marcher lordships were

abolished by the Act of Union in 1536. The manor of Llanblethian continued in existence and remained a possession of the Crown until Edward VI
granted it to Sir William Herbert, Earl of Pembroke, in 1550. Since that
date the manor has passed from the Herberts to their descendants the
Windsors and the Crichton-Stuarts, marquesses of Bute.

Boundaries

There seems to be no detailed account of the boundaries of the manor, but
from seventeenth-century surveys of adjoining manors it is possible to be
moderately certain of where they lay—with one important exception: it is
not possible to say where the boundary between Llanblethian and Llanquian ran. In general the southern, eastern and western boundaries were
the same as those of the parish, but on the north the lordship of Tal-y-fan
(out of which the manor had originally been carved) extended down to
Newton moors. The boundary from Maendy to Pantylliwydd is thus described in a survey of Tal-y-fan taken in 1602:

> . . . and along that portway [i.e. Heol Ffynnon Goeg] to a highway
> leading from Cowbridge to Lantrissent and so along the last highway
> till you come to a corner of a hedge that leadeth between the lands of
> Griffith Wylime and the lands of Lewis James' sons and also the lands
> of Evan Rosser and from thence along one hedge that directly meareth
> to one well called Ffynnon Sywyll and from thence along the water that
> runneth from the said well to one river called Ythavon [i.e. Ddawan,
> the Thaw] which river divideth and meareth between the lordship of
> Talyvan and the lordship of Penllyne being on the west part of the said
> lordship of Talyvan and so along the river upwards to a place called
> Rhyd Pant Llywith in the parish of Lansannor . . .

It is not easy to plot this boundary on a map, for who can now tell where the
lands of Griffith Wilym and Lewis James's sons once lay?

The Castle

It is not clear if there was a castle within the manor of Llanblethian in the
centuries immediately following the Norman conquest. Since the manor was
owned throughout the Middle Ages by the lords of Tal-y-fan the important
castle near Ystradowen may at first have been thought sufficient. Nevertheless, it is possible that there are remains of a medieval stronghold within
the hill-fort of Caer Dynnaf, overlooking the gorge of the river Thaw. An
eighteenth-century print shows a substantial ruin on this prominent site.
D. B. Hague does not consider the building to be medieval. However, the
author of the account of Caer Dynnaf in the *Inventory* of the Ancient
Monuments Commission refers unequivocally to a 'small medieval fortifica-
tion' which, he suggests, may have been the castle which Rice Merrick called
'Llygod' in his *Booke of Glamorganshires antiquities* (1578). Llygod was certainly in the vicinity of Cowbridge.

3. St Quentin's Castle, Llanblethian. The well-preserved Gatehouse was built in the early fourteenth century by Gilbert de Clare   *(Photo: Haydn Baynham)*

We are on much firmer ground with Llanblethian Castle itself. On the opposite side of the valley from the supposed Castell Llygod are the impressive remains of what for the last two hundred years has been called 'St Quentin's Castle'. There is documentary evidence of the date of its construction. Clearly it could not have been built by the St Quentins. At the inquisition into the estates of Earl Gilbert de Clare, lord of Glamorgan, who fell at Bannockburn in 1314, it was stated by the jurors that 'in the manor of Llanblethian there is a certain castle begun by the said Earl and it is worth nothing beyond reprise'. It seems clear that Earl Gilbert had begun either the building of a new castle or the remodelling of an old one—for Mr Hague suspects that the keep (now little more than a heap of rubble) may be of earlier date than the gatehouse which is so well preserved—sometime after he got possession of his inheritance in 1307; but in 1314, at the time of his death, the castle was still uncompleted. The architectural style of the gatehouse is consistent with its having been erected in the early years of the fourteenth century. Mr Hague mentions the possibility that the castle was *never* completed; this might explain the insignificant remains of the enclosure walls, especially on the south side, but equally likely is the explanation of the walls having been robbed by the local inhabitants for building stone. The late Miss Maud Gunter describes Castle Cottage and Porth-y-green as having certainly been built from this convenient quarry. Perhaps it is some confirmation of the castle's having been finished that in 1375 Edward Lord Despenser, lord of Glamorgan and one of the great magnates and military heroes of his day, died at Llanblethian—presumably in the castle—while on a visit to his Welsh estates[5].

In later centuries the castle, or rather the gatehouse, was kept in repair and used as a prison; a county coroner's roll of 1477 mentions a prisoner in Llanblethian castle; John Leland, the King's antiquary, writing about 1540, remarked that it was the prison for the lordship of 'Terstuard' (i.e. Tal-y-fan). The splendid gatehouse is now much in need of expert care and attention; it is still privately owned and, rather surprisingly, it has only grade 2 listing as a building of architectural and historical interest.

Land and Tenants

Llanblethian was not a particularly large or valuable manor. Unfortunately most of the accounts of it—which are fairly full for the late thirteenth and early fourteenth centuries—do not clearly distinguish between it and Tal-y-fan; the two were evidently administered as a single unit despite the obvious differences in land tenure and farming economy. The area of the manor of Llanblethian must have been much less than 2,000 acres, and much of that was ill adapted to intensive arable cultivation on account of the broken nature of the terrain.

What was the manor of Llanblethian, and how did it operate? Essentially a manor was an area of land cultivated by a community of tenants organised in a particular way and subject to a lord. Manors differed from one another in endless detail, but they had certain common features. The manor of Llanblethian was not untypical as far as the records existing can tell us. There were free tenants or freemen (they would be called freeholders in later times); it is not certain how many; they held their land from the lord of the manor and owed him a small, fixed rent and certain other dues. In 1307

---

[5] The remarkable effigy of Edward Despenser, surmounting his chantry chapel, may still be seen in Tewkesbury Abbey.

the rents of the free tenants of Llanblethian amounted to £3. 1s. 9d; if — as was later the case — they paid two pence an acre *per annum* for their land, they held only 370½ acres between them. Then there were the customary tenants or villeins, whose land was held of the lord in return for more or less onerous rents and services. In 1314 there were forty customary tenants who each owed the lord two plough-works at the sowing of wheat and oats, one harrowing-work and four hoeing-works; they had to mow 39½ acres of meadow and carry and stack the hay; they each owed about twenty autumnal works, which presumably meant twenty days' reaping, and in addition had to carry and stack the corn. The work thus demanded of the customary tenants was done upon the lord's home farm, his demesne. At Llanblethian in 1314 there were 255½ acres of arable land in the demesne; much of this probably lay in a triangle between the castle, Broadway, the St Athan road and the river Thaw. There was also meadow and pasture belonging to the demesne, probably lying in the valley below the castle. Although clearly the lord depended upon the work of his villeins, particularly for sowing and reaping, he also hired some workmen, referred to in the accounts as 'famuli'; their wages amounted to no more than £1. 13s. 4d. for the half year March to September 1316.

Among the details of manorial administration revealed in the inquisition of 1314 and in the half year's accounts of 1316 which have chanced to survive, we learn that there were three water mills, one windmill and one fulling mill belonging to the manor, and worth about £18 a year to the lord. (The mills were probably Llanblethian Mill, Town Mill and the Little Mill at Llanblethian on the Factory brook; the windmill stood on the demesne south of Broadway, and the fulling mill[6] was probably the Old Mill on the north side of Cowbridge.) There are minute details of the expenses of repairs to ploughs, carts, wagons, mills and buildings belonging to the lord' demesne.

Of the land in the possession of the free and customary tenants themselves the documents reveal little apart from its probable extent at the beginning of the fourteenth century of some thousand acres. There is no absolute proof that their lands were intermingled in common or open fields and in common meadows, yet this was the usual pattern on medieval manors in the Vale of Glamorgan as elsewhere. A sentence in the inquisition on the death of the Countess Joan de Clare in 1307 states that the demesne included 'various small pieces of [arable] land in various places which are worth *per annum* 20s'. This strongly suggests that part of the demesne was mixed with the lands of the tenants in open fields. The location of the meadows is easy; they were alongside the river Thaw and were the source of hay for winter fodder. (The meadows were of very limited extent, and it is significant that an acre

---

[6] The 'Lord's tucking mill' was still in existence at Cowbridge in 1630. In 1637 there was another tucking mill at Llanblethian; this later became the woollen factory. Tucking and fulling were much the same process of finishing woven cloth.

of meadow was valued at four times as much as an acre of arable land.)
Where were the large arable fields? The most likely areas are the gently slop-
ing ground between Cowbridge and the Stalling Down, the rising ground
south of the village of Llanblethian towards Llandough and Llanmihangel,
and the level ground west and north of the church, towards Llanfrynach,
Crossways and Marlborough Grange. There is no clue about how many
open fields there were, or how they were worked. Information about the
arable land in the demesne suggests that as little as one fifth was allowed to
remain fallow each year; the entry reads:

> [John Giffard, the bailiff, answers] for 18s. 4d. received from the
> pasture of 55 acres of arable land at Llanblethian which were not sown
> this year.

The Decline of the Manor
Very little can be said about how this particular manor changed in the later
Middle Ages, and how the elaborate arrangements and relationships within
it were transformed into those familiar in modern times. But the changes
undoubtedly occurred, and they were very far-reaching in their importance.
Probably the first thing which happened was that the lord of the manor
ceased to cultivate the demesne lands on his own account and either leased
them whole or let them in small tenements. The services formerly demanded
of the customary tenants were then no longer required to cultivate the
demesne, and the days' work so minutely itemised in the accounts of John
Giffard in 1316 were commuted to the payment of a rent. This is then the
origin of what in early modern times (and in this district right down to the
twentieth century) is called customary tenure of land, or copyhold. These
copyholders had as permanent an interest in their land as had freeholders
but their rents were larger.

A later phase of the decline of the manor was the enclosure of the large
arable fields. This seems to have taken place in the Vale of Glamorgan in the
late fifteenth and early sixteenth centuries. There was no formal rearrange-
ment of holdings as happened in the eighteenth-century enclosures in the
English Midlands; the scattered strips and pieces of land were merely
hedged around where they lay. The farms of sixteenth-century copyholders — rarely as large as fifty acres — were thus scattered rather than com-
pact and convenient holdings. This remained a feature of farms in
Llanblethian and may be clearly seen from a study of the Tithe Survey of
1840. But an important change had nevertheless come about: each farmer
now had his own farm which he worked as he chose, where formerly farming
had been a communal activity controlled by custom and by the mutual
agreement of the tenants of the manor.

What part in bringing about these profound economic and social changes
had been played by the disasters of the Black Death and the Glyndŵr
rebellion it is difficult to say in the absence of manorial records for the later
fourteenth century and for the early years of the fifteenth. In general it is

certain that they were powerful agents of change. The population of the Vale of Glamorgan was substantially reduced by the plague of 1348-9 and its later recurrences, and much land was waste because the tenants had died or because they had fled before the army of Owain Glyndŵr. There is no direct reference to the sufferings of the inhabitants of Llanblethian but it is obvious from the few surviving documents that the lord's income from this manor was substantially reduced in the later Middle Ages.

Another consequence of the economic upheavals of the hundred years or so from 1350 was that the distinctions between the English and the Welsh were gradually lost. Llanblethian manor had been populated largely by English immigrants who took at least the best land and the more prominent positions in the community. When the 'extent' of Llanblethian and Cowbridge was taken in 1296 following the death of Gilbert de Clare, the jurymen empanelled to answer the King's inquisition were named as follows:

John Rubey	William Keting
Richard Fitz John	John de Geteton
William Dolman	William Pryor
Alan Chyk	Michael le Tayleure
Thomas Randolf	William de Valence
John Galwey	John Galeraund
William le Prute	John Canty

The earliest surviving deeds of land in the parish of Llanblethian, dated in 1305 and 1317, mention the names of 28 persons many of whom would probably have been actually resident in the parish; only one of them had a Welsh name. This situation changed slowly. By the late fifteenth century there were several Welsh names in deeds and by the middle of the sixteenth century Welsh names were fairly numerous in both Cowbridge and Llanblethian.

The Manor of Llanquian
There is little to be said about this small manor; no accounts, no surveys survive. Its centre was a small castle set on a north-facing spur overlooking a secluded dingle to the east of the Stalling Down; only a few overgrown mounds mark its site today. The boundaries of the manor are uncertain, but it probably was of very limited extent since the farm of Llanquian Isaf (or Llanquian Fach as it is called now) was a freehold of the manor of Llanblethian. In a small field to the west of the castle may be seen traces of foundations which doubtless mark the site of the village of Llanquian, and on the south side of this field stands the derelict farmhouse once known as Llanquian Uchaf, now used as an outbuilding by the farmer of Hollybush nearby. Mr C. J. Spurgeon and Mr H. J. Thomas of the Royal Commission on Ancient and Historical Monuments in Wales believe that the farmhouse may incorporate the medieval chapel of St James. There is only a single documentary reference to the existence of a chapel at Llanquian, and that

4. A general view of the Stalling Down, the common waste of the manor of Llanblethian. The obelisk was erected in 1922 to the memory of officers and men of the Glamorgan Yeomanry killed in the Great War

(Photo: Haydn Baynham)

as early as the twelfth century. But the experts have discovered in the central part of the house the sawn-off stumps of two arch-braced roof trusses; a roof of this type in such a modest domestic building gives reason to suspect an ecclesiastical origin. Another instance of a medieval chapel being converted into a dwelling house was identified a few years ago at Llanwensan, near Peterston-super-Ely.

The names of the owners of the manor are unknown before 1262 when Philip de Nerber, lord of St Athan, was listed as lord of Llanquian, holding it of the lord of Llanblethian as half a knight's fee. There is a tradition recorded by G. T. Clark that the de Wintonia family held Llanquian before the Nerbers, and that their name survives at Pant Wilkin; there is, however, no documentary evidence to support this. The Nerbers remained in possession until the fifteenth century, and in the following century it belonged to the Carnes of Nash, from whom it was purchased by one Jenkin Williams. Williams's descendants were still in possession of the manor and estate of Llanquian (then about 275 acres) in the early nineteenth century.

The Borough of Cowbridge

About the middle of the thirteenth century Richard de Clare, Earl of Gloucester and lord of Glamorgan, founded a borough on the main road through Glamorgan, where it crossed the river Thaw. There seems to be no serious reason to doubt that, as a *borough*, Cowbridge goes no further back than 1250. And yet several historians, some of them scholars of considerable reputation, have antedated the foundation of the town. Dr Hopkin-James's *Old Cowbridge* contains the most elaborate and scholarly attempt to prove that, in the first place, Cowbridge was the Roman Bovium and that, secondly, there was a continuity of settlement at Cowbridge from Roman times to the present day. There may be something to be said in favour of Bovium (or Bomium, see pp. 14-18) but the dragging in—as he does—of Punctuobice from the Ravenna cosmography and equating it with Pont-y-fuwch[7], of Penychen (the bovine theme again here, since ychen means oxen), of Villa Fratrus from the *Book of Llandaff*, of the entry about the walling of Y Bont Faen from *Brut Aberpergwm*, and finally of early medieval references to Ecclesia de la Tawe, is only impressive until one begins a serious assessment. Punctuobice is identified by a recent scholar with Avonmouth; Villa Fratrus may refer to Cowbridge, but Aberthin seems the more likely place; the Aberpergwm version of the *Brut* is one of Iolo Morganwg's forgeries, and Ecclesia de la Tawe is quite without doubt Llansannor. Dr Hopkin-James's argument crumbles. It seems best to admit that with the fall of the Roman Empire in the fifth century, the Romano-British community at Cowbridge (whether it was called Bomium or not) dispersed because the trade and traffic which it had depended on ceased. It may well be that a small village continued to exist on the site between 400 and 1250, but we have no authentic knowledge of it.

The circumstances of the founding—or planting, to use the technical term—of the borough of Cowbridge within the bounds of the manor of Llanblethian were, in the first place political, but the fundamental motive of the founder was probably economic. The events which brought the lordship of Tal-y-fan and the manor of Llanblethian into the possession of Richard de Clare in the 1240s have already been mentioned (p. 24). This was the essential political prerequisite. The subsequent founding of a market town seems to have been a deliberate act of policy by Richard de Clare, with the intention of increasing his revenues from this part of his vast estates. A survey of the possessions of the Earl of Pembroke compiled in 1570 contains the only known reference to the foundation charter of Cowbridge:

> Note that Sir Richard Clare did grant unto Cowbridge all such liberties as Cardiff had by a charter bearing date the thirteenth day of March in the 38th year of Henry the Third [i.e. 1254].

What exactly was meant by a borough, and what were these liberties conferred by the Lord of Glamorgan? Professor Postan has described medieval towns as 'non-feudal islands in the feudal seas'. The inhabitants of a chartered town were known as burgesses; they were free men who owed no

---

[7] Pont-y-fuwch, the bridge of the cow, was not the bridge over the Thaw (that presumably was the stone bridge, y Bont Faen) but a smaller one over a brook near Llwynhelyg. That Punctuobice might be Cowbridge was suggested by Thomas Gale as long ago as 1699; the idea was enthusiastically adopted by local scholars such as John Walters who mentioned it in his *English-Welsh dictionary*.

feudal obligation to a superior lord, though they owed him their burgage
rents and certain other dues; they could buy and sell burgages and bequeath
them to their heirs, without the lord's consent or licence; they could decide
whom their children should marry; they were free from the tedious obligation to bake bread in the lord's oven, to brew ale in the lord's brewhouse and
from having to grind corn and to full and dye cloth in the lord's mills. The
burgesses had a monopoly of trade within their town and were exempt from
tolls charged at markets and fairs within Glamorgan. They enjoyed a degree
of self-government; a burgess had the right to be tried in the borough court
by a jury of his fellow burgesses, and in the course of time privileges of elec-
ting portreeves, bailiffs and aldermen were extended. Townsmen were thus
very much freer than were the inhabitants of manors, where there were
many restrictions even upon so-called free tenants. It was these advantages
that the Earl offered to confer upon men willing to settle in his new town of
Cowbridge. Although he thus surrendered important legal rights the lord in
return derived increased profits from burgage rents, from market tolls and
from fees paid at the holding of the borough court.

The scanty records from this early phase of the town's history fail to
disclose to us many of the things which we would like to know. For instance,
where did the pioneer burgesses come from? There were probably 59
burgesses in residence in 1262-3, but by 1295 there were apparently 233, or
rather the burgesses paid that number of burgage rents of one shilling each.
(It is not clear if each burgess paid one shilling, or if some paid more or less
than that amount.) After that there was a much more gentle growth of the
town, for there were 276¾ burgages in 1306 and again in 1314. The
number may possibly have been 293½ in 1316. In only half a century
therefore Cowbridge had grown into a town of considerable size for the
period. The evidence, such as it is, suggests that in 1300 Cowbridge was
among the largest and most flourishing towns in Wales; in fact, only Cardiff
was distinctly bigger. If a burgage can be taken to represent a single family
dwelling, then the population of the borough can hardly have been less than
1,200—roughly its size in the twentieth century. It is pretty certain that the
early inhabitants were Englishmen. All but two of the jurors who gave information in reply to the King's inquisitions in 1296 and 1314 had English
names, but they came from Llanblethian, Tal-y-fan and Cowbridge and
there is no way of distinguishing between those who were burgesses and
those who were manorial tenants. The earliest persons who can be identified
by name as inhabitants of the town are 'Johannes prepositus de
Coubrigge'—John, portreeve of Cowbridge—who is mentioned in a deed of
1305, and 'Amicia le Newelestar de Coubrugge' who granted a tenement in
Womanby Street, Cardiff, in 1310. Neither of these can tell us anything
about the nationality of the townspeople; Amicia's surname 'the Newelstair'
is more curious than informative—though it can scarcely be Welsh.

There is one specific reason for the success of the new borough in the first
half century or so of its existence, while so many boroughs founded by

over-optimistic kings and lords in the twelfth and thirteenth centuries were failures. Earl Richard had chosen a site which was convenient for trade, and one which was at the centre of a prosperous agricultural district. Several of the other boroughs in Glamorgan had grown up as appendages to important castles which had, of course, been sited for strategic, military reasons. Caerphilly, Llantrisant and Kenfig were inconveniently situated as market towns, their immediate surrounding country was not good farmland, and their situation adjoining enemy territory meant that there was constant risk of attack. Indeed the town of Kenfig — built largely within the outer bailey of the castle — was sacked by the Welsh on at least six occasions in a hundred and fifty years. Another important reason for the rapid growth of Cowbridge was probably this very fact, that it was, as far as we know, never attacked even though the records show that rebels did serious damage in the lordship of Tal-y-fan nearby in 1292-95 (the revolt of Morgan ap Maredudd) and in 1316 (the revolt of Llywelyn Bren)[8].

This brings one to a unique feature of Cowbridge as a town in the Marches of Wales — it had no castle. Llanblethian Castle, which was being built by Gilbert de Clare at the time of his death (1314) perhaps in order to provide additional protection for the borough, was within sight of Cowbridge, but half a mile away. It seems likely, however, that the town was provided with walls at its foundation, though experts date the surviving stretches of the wall and the south gate to the early fourteenth century. A further interesting point relating to the security of the town in the thirteenth and fourteenth centuries is that it is quite impossible that the entire population of 1,200 could have lived inside the walls. There were 276 burgages altogether but there could not have been more than about seventy actually within the gates. Many of the medieval burgage plots are still clearly marked on modern large-scale Ordnance Survey maps, especially on the northern side of High Street; on the southern side, and along Church Street, the pattern has been partly obscured by Old Hall and the grammar school. Clearly the town must have had suburbs outside both east and west gates by 1300 and in the early decades of the fourteenth century the whole length of the borough from the entrance to Llwynhelyg at the extreme west to Eastfield House at the extreme east must have been built up. John Leland, who was the first traveller to leave any description of Cowbridge, recorded that 'The great suburbe of Coubridge is cis pontem' (i.e. on this side of the bridge), referring to Eastgate or the East Village, but by his time, in the reign of Henry VIII, the town was very much smaller than it had been in the early fourteenth century.

Perhaps it is wrong to think of the town walls purely in terms of defence against military attack. Miss Hilary L. Turner would suggest that walls had an economic rather than a military purpose. She writes:

---

[8] The manor of Llanblethian was also one of the manors which Hugh Despenser claimed had been laid waste by his enemies in the so-called Despenser War of 1321.

At Cowbridge the enclosed area is only thirty-three acres, and the town
is situated not in a defensive position, but on the line of a main road;
thus as there seems to be no question of defence the walls must have
served to regulate ingress and egress and to facilitate the collection of
tolls.

One cannot agree that the walls of Cowbridge had no defensive significance,
but since Cowbridge was above all a place where markets and fairs were to
be held some weight must be allowed to Miss Turner's argument. One might
almost say that the walls enclosed the market rather than the town. In the
early centuries markets were probably held once a week but the records do
not actually specify this; certainly by Elizabethan times the market was being held twice a week, on Tuesdays and Saturdays. The fair is mentioned in
1296; in 1307 it is described as being held on the feast of the Exaltation of
the Holy Cross, that is 14 September, popularly known as Holy Rood Day.
(This was of course the feast of the dedication of Cowbridge church.) By
Elizabethan times there was also a fair on the feast of St John the Baptist
(Midsummer Day), the feast day of Llanblethian church, but there is no
reference to this fair having been held in medieval times.

Markets and fairs were the basis of the prosperity of Cowbridge in the
thirteenth and fourteenth centuries. But to the lord of the borough income
from the market tolls (from which the burgesses themselves were exempt)
was only a small item in the accounts, probably not exceeding £2 or £3 a
year. Yet in 1296 the annual value of the borough to its lord was estimated
to be £18 3s. 0½d., and in 1314 £25 6s. 11½d.; the actual income in six
months of the year 1316 (even though this was the year of Llywelyn Bren's
rebellion) was £12 14s. 4d. A decline to £20 0s. 6d. is recorded by the following year, 1317. The bulk of the income came from burgage rents, but the
'prise of ale' was always an important source of revenue—the duty paid to
the lord upon the brewing of ale. The holding of the borough court brought
in a further pound or two each year. The greater part of this money did not
actually go into the earl's treasury, however; in 1289 Earl Gilbert de Clare
had assigned £14 12s. 7½d. a year from the profits of the borough of
Cowbridge to the Abbot of Neath in exchange for extensive lands in the
neighbourhood of Neath.

The only clue to the economic prosperity of the burgesses themselves in
the first fifty or sixty years of the borough's existence lies in the impressive
growth in their number. We have no specific knowledge of how wealthy they
were, and little even of what trades and crafts they followed. There are
references in the Ordinances of Cowbridge, which may have been promulgated in the fourteenth century, to butchers, tanners, bakers, brewers,
tapsters and tavernkeepers. Clearly many of the burgesses, in medieval times
as well as much later, also kept livestock; they were forbidden by the
Ordinances to allow their animals to roam the town's streets. There is no
known reference to the existence of a 'guild merchant' in the town though

5/6. Two views of the best surviving stretches of the medieval town walls of Cowbridge,
thought by experts to date from about 1300

(Photo: Haydn Baynham)

there almost certainly was one; the guild would have been the association of the burgesses for the regulation and control of the market. (Only in larger towns were there separate guilds for individual trades and crafts.)

We can, however, in a general way, trace the progress of self-government within the town. The possession of certain rights of self-government was, of course, one of the distinguishing marks of a borough. The charter of 1254 had granted to the burgesses of Cowbridge the liberties enjoyed by the burgesses of Cardiff. The constable of Cardiff Castle was to be mayor of Cowbridge; he was appointed by the lord and held office during the lord's pleasure. The burgesses had the right to elect their portreeve and bailiff (or catchpole), who, together with the constable, were magistrates of the town, presiding over the borough (or hundred) court. Because none of the medieval charters has survived it is difficult to be precise about the powers and duties of the officials and of the court. Neither is it quite clear whether the succession of charters granted to Cardiff applied to Cowbridge — which is not named in them — by virtue of the original grant by Richard de Clare of 'all such liberties as Cardiff had'. It was claimed in the sixteenth century that Hugh Despenser 'did increase the liberties granted by Clare'; but whether this was done by implication by his Cardiff charter of 1340 or whether he granted a separate one to Cowbridge (as his son did to Kenfig) is obscure. Certainly more important was a charter of Richard Nevill[9] dated 12th December 1460, and confirmed by his son-in-law, George Duke of Clarence, in 1473. An abstract of this document was included in the Pembroke survey of 1570, from which it appears that Nevill allowed the creation of a bench of twelve aldermen; on the death of an alderman 'the other aldermen shall choose another in his place'. The charter permitted the burgesses to choose four of their number out of whom the constable was to appoint two bailiffs to serve as magistrates for the year. In this charter of 1460 we have the origin of the Court of Common Council which, under the presidency of the bailiffs, was to manage the affairs of the borough of Cowbridge down to the year 1886[10]. Whereas previously the town was governed by the body of burgesses meeting in the borough court under the presidency of the constable or the portreeve, now comes an important step whereby the more prominent burgesses become aldermen and establish a self-perpetuating inner group who really control the business of the borough. The fact that the constable or mayor was normally resident in Cardiff would probably have meant that

[9] Richard Nevill is often referred to as Warwick the Kingmaker for his part in the dynastic troubles of the Wars of the Roses. He ruled Glamorgan in the right of his wife, Lady Anne Beauchamp, from 1449 to 1471. His two daughters and co-heiresses, the Ladies Isabel and Anne, were married to George Duke of Clarence and Richard Duke of Gloucester respectively, both brothers of King Edward IV. Richard established his claim to Glamorgan when the Nevill estates were partitioned in 1474; he later succeeded to the throne as Richard III.

[10] The Court of Common Council did not exist under this name until the charter of 1681 (see p. 55). when the bench of capital burgesses was created.

the bailiffs and aldermen of Cowbridge were fairly free from the direct interference of the constable and of the lord himself.

The law which the dignitaries and their courts had to enforce was not so much the English common law or even the law of the March (though this would have been a part of the business, especially where actual crime or disputes over property were concerned) but the ordinances of Cowbridge itself. By a lucky chance the Ordinances—or bye-laws as we should say—have survived in a document written down in the year 1610, with some later additions[11]. They were already old in 1610 and in that year the bailiffs and aldermen consented to their being newly written 'word by word agreeable to the old decayed roll'. The laws compare very closely with those set forth for the borough of Kenfig in 1330 (though these are only known in a copy made in 1572) and it may well be that Cowbridge's ordinances had also been promulgated as far back as the fourteenth century. Assuming that the Cowbridge laws are basically of that date, we get nearer to a picture of life as it was lived in the medieval borough by studying them than we can in any other way. The ordinances were primarily concerned with the regulation of the market and the trades carried on within the borough, but they also regulated public order, public health, the conduct of legal business and the admission of burgesses to their privileges. A few examples must suffice. First, the regulations relating to the butcher's trade: butchers might not slaughter animals nor scald meat in the High Street; they might not throw heads, feet or other garbage into the street; all meat had to be sold in the shambles; no butcher could trade on a Sunday and butchers who were not burgesses could sell meat only on market days. Public order was provided for in a dozen ordinances; the twentieth stated that every inhabitant should have a 'defencible weapon' so that he could come to the aid of the magistrates for the defence and good order of the town. Public health was protected by several ordinances such as the twenty-fourth which forbade anyone to 'cast no dust, dung, nor no other filth in the streets nor in the town ditches, nor within forty foot of any [of] the four gates of the said town, or any part of the walls thereof'. The twenty-third ordinance allowed the building of privies and pigsties only in gardens, while the forty-eighth prohibited anyone from making a dunghill anywhere within the borough where it might be to the annoyance of any man or to the inconvenience of any of the streets of the town. The semi-rural character of the town is brought out in several of the ordinances which refer to the keeping of livestock in the town; if any swine were found in the neighbourhood of the town cross their owner was to be fined; no one was allowed to drive animals into the town ditches; cows might not be milked in the High Street and no one should allow his beasts to 'abide in the high street nor in no other street by night nor by day'. Two final quotations, from the forty-seventh and nineteenth ordinances, must be allowed to conclude this brief summary of the quaint, but

---

[11] The text is printed in *Old Cowbridge*, pp. 25-39. The document, written on a roll of parchment, is now preserved in the Glamorgan Record Office together with the other records of the borough.

remarkably comprehensive, code of laws under which the townspeople of Cowbridge were governed in medieval and Tudor times:

> No manner of burgess, chencer[12], nor inhabitant of the said town shall keep no licentious naughtypacks[13], bawdry, or suspected harlots, vagabonds nor loiterers in their houses, upon pain of ten shillings.

To ensure further that virtue and good order prevailed it was ordained that

> No manner of person shall play at dice, cards, bowls, nor other unlawful games, within the said town . . . upon pain of amercement of twelve pence upon him that owneth the house that such play is kept in. And the players to be brought to prison and amercement to the Lord. And also that there be no tennis playing within the High Street upon pain of 3s. 4d. to be levied upon every of them that playeth.

Late Medieval Cowbridge

The rapid growth of the town up to at least 1316 has been described, and a population of at least 1,200 has been suggested. The records of medieval Cowbridge are so few in number that it is not possible to plot the course of the town's growth after that date (if indeed it grew after that date) neither can the precise time when its decline set in be pinpointed. The annual value to the lord was estimated at £18 3s. 0½d. in 1296, at £25 6s. 11½d. in 1314; six months of 1316 brought in £12 14s. 4d.—but the slight fall that this represented could be interpreted as only a temporary one because of the war. In 1317, however, the estimated value was set at only £20 0s. 6d. Had the town's prosperity begun to ebb already? Perhaps the dislocation and destruction of Llywelyn Bren's rebellion had a lasting effect upon the economy of the rural hinterland, especially upon Tal-y-fan and Ruthin to the north of Cowbridge, and this injured the trade of the town itself. At the inquisition on the death of Lord Hugh Despenser in 1349 the burgage rents numbered only 151, not many more than half the number of thirty-three years before. By 1376 there had been something of a recovery, for then the lord's income from the borough was set at £14 7s. 7d. To account for these figures we have to go to textbooks of national history, for there are no local records to enlighten us. Medieval historians recognise that a general contraction in the economy took place in the fourteenth century, bringing to an end a period of agricultural and commercial expansion and of population increase. It is now thought that economic decline set in as early as the 1320s, but the importance of the coming of the bubonic plague in 1348 cannot be overstated. There is little explicit evidence of the 'Black Death' in Glamorgan, but the effects of it are plainly visible in the seigneurial records.

---

[12] A chencer was someone who was licensed to trade in the borough but who was not a burgess.

[13] A naughtypack was a person of bad character, either man or woman.

The burgesses of Cowbridge paid only 151 burgage rents in 1349 where in 1314 they had paid 276. The devastating effects of the plague are most clearly seen in Monmouthshire; for example, in the hamlet of Tregoythel in the lordship of Abergavenny all the customary tenants died; rents received from many manors were only fractions of what they had formerly been. Even the revenue of Cardiff in 1349 was less than half of what it had been in 1316. We need look no further to explain the shrinkage of the population of Cowbridge in the fourteenth century. If the population was indeed as great as 1,200 at the beginning of the century then it was not until the 1870s that this level was regained—more than five hundred years later. We lack the detail of this human tragedy, but there can be no doubt that the visitation of the plague in 1348-9 was a catastrophe entirely beyond our own experience. The slight recovery observable by 1375 may have been set back by further outbreaks of the pestilence in the second half of the fourteenth century, and possibly also by the havoc known to have been caused in some places in Glamorgan (in Cardiff particularly) during the revolt of Owain Glyndŵr[14] in the opening years of the fifteenth century. The population of Cowbridge cannot be even guessed at until 1546; in that year it is unlikely that there were as many as 500 people living in the town.

However, that Cowbridge enjoyed a degree of prosperity, albeit on a much reduced scale, in the later fifteenth century is suggested by one or two facts. In 1460 the Lord of Glamorgan, as we have already seen, granted a new charter to the town with significant new privileges, especially the permission to elect alderman and bailiffs. There is evidence that the vesting of authority in this narrow caucus of 'the most sufficient and discreet' of the burgesses reflected the fact that wealth had become markedly uneven in its distribution amongst the townspeople. We know of several prosperous burgesses from the fifteenth century—Howell Carne, ancestor of the gentry families of Nash and Ewenny; possibly William Prior, founder of a chantry in the church; Hywel Prains or Pranche, to whom the Welsh poet Lewis Glyn Cothi (*fl.*1447-86) addressed two *cywyddau*. (Anyone wishing to read these poems will find the text in *Old Cowbridge*, pp. 286-8, and a translation in W. G. Wrenche, *Wrenche (Pransiaid) and Radcliffe: notes on two families of Glamorgan*, pp. 22-4.) It is impossible to extract much of historical value from the poems, though clearly Hywel Prains was a Welshman—a native of Tir Iarll or Llangynwyd—and this points to an interesting fact about late medieval Cowbridge: that Welshmen were now becoming burgesses, and prosperous ones at that. Hywel is called 'marsiant mawr', a great merchant:

---

[14] Local traditions of a battle on the Stalling Down about 1400-5, after which Glyndŵr ravaged many local castles, villages and churches, have little basis in truth, and may indeed have been invented by Iolo Morganwg. See *Old Cowbridge*, pp. 76-7 and 312.

O'i rodd iawn a'i rwyddineb
o'i ras i huw yr a'r Sieb
A fu un yn y Venis
byw yn y wal na bai'n is
Cannings ieuangk a enwir
neu whidintwn ydyw'n tir

(Roughly translated: On account of his true gift and his largesse Cheapside of its grace will go to Hywel. Did anyone live in the city of Venice that was not inferior to him? He is called the younger Canynges, or Whittington is he in our land.) In the second *cywydd* the poet calls Hywel 'Brig y dref foneddigaidd'—the crest of the gentlemanly town. The Welsh poets traded in this kind of hyperbole, but there must have been a grain of truth, Hywel Prains must have been both rich and generous to have elicited such fulsome praise and comparison with the famous Canynges of Bristol and Sir Richard Whittington, Lord Mayor of London.

The Church of Llanblethian with its Chapels

The earliest reference to the existence of a church at Llanblethian is in an undated charter of Nicholas ap Gwrgant, Bishop of Llandaff from 1148 to 1183. The bishop confirms to the abbey of Tewkesbury all the churches and other property which it had in his diocese. Among them were:

> The church of Llanblethian, with the chapel of St Donat, the chapel of St James of Llanquian, the chapel of Llansannor, with their remaining appurtenances. This chapel was dedicated and permission given for the burial of bodies, provided it should not be to the damage of the church of Llanblethian, to which it belongs by parochial right.

In this document two important facts are recorded: that the church of Llanblethian had become a possession of Tewkesbury Abbey by the second half of the twelfth century, and that there were attached to the church of Llanblethian the chapels of Welsh St Donat's, Llanquian and Llansannor. Llanblethian was thus the mother church of a large part of the commote of Tal-y-fan; two other churches in the commote (Ystradowen and Pendoylan) belonged to the cathedral chapter of Llandaff, while another church, that of Llanhari, was an independent rectory. Llansannor too had become a rectory by the middle of the thirteenth century, but Welsh St Donat's remained attached to Llanblethian until the twentieth century. The document quoted above is the only one extant that mentions the existence of the chapel of St James at Llanquian[15].

---

[15] See p. 30-31.

In 1254 the 'church of Llanblethian with its chapels' was valued at eighteen marks, or £12, while the vicar's stipend was a mere forty shillings. The larger sum would have gone to swell the coffers of the abbot of Tewkesbury who appointed a vicar (the word means deputy) to perform the services and other spiritual duties in the parish on his behalf. In 1254 Llansannor, referred to as 'Ecclesia de La Tawe', was separately valued at £3; it would be interesting therefore to know which were the chapels of Llanblethian by that date. Welsh St Donat's was certainly one of them, but was Llanquian chapel still in existence, and, even more important, had the chapel of the Holy Cross at Cowbridge yet been founded? (1254 was of course the year of the first charter of the borough.)

7. The Parish Church of St John the Baptist, Llanblethian, the mother church of Cowbridge. Although its origins lie in the remote Dark Ages, the present building dates from the 13th-15th centuries   *(Photo: Haydn Baynham)*

There seems to be no written reference to the church at Cowbridge before 1443 when a deed was drawn up 'in the chapel of the Holy Cross of Cowbridge'. That the building was already nearly two hundred years old by then is, however, fairly certain. The probability is that a chapel was established at Cowbridge soon after the borough was founded, or at least as soon as it began to show signs of rapid growth in the late thirteenth century. What, in the absence of documents, is to be learned from the fabric of the building itself? The building as it exists today displays a variety of styles of architecture, and it has evidently been altered and extended at different times. On balance opinion seems to be that the nave and chancel are basically late thirteenth century (there is a particularly fine piscina of this period in the south wall of the chancel), the tower perhaps early fourteenth century, and the arcade and south aisle of the nave are fifteenth century (the erection of this being traditionally attributed to the generosity of Lady Anne Nevill).

By the end of the Middle Ages Cowbridge church had become much larger than the parish church or mother church at Llanblethian, though some effort was made to enhance the dignity of the latter. The south transept, or rather chapel, at Llanblethian with its crypt[16] seems to have been added on to a mainly thirteenth-century building early in the fourteenth century; the imposing tower, of simplified Somerset type, was added in the fifteenth century. (Tradition again attributes the building of this tower to Lady Anne Nevill.) It may be that in order to show their superiority over the villagers of Llanblethian the townspeople of Cowbridge added a spire to the tower of their church at this time. (Dr Hopkin-James recounts the evidence and the traditions relating to the spire in *Old Cowbridge*, pp. 143-4.) The enlargement of Cowbridge church and the building of a tower at Llanblethian and spire at Cowbridge probably betoken an increasing prosperity in the district in the later fifteenth century.

There were other developments about this time in the services of the church at Cowbridge. In 1484 Richard III, as lord of Glamorgan, issued a charter by which he assented to a request from the burgesses and inhabitants 'of our town or borough of Kowbrygge' that they should be allowed to have a chaplain in the chapel of the Holy Cross to administer the sacraments. This provision of a chaplain seems to have been continued until about 1550, when one Richard Eles was in receipt of a salary of £4 a year.

Attached to Cowbridge church also was a chantry priest. The chantry was founded by a burgess, one William Prior, who endowed it with land and burgages which, in 1546, brought in a rent of £11 15s. 11d. Out of this

---

[16] The crypt was rediscovered during repairs to the church in the 1890s. The whole chamber was filled with the remains of about 250 persons together with portions of stone coffin lids. The bones were then reinterred in a large grave in the churchyard. Marianne Robertson Spencer recorded a much embroidered account of the skeletons in the crypt in her book *Annals of South Glamorgan*, p. 148; she seems to suggest that they were the bodies of those slain in a battle on the Stalling Down about 1400 (see note on p. 40).

8. Church of the Holy Cross, Cowbridge, built in the 13th century as a chapel of ease for
the townspeople   *(Photo: Haydn Baynham)*

income the priest received a stipend of £6. His duty was to say daily prayers
and masses for the repose of the soul of the founder, but especially to mark
the anniversary of his death (and probably that of his wife) with a solemn
celebration called an obit. For the two annual obits the sum of £1 16s. 8d.
was provided out of the endowment controlled by the feoffees, the vicar of
Llanblethian and two burgesses of the town. Part of this sum was given away
in doles to the poor. There was no requirement that the priest should be a
schoolmaster (as Dr Hopkin-James supposed), though it is, of course, quite
possible that he taught a school to supplement his income. It is not really
clear when the chantry was founded; there was a prominent inhabitant of
Cowbridge or its neighbourhood called William Prior living in the early
fourteenth century, but there is no reason to suppose that it was he who was
the founder. A man living in the late fifteenth century seems rather more
likely, the earliest hint of the existence of the chantry being contained in a
document of 1487 in which the feoffees of William Prior granted some
property in Cowbridge to one John Thomas son of John ap Evan ap
Thomas. The chantry was suppressed and its endowment was appropriated
to the Crown in 1548. The priest was granted a pension of £5, and in 1550
the King sold the former property of William Prior to Sir William Herbert,
soon to be created Earl of Pembroke.

There seems to be no doubt that 'Prior' was William's surname and not an ecclesiastical title; he was not 'William the Prior', as Dr Hopkin-James would have us believe, and there was no priory in Cowbridge in spite of Iolo Morganwg's including it in several lists of religious houses in Glamorgan. (Hopkin-James's object was, of course, to prove that the grammar school had its origin not in Sir Edward Stradling's foundation of 1608 but in a medieval priory-cum-chantry. Mr Iolo Davies has finally exposed the falsity of this idea in his book *A certaine schoole*, pp. 348-350.)

By the end of the fifteenth century the parish church at Llanblethian was served by a vicar and the chapel at Cowbridge by a chaplain and a chantry priest. The buildings in which they offered up the mass would have been recognisably those which stand today, though the decoration and furnishing would have been very different. Llanblethian church had two altars, one of them in what is now the south transept; it had a rood-screen and loft of some kind, but only the upper and lower doorways to the staircase now remain. At Cowbridge there were three altars — the high altar, an altar in the chapel on the north side of the chancel (probably the altar served by the chantry priest), and an altar at the east end of the south aisle of the nave (where the organ now is); the last named was probably the altar of St Nicholas mentioned in a clause of a mortgage deed of 1516 which allowed the redemption of the mortgage by repayment in gold marks and groats 'in the Rood Church of Cowbridge, upon the altar of St Nicholas, between the rising of the sun and the going down of the same'. The present screens[17] were erected about 1850 but they undoubtedly replaced an earlier rood-screen and loft which possibly closed off the east end of the south aisle as well as the chancel itself; the loft was probably reached by a stair in the south-west pier of the tower crossing. Since the Rood — the representation of the crucified Christ flanked by St Mary and St John — gave the church its name, it seems reasonable to suppose that the screen was surmounted by such a representation. The rood was probably cut down and destroyed about 1540.

In 1553 'a little before the death of King Edward the sixth', commissioners appointed by the King's Council came to Llanblethian and Cowbridge to confiscate any plate, vestments and ornaments which the religious changes of the Reformation had rendered unnecessary (at least this was the government's excuse). The local commissioners were Sir Edward Carne, Robert Gamage and William Bassett, prominent members of the neighbouring squirearchy. From Llanblethian church they took

> a chasuble of crimson velvet with the alb, a chasuble of purple velvet with an alb, an old cope of red chamlet with flowers, a latten [i.e. brass] cross with the images of Mary and John gilded, a banner of green silk of a yard long belonging to the same, two latten candlesticks and a holy water pot.

---

[17] The screen separating the nave from the choir was removed a few years ago, but that between the choir and the south aisle remains.

From Cowbridge church they had a much richer haul:

> a cope, a chasuble and two tunicles of green velvet, a chasuble of purple velvet, a chasuble of red velvet, a chasuble of blue silk, a chasuble of white satin, a cope [of] red damask, a cross of latten gilt and the foot of the cross, a pair of candlesticks, a censer, a basin and holy water pot of latten, a diaper napkin, whereof they [the vicar and churchwardens] say there was no part sold neither yet otherwise restored to the said town.

These catalogues of the royal commissioners' loot add some colourful details to our knowledge of the churches and their services in late medieval times. Many of the valuables seem to have been embezzled by the commissioners and their servants, for only a small quantity was publicly sold. In 1556, after repeated enquiries from Queen Mary, the commissioners admitted liability for a mere £15 for goods sold from the eastern hundreds of Glamorgan, though the goods, plate, jewels and ornaments of Llandaff Cathedral alone were said to have been worth £2,000 or £3,000.

During the same period of official spoliation of churches it is probable that any wall paintings there may have been in Llanblethian and Cowbridge churches were covered with whitewash. The evidence for this disappeared at Cowbridge when the church was restored in 1848-53. At Llanblethian in 1898, when the plaster was stripped and the stone walls exposed, one small fresco was found, a representation of some of the instruments of Christ's passion, namely a saw, sword and scourge depicted in red and yellow. Drops of blood of a dark red were painted under the teeth of the saw, the point of the sword and the lash of the scourge. There is no information about whether the churches lost medieval stained glass from their windows at the Reformation or during the Civil War and Commonwealth.

PART III

Early Modern Times, 1536-1900

Introduction: The Union of England and Wales

Until the series of acts of Parliament in 1536-43 which we know as the 'Acts of Union', Glamorgan was governed as a private estate, almost as a separate kingdom, by its lords and their officers. The lordship of Glamorgan like the rest of the Welsh Marches, was notoriously lawless, its administration corrupt and ineffective. In the 1530s King Henry VIII's government was faced with the tremendous political problem of the Reformation—the break with the Roman Catholic Church. In order to ensure the smooth acceptance of this policy the King and his chief minister, Thomas Cromwell, thought it expedient to reform the government of Wales by bringing it into line with the pattern familiar in England. For the future the county of Glamorgan was to be ruled by sheriff and deputy lieutenants and by magistrates meeting in quarter sessions. They would be chosen and appointed by the king from among the leading gentry families like the Herberts, Stradlings, Carnes and Bassetts. The English common law was to be enforced by the king's judges in the Great Sessions (or Assizes), or by the Court of Star Chamber in London and the Council of the Marches sitting at Ludlow. An important new privilege extended to the county was representation in Parliament at Westminster, the right to elect one member for the county itself to be chosen by the freeholders and another for the boroughs to be chosen by the burgesses. By these statutes of Henry VIII's reign the basic structure of local government and law-enforcement was established in Glamorgan and it was not substantially altered until the late nineteenth century.

The Tudor and Stuart Periods, 1536-1714

The town of Cowbridge was one of the beneficiaries of the royal policy which brought about the union of England and Wales. Its importance and dignity were much enhanced by its new status as one of the 'contributory' boroughs which, together with Cardiff, had the right to elect a member of Parliament. (In practice there was rarely a poll of the burgesses and the election was determined by the lords of the several boroughs. The member chosen usually belonged to one of the county families of Glamorgan.) The dignity and prosperity of the town were further promoted by its becoming the venue of the two new courts, the Great Sessions and the Quarter Sessions, both being held in Cowbridge once a year. On those occasions the 'county' would come to Cowbridge, and with them all who had business in the courts.

Although raised in dignity and importance by becoming one of the county towns of Glamorgan, Cowbridge's basic trade and wealth still depended upon the exchange of livestock and produce in the markets and fairs. The Elizabethan historian of Glamorgan, Rice Merrick, tells us that there were two weekly markets, on Tuesdays and Saturdays, and that there were two annual fairs, at Midsummer and on Holy Cross Day (14th September). The town remained, however, very small—hardly a town at all by present-day standards. The poet, Dafydd Benwyn, could write in his 'Poem in praise of the town of Cowbridge' of Babylon, Nineveh, Troy and Paris, but we find in more sober documents that in 1546 there were only 300 'houseing' people, that is people of an age to take Holy Communion— probably those aged 14 and over. The entire population at that time can hardly have numbered more than 450.

In 1543 the government levied a tax called a lay subsidy for the first time in Glamorgan. (This was one of the disadvantages of union with England!) In Cowbridge 68 people were taxed a total of £9 10s. 0d., a much smaller sum than the inhabitants of Cardiff or Swansea were called on to pay, but considerably more than Neath. The average tax was 2s. 1d. per person, yet one man, Roger Carne (whom we shall meet again) was assessed at £2 10s. 0d., and Elizabeth Bassett and John Rice at £1 6s. 8d. each. The great majority of the taxpayers had to find 4d. or less. Only people owning goods or land worth £1 were liable to pay the subsidy; we have no means of knowing how many were exempt on account of their poverty, but in many English towns they were as many as one third (and in some places even more) of the total. Given that one person in three was too poor to be taxed there would have been about 100 households in the town in 1543, which more or less confirms the estimate of 450 inhabitants made in the previous paragraph. In the parish of Llanblethian only 17 men were taxed in 1543, being required to pay a total of £1 9s. 4d. of which one man, John Turberville, paid £1 and Hywel ap John, ancestor of the Williamses of Aber-thin, paid 4s. 1d. Eleven of the taxpayers in Llanblethian paid only 2d. each. There were thus far more wealthy men in the town than in the sur-rounding rural parish. One interesting feature of the lists of names is that English surnames were still numerous though they were no longer over-whelmingly so; we find curious names like Gylinger, Flomaker, Bede and Mappe, alongside the more ordinary Smith, Taylor, Glover and Coke. But there were many men with names like David, Morgan and Rice, and six ac-tually still had the 'ap' in their names, John ap Rice and Llywelyn ap Richard for example. Welshmen were moving into the town.

Although the town was so small in the mid-sixteenth century and its tax-able capacity so low, there is every reason for believing that its prosperity was growing in the later sixteenth century, and probably its population too. The hearth tax assessment of 1670 allows another guess to be made at the number of the people; there seem to have been 87 occupied houses liable to the tax, 40 houses exempt from the tax because their occupants were too poor, and 17 vacant houses. There were perhaps something like 570 in-habitants in the town at that date; a similar calculation for the parish of Llanblethian gives a total of 540, but this is a little difficult to credit.

Further indications of prosperity and growth are seen in the histories of particular families and in the rebuilding of many houses along the High Street. The only Cowbridge families of the sixteenth and seventeenth cen-turies of whom much is known are the Seyses and the Carnes. A collection of deeds relating to the former is preserved among the Fonmon Castle archives, now in the Glamorgan Record Office. The earliest member of the family at Cowbridge was David ab Ieuan Sais (also spelt Saice, Sayes and Seys), mer-chant and alderman; despite his name, David son of Ieuan the Englishman was probably a Welshman from the hill country of Glamorgan, or possibly from the Border Vale. In the 1520s he and William ap John of St Hilary bought part of the manor of Eglwysbrewis, and David Seys alone bought land in Ruthin, Pendoylan and Talygarn. His two sons were also residents in Cowbridge even though both were usually described as yeomen, but his grandson, Roger Seys (*c*.1539-1599) became a successful lawyer and wealthy squire of Boverton Place. The most important family in the town and in the parish of Llanblethian seems to have been that of Carne. The Carnes first appeared in this locality in the first half of the fifteenth century; about 1430 Howell Carne of Cowbridge married Tibbet Giles, heiress of John Giles of Nash, and from that time until 1951 Nash was the main residence of the family. Many of the deeds still exist whereby Howell Carne and his grandson acquired property in Cowbridge, Llanblethian and other places in the Vale. Their town house was Great House in the High Street, or rather 'in the market place' as it was described in the sixteenth century; the existing façade of Great House is seventeenth century but this conceals a con-siderably older building. In the seventeenth century the Carne family leased a substantial part of the demesne lands of the manor of Llanblethian from the Earl of Pembroke; in 1668-69 Thomas Carne of Nash purchased the freehold of what came to be called Llanblethian Farm. Various members of the family continued to live in Cowbridge, for example Roger Carne, the wealthiest man in the town in 1543; he was a younger son who became the first clerk of the peace for Glamorgan. He died in 1550 a man of some wealth, but nothing like as successful as his distinguished brother Sir Edward Carne of Ewenny, whom Queen Mary sent as ambassador to the Holy See. William Carne of Nash (d.1582) and his wife were apparently buried in Cowbridge, for their son Sir Edward Carne of Nash erected a monument to them which is by far the most impressive one in the church.

The later Carnes of Cowbridge were Edward, one of the younger sons of this Sir Edward, and his descendants who held office as aldermen and bailiffs down to the middle of the eighteenth century. In 1763 the Rev. John Carne of Nash sold the Great House to the Rev. Daniel Durel, master of the grammar school.

Members of the Carne family were evidently at the heart of a series of affrays which disturbed the peace of Cowbridge and elsewhere in the Vale in the reign of Henry VIII. We know of the events of 1537 and 1540 only from documents prepared by opponents in lawsuits which were brought before the Court of Star Chamber; it is difficult therefore to know where, among the conflicting statements, the truth lies. The first incident occurred in February 1537 when William Carne of Cowbridge was attacked by three of Sir Rice Mansel's servants who had lain in wait in the house of Dafydd Thomas Lloyd in Cowbridge; Sir Rice claimed that this had been done without his knowledge. Carne further accused Sir Rice of attempting to overawe a court being held in the town by Roger Carne, presumably as bailiff. Mansel's reply to this charge is worth quoting at some length for the glimpse it gives of the way gentlemen behaved in the time of Henry VIII.

> On the 8th of May last, being the hundred [i.e. court] day kept in the town of Cowbridge, [this] deponent [i.e. Sir Rice Mansel] and his wife, with 15 or 16 servants, was riding to a house of this deponent's ten miles distant from his said place, at what time he came through the town of Cowbridge he alighted off his horse, and took two of his servants with him, and no more, and went to the Court there holding by Roger Carne for a matter [i.e. case] of this deponent's, where he could not be admitted to his attorney unless he had once personally appeared . . . and saith that he had a coat of armour on his back, and five or six of his servants likewise having some bows and arrows, some javelins, and some crossbows of this deponent. That he came not to the town of Cowbridge to the intent to hurt or displeasure the said William Carne; and saith that he and his said servants [wore] such coats of ferre [i.e. iron?] because the said Carne hath threatened this deponent and his servants.

In October 1537 George Herbert, younger brother of the William Herbert who was created Earl of Pembroke in 1551, was travelling from Abergavenny to Swansea with a retinue of armed attendants. He turned aside from the main road to spend the night at his mother's house at Penmark but sent eight of his servants on to Cowbridge to lodge at an inn. No sooner had they arrived at the hostelry of Lewis ap Richard[18] than a commotion arose.

---

[18] Lewis or Llywelyn ap Richard is almost certainly the leading Welsh poet of his day, better known as Lewis Morgannwg. According to the Rev. Thomas Wilkins of St Mary Church, Lewis lived by the cross in Cowbridge, which could mean that he kept the inn now known as the *Duke of Wellington*, formerly the *Black Horse*. Documents show that he was an alderman of Cowbridge by 1535 and that he was still alive in 1570. Lewis is another example of a Welshman moving down from the hill country of Tir Iarll (the Earl's land — modern Llangynwyd) and doing well for himself in the town.

Herbert's servants claimed that Roger Carne and a great number of townsmen, with swords drawn, attacked them, calling them knaves. Arrows were shot into and out of the house. The men were overpowered and so many as could be accommodated were locked up in the town dungeon. Roger Carne claimed that he had been attacked and wounded at George Herbert's orders, and that this was not the first time that Herbert had sent his men into the town with intent to do him harm. Herbert, of course, denied the accusations. The predicament of the bailiffs of Cowbridge when faced by disorder on this scale was made worse — indeed insult was added to injury — when they applied to Sir Rice Mansel at Beaupre to 'set an order in the matter'. As it happened, George Herbert was dining with Sir Rice when the bailiffs arrived; he replied to their request that he discipline his servants by boasting that if he and sixteen of his men chose to enter Cowbridge they would pit themselves against all the inhabitants of the town.

The feud between the Carnes and the powerful Herberts and Mansels was not yet done. In January 1540 John Carne was supervising the ploughing of some land called 'Pyssherley' or 'Parisshely', in the parish of Sully, the ownership of which was disputed between himself and Walter Herbert, the deputy constable of Cardiff Castle, a cousin of George Herbert's. Some servants of Walter Herbert's appeared in the field and demanded of the ploughman, 'Thou thief, what doest here in my master's close ground', and then struck him. Carne went to his servant's aid and was struck a blow on the head with a bill; the men made good their escape, but John Carne soon died. Justice was not to be had in Glamorgan where the criminals were protected by the most powerful family in the county, so Carne's widow was obliged to file a complaint in the Court of the Marches at Ludlow, and later to petition the Court of Star Chamber.

Gradually the beneficial effects of the reforms brought in by the Act of Union were felt in Glamorgan. The old seigneurial order was replaced by magistrates, judges and courts all owing their appointment to the King. Nevertheless it was generally the same men as before who held office under the new régime and it was several generations before the old violence, lawlessness and corruption were finally replaced by peace and good order. Only one more affray in the streets of Cowbridge is recorded. In February 1576 a battle was fought between the followers of several of the local gentry; what exactly happened and what was the cause of the dispute is not at all clear. But several men, including a petty constable, were injured and the Council of the Marches complained that the affray was 'a great disquiet to the whole country[19] and (as it is thought) likely by parts taking to work division in the country to renew their wonted malice and outrages'. There were certainly several notable feuds among the gentlemen of Glamorgan in the 1570s, and the incident at Cowbridge evidently arose from one of these.

---

[19] By 'country' sixteenth-century people meant their district or county.

9. The *Bear Hotel*, up to 1850 the main coaching inn of Cowbridge. Its 18th century
frontage conceals a partly medieval interior

(Photo: Haydn Baynham)

10. The *Masons' Arms*, a partly medieval building built into the town wall. The west
gate of the town stood here until 1753

(Photo: Haydn Baynham)

There was also a fairly general discontent among the leading families with the enormous power and influence wielded in Glamorgan by the ramified Herbert clan.

After 1550 the Herberts, or rather William Herbert Earl of Pembroke and his descendants, were of course lords of the manor of Llanblethian and borough of Cowbridge. In the absence of any of the borough records for this period it is very difficult to discover what sort of influence they actually exerted over the affairs of the town. Under the medieval charters they continued to appoint the constable or mayor, but this official probably had little to do with the town. There is, however, the possibility that the two silver maces, which symbolised the authority of the borough magistrates, were presented to the town by Mary, widow of the third Earl of Pembroke and sister of Sir Philip Sidney; they bear the date 1606 and the heraldic emblems of the Herberts and Sidneys.

Little is recorded about Cowbridge in the seventeenth century; there seem to have been few stirring events, and even the Civil War had little impact here, though armies on both sides must have passed through the town from time to time. Several of the local gentry took a part in the Civil War, on the King's side. Especially prominent was Sir Richard Bassett of Beaupre who was knighted by the King at the siege of Gloucester in 1643 and who was briefly and ignominiously governor of Cardiff Castle in 1645. Judge Jenkins of Hensol, one of the most redoubtable defenders of the royalist cause, was buried in Cowbridge church in 1663, and his monument may still be seen there.

Perhaps nothing is better proof of the quietly advancing wealth and prosperity of the town and district in the sixteenth and seventeenth centuries than the rebuilding of houses which took place at that time. There are traces of medieval architecture in the *Bear Hotel* and the *Masons' Arms Inn*, but many buildings along the main street of Cowbridge prove to have been erected between 1560 and 1700, though it is true that the general impression of the street is Georgian. Several farmhouses in Llanblethian parish are also of this period, for example Breach, Pant Wilkin and Maendy Ganol. The most distinguished house of the period is, however, Great House or Tŷ Mawr, Aberthin, which experts now tell us was built between 1625 and 1650. The curious gatehouse is also of this date. Until fairly recently the initials RW and date 1658 appeared on a sundial on the porch of Great House; this commemorated Robert Williams, a barrister, the son of William Thomas, the probable builder of the house. Very little is known of this family who were distant kin of the Gwyns of Llansannor; an heiress carried their estate to the Mathews of Castell-y-mynach, and their heiress in turn to the Lords Dynevor. In 1671 the house was assessed at ten hearths which made it by far the largest in the parish, for Great House, Llanblethian, was not built until 1702.

An instance of the commercial importance of the town of Cowbridge occurs in 1669. In that year William Bassett, a mercer, issued a half-penny

11. Tŷ Mawr, Aberthin, a fine house built in the reign of Charles I for William Thomas, an ancestor of Lord Dynevor   *(Photo: Haydn Baynham)*

12. Great House, Llanblethian, built about 1700 for Thomas Wilkins, a lawyer and official of the Court of Great Sessions

(Photo: Haydn Baynham)

brass token bearing the inscription WILL: BASSETT. MERCER / HIS HALFE PENY on one side, and IN. COWBRIDGE. 1669 on the other. This is the only token known to have been minted for a Cowbridge tradesman, though several are known for Neath, Swansea and even Llantwit Major. The tokens were privately minted to supply the need for small change, in the absence of an official copper coinage before 1672.

A final recognition of the town's status and dignity was accorded in 1681. King Charles II granted a charter of incorporation to the bailiffs, aldermen and burgesses of the town of Cowbridge, the town being described in the long Latin document as 'very ancient and populous'. Henceforth the bailiffs, aldermen and burgesses formed a corporation having its own seal and the right to own property. The mayoralty of the town was separated from that of Cardiff and was vested in the Constable of the Castle of Llanblethian, though the appointment remained in the gift of the lord of the manor and borough. The mayor, together with the two bailiffs, would be magistrates for the borough with the power to hold a court every third week and also a court of quarter sessions. The burgesses were authorised to elect twelve of their number to be capital burgesses, to join with the aldermen to form the Court of Common Council, the new governing body of the town. The bailiffs were still to be chosen by the aldermen with the approval of the mayor; vacancies on the aldermanic bench were to be filled from among the capital burgesses, and vacancies among the capital burgesses were to be filled by the surviving capital burgesses from among the body of the burgesses of the town. The charter named the first of the new bailiffs, William Bassett and Richard Phillips, and the new aldermen: Edward Carne, John Morris, William Miles, William Fream, Lewis Evor, John Powell, Richard Lloyd, Edward Bates and John Miles.

Since vacancies were filled by the choice of the surviving aldermen and capital burgesses, the Corporation was a very exclusive body, very little responsive to the wishes of the town at large. It also became the common practice to limit membership of the Corporation to particular families. The Carnes were an obvious case; the Bateses were even more tenacious and remarkable for their continuity of tenure over many generations. The Edward Bates nominated an alderman in 1681 is the earliest member of the family known to have lived in Cowbridge. He was in the town by 1670 and may well have been a medical man like his descendants, for many of them served the neighbourhood in this capacity until Victorian times; their hold on the office of alderman was, however, broken when some members of the family became Roman Catholics.

The Founding of the Grammar School
Sir Edward Stradling of St Donat's died on 15 May 1609 leaving unfulfilled his intention of setting up a school at Cowbridge in a building which he owned on the north side of the market place called Prior's Tower. Iolo Morganwg created a much more romantic and ancient beginning for the

13. The Grammar School, with the medieval south gate referred to by Leland as the 'Mill Gate' (Porth Melin). The present school buildings were erected in 1847-52 on the site of the original school built by Sir John Stradling early in the 17th century

(Photo: Haydn Baynham)

school which, he claimed, had originated from the famous college of St Illtyd at Llantwit Major. Local antiquarians seized upon Iolo's notion with enthusiasm — we have the long poem in praise of the school written by one of his protégés, Iolo Fardd Glas, a cooper from Aberthin. And, of course, we have the remarkable work of Dr L. J. Hopkin-James, to which reference is so frequently made in the present book. In addition to a learned review of the Illtyd tradition, which he elaborated with his own conjectures, Hopkin-James traced the history of the school through the (supposed) medieval priory and the chantry down to the time of Henry VIII. Tradition continued to the effect that the school had fallen into disuse at the dissolution of the monasteries and chantries to be revived early in the reign of Queen Elizabeth, and then to be re-endowed by the Stradlings early in the seventeenth century.

Mr Iolo Davies, in his history of the grammar school, has shown once and for all that this 'tradition' is what he calls an 'audacious fiction' concocted by Iolo Morganwg in the eighteenth century. The simple, unembroidered facts are that old Sir Edward Stradling had intended founding a school where youths might be 'instructed in the rudiments of grammar'. His intention was to 'place this school in the very front and face of this town, that is in that lofty tower which is situated almost in the middle of the market place, and as it were in the passage of all those who come to this market'. Sir Edward, on his deathbed, asked his heir to complete the setting up of the school. This Sir John Stradling did, but he preferred the secluded spot between the church and the town wall where the school stands to this day. What is known of the founding of the school comes from the remarkably competent Latin speech delivered in September 1618 by Evan Seys of Boverton, then fourteen years old, when Sir John Stradling visited the school. Mr Iolo Davies surmises that the speech had in fact been written by the Rev. Walter Stradling, the first headmaster and one of the baronet's poor relations; he certainly added a final paragraph of an extreme obsequiousness.

Very little is known of the history of the school in the seventeenth century. It was almost certainly very small; the founder had probably provided for free education to be given to ten poor boys from the town, but in order to maintain himself the master had to take in fee-paying pupils to supplement the meagre £20 a year allowed him from the endowment. Since it could be said that the education of the poor boys was the primary object of the foundation, the name 'Free School' attached to it for long before the more familiar 'Grammar School', came into common use in the nineteenth century.

Probably the most distinguished 'old boy' of the school is Sir Leoline Jenkins. Llywelyn ap Jenkin (to give him his original Welsh name), the son of Jenkin ap Llywelyn a yeoman of the parish of Llanblethian, attended the school from about 1635 until he went up to Jesus College, Oxford, in 1641. Sir Leoline was apparently born at Talygarn, in the parish of Llantrisant, and tradition describes his daily barefoot walk to school. On frosty mornings he would rouse up the cattle in the fields to warm his feet in the places where they had lain. But this is not an indication of poverty. His father was described as 'an honest, prudent, industrious man of about £40 a year'; he was thus a fairly well-to-do farmer who seems to have lived, at least in his later years, at Maendy. Sir Leoline's distinguished career took him from the principalship of Jesus College to Parliament, to an embassy at the Hague, to the Court of Admiralty and finally to the Privy Council and the Secretaryship of State. In an age of corruption he gained the commendation of Samuel Pepys, John Aubrey and Gilbert Burnet for his probity. His lasting contribution was to the building up of international law while he was judge of the Admiralty Court. He died a bachelor in 1685.

Sir Leoline ranks as the second founder of Cowbridge School, for shortly before he died he purchased the school premises from the Stradlings. His will was the foundation charter of the school for the following two hundred years or so. Ten poor boys would continue to be educated free of charge, and a further five called pensioners or monitors were to receive their schooling free and were to be given £6 a year for four years. To encourage them to proceed even further with their studies, the will established two scholarships and an exhibition at Jesus College for boys who had been pensioners at Cowbridge.

A portrait, now dark with age, hangs in the headmaster's study. It is presumably the one referred to in the will of Evan Jenkins of Maendy (the great man's brother), dated in 1702:

> I give and bequeath my dear Brother's picture to the Free-School of Cowbridge and that it may be fixed up in the said School and all my books which are useful for the said School.

The Georgian Era, 1714-1830

The prosperity and importance of Cowbridge had been growing since the sixteenth century; the town enjoyed its heyday in the hundred years or so that the first four Georges occupied the throne. As we have seen, the best estimate of the population of Cowbridge that it is possible to obtain for the seventeenth century is 570, in the year 1670. The first reliable figure that we have for the eighteenth century is 705, from what was evidently a careful count taken and recorded in the parish register in 1781. At the time of the first national census in 1801 there were 759 inhabitants in the town and 475 in the parish of Llanblethian. In the first few decades of the nineteenth century the population increased quite rapidly, reaching 1,107 in Cowbridge and 703 in Llanblethian by the time of the census of 1821.

Though still a small town by any standard, its population had more or less doubled since 1670, and by 1821 it was approaching the level of the early fourteenth century. Many new houses must have been built to accommodate the extra people. There is no detailed map of Cowbridge earlier than 1840 so we cannot easily trace the history of building, but it would seem likely that it was between 1750 and 1850 that the houses along Eastgate became more or less continuous and that Westgate was being developed to some extent. Another feature was the in-filling of the area within the old walls with small courts—such as Verity's Court—approached by narrow passages and under archways. Many of the wealthy of Cowbridge, living in the houses flanking the High Street, rebuilt or renovated their properties and provided them with well-proportioned façades, and a few with elegant porticos like the surviving one at Caecady House. Many of the buildings in the street still reflect Georgian prosperity and taste.

Some of the descriptions of the town which visitors and tourists have left us provide a valuable corrective, however. In the summer of 1775 Francis Grose travelled from London to Glamorgan in search of material for his book, *The antiquities of England and Wales*. In his diary he recorded that Cowbridge consisted of a single street of houses, 'some good but the major part only thatched cottages not unlike an Irish town.' A tourist known only by the initials C.C. visited Glamorgan in the summer of 1789. His account of Cowbridge is rather less perfunctory than Grose's:

14. Caecady House, once the town house of the squires of Caecady, Welsh St. Donat's

(Photo: Haydn Baynham)

Cowbridge is distinguished by its grammar-school, which is the most flourishing of any in Glamorganshire. The school-room is a handsome stone building, at the back of the master's house. The town-hall, in which the assizes for the county are sometimes held, is a tolerable building; but, as it stands in the high street of the town, it inconveniently narrows a part of it. The church is a heavy, ill-built structure, with a tower resembling that of a castle. There are many good houses in this town; but they are frequently disgraced by the immediate propinquity of wretched hovels.

A third account, by Edward Donovan, published in the year 1805, adds little, but confirms the general opinion of the appearance of Cowbridge at this period in its history. He and his companions approached the town from the direction of Cardiff:

The cluster of indifferent little cottages at the first entrance, present no very favourable indication of its opulence, but we had scarcely proceeded more than half way down the main street, before we began to perceive it to be a place of business, and some respectability.

The tourists were only one small category of people who were travelling the county in ever-growing numbers in the second half of the eighteenth century as the trade and industry of Glamorgan advanced. In 1764 some of the more enterprising landowners and others in Glamorgan obtained an Act of Parliament to set up a turnpike trust. In return for the right to charge tolls the trust undertook to make a road from Cardiff to Swansea, following the line of the existing road. In 1769 Arthur Young, the agricultural writer, testified to the fact that the road to Cowbridge was 'exceedingly good'. Toll gates were set up at either end of the town of Cowbridge and outside the ancient south gate on the road towards the mill. It was in order to facilitate the passage of traffic along the road that the east gate in the town walls (which stood between the *Horse and Groom* and the *Master Brewer*) was pulled down; it was apparently still standing in 1768, but had gone by 1775. (The west gate, by the *Masons' Arms*, had been pulled down in 1753 by Thomas Edmondes of Old Hall with the consent of the Corporation and of Lord Windsor.) The cross, the town hall and the market house, standing in the middle of the street, remained, however, serious hindrances to traffic through the town. In 1786 the mail coach began to run from London to Swansea three times a week; it changed horses at the *Bear Inn*, then kept by Christopher Bradley. The Bradleys were long connected with the coaching business in Cardiff and Cowbridge, and when Christopher moved from the *Bear* in 1804 he announced in the newspapers that he would continue the hiring of post chaises from his own house in Cowbridge, to the great chagrin of Michael Glover, the new landlord of the *Bear*[20]. Competition among the

---

[20] The story of this rivalry is told by Herbert Williams in his book *Stage Coaches in Wales* (1977), pp. 41-2. The post chaise was a carriage available for hire from one staging post to the next.

15. Verity's Court, now picturesque but one of the parts of Cowbridge criticised by the
inspector of nuisances in 1853   *(Photo: Haydn Baynham)*

leading innkeepers of Cowbridge was evidently very keen, for in 1785 the new licensee of the *Spread Eagle* was also advertising post chaises, in language which is worth quoting:

> If the best of wines, spirits, cyders, and malt liquors, with neat post chaises, and able horses, and obliging servants in all departments, and the most unremitting attention and assiduity to merit the countenance of the Nobility and Gentry passing thro' Cowbridge, can be called accommodation, they may be assured of receiving it from their most obedient and most humble servant, William Rees.

In 1796 the Corporation petitioned the Post Master General for the opening of a post office in the town; Mrs Cole was appointed postmistress in the same year.

Markets and Fairs
The increasing trade and prosperity of Cowbridge in the eighteenth century was, thus, partly the result of a greater volume of traffic using the improved road. More fundamental to the economy of the town were, as they had always been, the fairs and markets. In the sixteenth and seventeenth centuries there had been two annual fairs, at Midsummer and on Holy Rood Day (14 September), but the royal charter of 1681 appointed 23 April[21] as a fair day and the Holy Rood fair (probably dating back to the founding of the borough in the middle of the thirteenth century) fell into disuse. According to the diarist, William Thomas of Michaelston-super-Ely, Thomas Edmondes of Old Hall started a fair at Michaelmas (29 September), having somehow managed to transfer it from Ogmore:

> in 1752 he bought Brogwr's fair and brought ye same to Cowbridge which is still kept then at Michaelmas.

In 1789 the *Glocester Journal*, one of the weekly newspapers circulating in Glamorgan at that time, carried an announcement that a fair would be held on 24 March for the sale of cattle, horses and sheep, and that it would be continued annually on the Tuesday before 25 March. John Franklen of Llanmihangel is said to have been the prime mover in starting this fair in order to give farmers the opportunity of raising cash to pay their Lady Day rents. In the course of time 'March Fair' became the most important event in the commercial calendar of Cowbridge. By the end of the century there were thus four annual fairs held in the town. No description of an eighteenth-century fair seems to have been preserved, but it is reasonable to surmise that the main street of the town between the two ancient gates, and especially around the cross, the town hall and the market house, would have been crowded with country people and their animals and produce, with traders and dealers of all descriptions, with farm labourers and domestic

---

[21] When the calendar was altered in 1752 this was moved to 4 May.

servants anxious to be hired, and with people simply out to enjoy a holiday. At the end of each fair day there would be dancing in the numerous public houses of the town.

Several times in the year there were also what were called 'great markets' or 'high markets' which were something between a fair and an ordinary market. On other Tuesdays in the year the normal market for cattle and produce would be held; contemporary sources describe the Cowbridge market as 'plentiful' or 'good'. The market too was held in the High Street, but in 1806 a sheep market was constructed in the town ditch adjoining the wall and the *Masons' Arms*.

The Sessions

In addition to the serious business of the markets and fairs, Cowbridge in the eighteenth century added to its wealth and dignity by being host to the 'county'. The quarter sessions were held in the town each year in the week after Easter bringing hither the magistrates to transact the affairs of the county, and to try minor offenders and debtors. Throughout the eighteenth century also the king's judges came to the town once a year to hold the great sessions, in which the more serious civil and criminal cases would be tried. For about two decades, in the 1770s and 1780s, the judges held two courts at Cowbridge, in April and August, but from about 1800 the great sessions were removed from Cowbridge altogether and were held only at Cardiff and Swansea. On these occasions Cowbridge would be full of people of all sorts, ranging from the leading men of the county down to the unfortunates who had fallen into the clutches of the law. Sentences were savage for what we would regard as quite trivial offences; for example, the Rev. John Carne of Nash attended the quarter sessions in April 1770 and noted in his diary:

> We ordered a man to be transported for 7 years for stealing two hand-kerchiefs & a bit of ribbon. A severe sentence!

For stealing very little more the man might have been tried at the great sessions and then hanged on the Stalling Down. Technically it was 'grand larceny' to steal anything worth more than a shilling, and grand larceny carried the death penalty. In practice goods were often undervalued; the thief might then be convicted of petty larceny and be sentenced to be whipped or transported.

Quarter sessions were generally held in the comfortable and informal surroundings of the *Bear Inn*, but the pomp and ceremony of the great sessions required the more suitable setting of the town hall which was presumably properly furnished as a court room. The Corporation was frequently at the expense of repairing and improving the building mainly, it seems, lest the judges should decide to remove the sessions to one of the other towns in Glamorgan. In 1778 £100 was spent for 'repairing, widening and raising the Town Hall' and in 1782 additional rooms were built on to the east end, with a new shambles (or open-air meat market) beneath. There was constant

expenditure on painting, whitewashing and minor repairs. In 1774, when
he preached in the town hall, John Wesley noted in his journal that it was
the neatest place of its kind he had ever seen; 'Not only the floor, the walls,
the ceiling are kept exactly clean but every pane of glass in the windows.'

In the 1820s it was decided that the old town hall, together with the
market house (or weigh house) and the cross, would have to be demolished
in order to widen the High Street. Presumably the hall and cross (the history
of the market house is much more obscure) had stood in their prominent
positions ever since the founding of the borough, but busy nineteenth-
century traffic required a clear, broad road. A subscription was opened with
the object of acquiring the house of correction from the county magistrates
and enlarging this as a new town hall and market place. The work was completed in 1830 and the freedom of the town, enclosed in a box made of oak
taken from the old town hall, was presented to Isaiah Verity for his skill and
care in superintending the building operations.

House of Correction

Very little is known of the early history of the house of correction, or
Bridewell as it was often called. Each county was required to have such an
institution for the correction of idle and disorderly persons, where they

16. The Town Hall, built on the site of the House of Correction in 1830 to replace the old
town hall which had stood in the middle of the High Street near the junction with
Church Street   *(Photo: Haydn Baynham)*

might be set to work to earn their keep and to reform their characters. The original Act of Parliament was passed in 1576, but there seems to be no reference to the Cowbridge Bridewell before 1725; this is probably because the records of the quarter sessions for Glamorgan only survive from 1719 onwards. By the eighteenth century there was little difference between a house of correction and a gaol; a magistrate would often commit a person to Bridewell for some misdemeanour. A list of prisoners in Bridewell in 1729 gives some idea of the sort of offences which might lead to confinement there:

> Rebeka the wife of Thomas Thomas of Penmark committed by the worshipful George Howells Esq. for milking the cows of Madam St John.
> William Mireck son of David Mireck of Llantrisant committed by the worshipful William Bassett Esq. for being a person visibly disordered in his senses and has lately behaved himself disorderly to several persons.
> Jane William of the parish of Llanblethian committed by the worshipful William Bassett Esq. upon suspicion of stealing and taking away one blanket from the hedge of Margaret Butler.

A list of twenty-seven inmates in 1793-4 shows that ten had been committed for vagrancy and that four were illegitimate children (this was their 'crime'); four others had been imprisoned for leaving their work, two men had abandoned their families, someone else had been convicted of an unspecified felony, four had been imprisoned for breach of the peace, one had sold ale without a licence and one, John Hughes by name, is mysteriously described as an 'alien'. Few of them stayed inside longer than a month. The house of correction was thus part workhouse and part gaol. Dr Hopkin-James records some memories of the place that had been handed down to old people living about 1920. One person remembered hearing that gangs of prisoners from Bridewell used to work in the neighbourhood under the supervision of the turnkeys and governor armed with muskets. Another informant told Hopkin-James that he had known an old woman who remembered seeing a female taken out of Bridewell, naked to the waist, and beaten the length of the main street and back again by one of the turnkeys.

The eighteenth-century Bridewell may well have been an old building; in July 1751 the justices meeting in quarter sessions received a report on its state:

> Over the strong ward the boards are rotted and dangerous to tread on and the roof ready to fall, without rafters of one side, and the top stands upon props and ready to drop down, and [the] next room over the dwelling house without one sound board, and another chamber without gyves [i.e. fetters] having fallen down and rotten, two doors and three door frames wanted, and not a tolerable room in the house to live in, nor as much as a necessary place to ease their bodies.

Robert Lougher and Richard Deere, the mason and carpenter making this report, offered to make good the defects for £15!

The house of correction was rebuilt in 1806[22], and the façade was substantially preserved when the building was enlarged in 1830. The row of cells opening off a corridor leading from the council chamber is also probably a surviving part of the house of correction. It is unlikely that many people in Cowbridge would have regretted the news that the county magistrates had decided to remove the house of correction to Swansea and that the building would become the town hall.

Social Life

There was a lighter side to the solemn meetings of judges and juries and county magistrates. The weeks of their respective sessions were among the high spots of the social calendar in Cowbridge, and in the county at large. The gentry families of the neighbourhood would come to town during sessions week, and at other times, to attend the assemblies, dinners and balls, the horse races and performances by strolling players and other entertainers. The diaries kept by the Rev. John Carne of Nash[23] and by a fifteen-year-old pupil at the grammar school, Daniel Walters, son of the Rector of Llandough, in 1777-8 give us an outline of the main social events of the year, as well as fairs and high markets. On such occasions the school was almost invariably granted a 'playday'. On 2 August 1777 Daniel noted that Judge Williams[24] arrived to hold the great sessions. Two days later his brother went to the play at Cowbridge, and on the 7th he, his brother and Popkin, his father's pupil, went to the ball. On another occasion the young diarist records that he saw a play acted by Mr and Mrs Elrington; this was probably the Richard Elrington who is known to have been the manager of a not very distinguished troupe of players who were touring South Wales in the 1750s. And for at least a week in January 1778 mountebanks were in town. Daniel writes:

> The Mountebanks in general are mean, cheating Rascals, who go about the Country to take poor People's Money, give them nothing for it but a little Plaister. In short, they are no better than Thieves.

He is presumably quoting one of his elders, the master of the grammar school perhaps, or his straight-laced father, the Rector. The mountebanks were itinerant cheap-jacks and sellers of quack remedies, usually assisted by a clown or fool known as the merryandrew. They had indeed a universal reputation for sharp practice.

---

[22] See the sketch in John Richards, *The Cowbridge story*, p. 67.

[23] Carne's diaries for 1762, 1764, 1765, 1769, 1770, 1771, 1773, 1789 and 1797 are preserved among his family's papers in the Glamorgan Record Office.

[24] This was John Williams of Bodelwyddan who was for many years chief justice of the Brecon circuit.

17. The Eagle Stores. In the 18th century this was the fashionable *Spread Eagle Inn*. The wing at the back was the town's assembly room which later became the famous Eagle Academy   *(Photo: Haydn Baynham)*

The Rev. John Carne was a regular subscriber to the Assemblies which were held monthly in the winter, and in 1765 he records the payment of 10s. 6d. to a 'Musick Club'. In January 1789 he notes:

> We went to Cowbridge where Dr. Throckmorton & myself were stewards for the night. A very small meeting owing to the very cold weather. The Sieur Rea[25] exhibited his legerdemain. My subscription to the Assembly for the Season £1-1-0.

The Assembly Room was in the *Spread Eagle Inn* and it was the focal point of the social life of the gentry of Cowbridge and district. In 1758 John Wesley preached twice in the 'new Assembly Room', so we may assume that it dated from about that time.

We learn of other dramatic entertainments witnessed by the citizens of Cowbridge earlier in the century from the letters of the schoolmaster, Daniel Durel. On one occasion, in August 1745, there was more than the anticipated excitement:

[25] Le Sieur Rea was an Irishman who had adopted a French title for professional reasons. He was a well-known entertainer touring South Wales from the 1770s.

Just as ye shew was ending, and ye people getting up to go away the
beam which supported the room gave way, and the floor falling to
pieces, my poor little girl[26] (who was in a very dangerous place) and
the rest of the company fell all together into ye under room 9 foot high.
Several were bruised or wounded; but I thank God nobody was killed,
and she received only a slender bruise on her shin bone.

The date of Cowbridge race week in the 1760s and 1770s varied between
June and October; sometimes there were two race meetings in one year.
Later in the century the Glamorgan races were held in July, in alternate
years on the Stalling Down and the Great Heath outside Cardiff. A lengthy
notice appeared in the local and London press in 1769 announcing the
forthcoming three-day event to be held on the Stalling Down. Purses of £50
were offered on each of the days for the horse that won the best of three
heats. Evening entertainments included dinners and balls at both the *Bear*
and the *Spread Eagle*. The Rev. John Carne was a regular racegoer, atten-
ding twice in the summer of 1765; in September 1770 his expenses at the
Cowbridge races were £28 — a huge sum, much more than a labourer's
wages for a whole year. In the following year, however, he won about ten
pounds; 'which defrayed my expenses', he noted.

Another important event was the Mabsant or Revel, in the last week of
August. Squire Carne took his wife to Cowbridge mabsant in 1765 and spent
£1 1s. 0d. The mabsant was a popular festival, originally religious but by the
eighteenth century entirely secular. An advertisement in *The Cambrian* in
1817 gives a good idea of the nature of the entertainments offered:

> Rural sports and festivities at Cowbridge during the Revel Week on
> 28-30 August. On the Stallion Down, Galloway and pony races for
> different prizes, foot races, a race for a pig, running in bags &c &c.
> After every day's sports, dancing will commence at the Town Hall,
> White Hart and Black Horse at seven o'clock. NB. There will be a
> famous foot race between the Welsh Abraham Wood and the noted
> Abbey Man, for 20 guineas each. Ball playing every day.

Llanblethian and Aberthin, like almost every village in the Vale, also had
their mabsants, though these were much less elaborate than Cowbridge's.
Dancing was the main attraction in these festivals and was evidently the
main form of recreation enjoyed by the villagers throughout the year. At
Llanblethian there was even a special building for dancing called a 'pabell',
the Welsh for pavilion. David Jones of Wallington took down a description
of it from an old woman whom he interviewed in 1882:

> Outside the 'Picton' she said there was a *Pabill* for dancing in. It was a
> rudely-built structure, posts, with wattled sides and thatched. The
> young people of the village would meet twice or thrice a week for

---

[26] Durel's daughter Susanna, aged about ten at this time. She married John Franklen of Llanmihangel in
1765.

dancing. The paraphernalia of the *Morris Dancers* was kept in this 'Pabill'—*morris dancing* being then quite a recognised public amusement and frequent exhibitions of it were made about the country. The 'Pabill' at Llanblethian was accidentally burnt down. There was another like it at Penmark.

The races and revels were popular with both rich and poor, but much of the social life which we have described was available only to those with money to spare. Indeed, the wealthier inhabitants of the town and district had made every effort to provide themselves with what they thought to be the essentials of 'polite life'. An advertisement in the *Glocester Journal* in 1770 (admittedly inserted by someone trying to sell a house) went so far as to claim that Cowbridge possessed 'an exceedingly polite and social neighbourhood'. Iolo Morganwg, in a mood of social criticism which was not infrequent with him, poured scorn on the townspeople's social pretensions— 'aping they know not what'. An even more scurrilous attack upon the reputations of prominent citizens is contained in his well-known poem, 'Cowbridge Ale Triumphant', or the 'Cowbridge Topers'. Aldermen, doctors, attorneys, sundry tradesmen, and even their wives, are mocked for their prowess—'A glorious race of drinkers'. In subtler vein, John Walters, the brilliant eldest son of the Rector of Llandough, portrayed the gossiping town in a poem written about 1780:

> Yet happy town! thro' all the circling year
> They'll find no dearth of conversation here,
> Where still so many love to pry and prate,
> And one Night furnishes three months with chat.[27]

A generation earlier, Daniel Durel had had much more abusive things to say of Cowbridge:

> It is such an idle and wicked town, where there are Rakes able to corrupt almost an Angel, and continually doing mischief among my scholars.

No doubt the schoolmaster was feeling especially aggrieved about something when he wrote this, for one must believe that he exaggerated.

Having attended the sessions and indulged themselves in such social pleasures as Cowbridge afforded, the gentry often took the opportunity of conducting a variety of public business in the town. It seems fairly clear that Cowbridge was widely regarded as the most convenient of the four principal towns of Glamorgan—the others being Cardiff, Neath and Swansea—in which to hold meetings of the gentlemen of the county and of the clergy of

---

[27] The whole poem, written in the style of Alexander Pope, is printed in Iolo Davies, '*A Certaine Schoole*', pp. 375-6.

the diocese of Llandaff. The *Glocester Journal* carried reports and adver-
tisements of a whole range of meetings held in one or other of the principal
inns of Cowbridge. We read of the Society for the Relief of Widows and
Orphans of Necessitous Clergymen in the Diocese of Llandaff which met at
the *Spread Eagle*, a meeting of gentlemen and freeholders at the *Bear* to
petition Parliament for a renewal of the county's turnpike trust act; there
were weekly meetings alternately at the *Bear* and the *Dragon* of the Society
for the Apprehending and Prosecution of Felons within the County of
Glamorgan. These were all found in the 1780s. A more significant meeting
was that which took place at the *Bear* on 28 October 1772 when the county
grandees under the chairmanship of Thomas Mansel Talbot of Margam
founded the 'Glamorganshire Agricultural Society, for the Encouragement
of Agriculture &c.' John Franklen of Llanmihangel, farmer and land agent,
was undoubtedly the 'great motive power in the Society', as its historian,
John Garsed, said; he was the treasurer of the Society for half a century and
even the hypercritical Iolo Morganwg agreed that Franklen had been 'the
principal means of introducing the modern improved system of agriculture
into this county'. The Society offered prizes for the best livestock, for the best
field of turnips (the cynosure of eighteenth-century agriculturists) and for
bringing rough land into cultivation. Special meetings of the Society for the
exhibition and judging of stock developed into the annual show which was
held at various centres in the county—more often than not at Cowbridge
itself—through to the end of the nineteenth century. (The Vale of
Glamorgan Agricultural Society, which supplanted the Glamorgan Society,
has held its annual show at Cowbridge or Penllyn since 1892.)

Schools, Books and Printing
In addition to its economic, administrative and social importance, there was
a side to the life of eighteenth-century Cowbridge which, difficult to define
in a single word, included intellectual, scholastic and literary activities cen-
tring upon the schools, the library, the book societies and the printing press.
   By 'schools' one means principally the Free School or Grammar School.
During the period 1714-1830 the grammar school was in a more or less
flourishing condition under a succession of remarkable headmasters, the
Rev. Robert Powell (1704-21), the Rev. Daniel Durel (1721-63), the Rev.
Thomas Williams (1764-83) and the Rev. Dr William Williams
(1787-1847—an amazing reign of sixty years). Between the two Williamses
came the brief headships of the distinguished Walters brothers, John and
Daniel, whose names have already been mentioned in these pages. The story
of the school is fully told in Mr Iolo Davies's excellent book, '*A Certaine
Schoole*', published in 1967, and readers are warmly urged to refer to it for
the detailed picture which is given there—especially of Durel whose personality comes so clearly through his many surviving letters. During Durel's
later, crotchety years the school seems to have declined in reputation and
numbers which angered the tradesmen of the town who looked to the school

as an important source of income. In a petition for his resignation they claimed that in Robert Powell's time there had been between sixty and a hundred boys in the school, bringing the town £1,000 a year from boarding and clothing. Among the pupils at the school were the sons of many of the gentry families of South Wales in addition to the poor scholars from Cowbridge district educated under the provisions of Sir Leoline Jenkins's will. For example, an account survives of an incident in which a seventeen-year-old pupil, John Williams, son of the squire of Abercamlais in Breconshire, was rumoured to be in love with Miss Carne of Cowbridge. John admitted to his headmaster

> that he had talked with her through the surgery window and had walked down to the Mill and back with her, but had only talked of trifling matters and nothing of love.

The Free School was, however, not the only school in the town. Information about the numerous private-venture schools and of the famous Eagle Academy is much too slight and fragmentary for an adequate account to be given. In Durel's time 'Mr Pearson ye writing-master' was called in to the grammar school to provide instruction in penmanship and arithmetic—since Durel taught only Latin and Greek, with perhaps a little Hebrew. Mr Pearson probably had his own private school in the town. In 1771 there is reference to 'Mr Thomas Roork, Master of the boarding and writing school at Cowbridge'. Whether Pearson's and Roork's schools can be thought of as forerunners of the Academy is not clear, neither is it exactly certain when the Academy first opened. The *Spread Eagle* was one of Cowbridge's leading hostelries in the 1780s but by the beginning of the nineteenth century its premises had become the home of the Academy presided over by Mr Thomas Williams and Mr Thomas Rhys. The obituary notice of Thomas Williams printed in *Y Gwron Cymreig* for November 1839 is worth quoting (in translation):

> There died on the 24th October in this town aged 81 Mr Thomas Williams who kept the Eagle School for many years; and it is likely that no other school in the kingdom had greater renown: from it came a very great number of well-informed and reputable scholars, who will hear this news with sadness and deep grief.

In the late 1790s we read that Thomas Rhys—who appears to have had charge of the junior or infants section of the school—went to St Hilary to teach handwriting to John Montgomery Traherne and his sisters, and about 1812-15 John Sterling[28] attended the school. Sterling published his recollections of his early days in Llanblethian and Cowbridge, of which the following passage is a sample:

---

[28] John Sterling (1806-1844) became a well-known writer, man of letters and central figure of the 'Sterling Club'. The Sterling family lived in Llanblethian from 1809 to 1815.

At the entrance of the little town stood an old gateway, with a pointed arch and decaying battlements. It gave admittance to the street which contained the church, and which terminated in another street, the principal one in the town of C---. In this was situated the school to which I daily wended. I cannot now recall to mind the face of its good conductor, nor of any of his scholars; but I have before me a strong general image of the interior of his establishment. I remember the reverence with which I was wont to carry to his seat a well-thumbed duodecimo, the *History of Greece* by Oliver Goldsmith. I remember the mental agonies I endured in attempting to master the art and mystery of penmanship; a craft in which, alas, I remained too short a time under Mr R--- to become as great a proficient as he made his other scholars, and which my awkwardness has prevented me from attaining in any considerable perfection under my various subsequent pedagogues. But that which has left behind it a brilliant trait of light was the exhibition of what are called 'Christmas pieces'; things unknown in aristocratic seminaries, but constantly used at the comparatively humble academy which supplied the best knowledge of reading, writing, and arithmetic to be attained in that remote neighbourhood.

Thomas Carlyle, Sterling's famous biographer, visited the district in the 1840s in search of background material—his description of Llanblethian as 'a little sleeping cataract of white houses, with trees overshadowing and fringing it' is still well-known, and still appropriate. Carlyle learnt that Thomas Rhys was yet alive and was remembered by his pupils as a worthy, ingenious and kindly man who wore drab breeches and white stockings. Thomas Rhys died in 1851 and was buried in Llanblethian churchyard.

The grammar school, the Eagle Academy and the other private-venture schools of the eighteenth and early nineteenth century provided sound education for pupils of all ages, for the sons of farmers and tradesmen who wanted a good 'commercial' education, and for the sons of gentlemen who were to learn Latin and Greek in preparation for the universities. A rather more exotic note is struck by an advertisement inserted in *The Cambrian* (the Swansea newspaper) in January 1815:

> Cowbridge French Academy will re-open on Monday 30th inst., where Ladies & Gentlemen will be taught to speak and write this beautiful language with purity and correctness, by Mr Bates, late of Douay College, French Flanders. Terms per quarter 10/6—Entrance 10/6—Private tuition in town and country on moderate terms.

The schooling of the children of the poor was not yet something given serious consideration except by a few pious individuals. Francis Wyndham (1670-1716) founded a charity school in Cowbridge under the auspices of the S.P.C.K., but nothing is known of this school apart from the mere fact of its existence. The famous 'circulating schools' of Griffith Jones of Llanddowror were held in the parish of Llanblethian on at least ten occasions (sometimes in the village, sometimes at Aberthin or Trerhingyll) between 1739 and 1760, but it is very difficult to assess the impact they may have had on the literacy of the poor.

The educated men of the town and neighbourhood were the gentry and members of the learned professions — clergymen, physicians and lawyers; most of the gentry doubtless spent their leisure in pursuit of foxes rather than in adding to their stock of learning. In 1711 the Society for Promoting Christian Knowledge decided that Cowbridge would be the most suitable place in which to deposit a collection of books intended principally for the use of clergymen and schoolmasters of the diocese of Llandaff, or especially of those living within ten miles of the town. Francis Wyndham of Clearwell, Gloucestershire, seems to have been the person instrumental in obtaining this benefit for the town and district; he belonged to the family of Dunraven Castle, and his father Serjeant John Wyndham had lived in what is now called Woodstock House in Cowbridge. There are two sets of instructions extant which give some idea of the problem of conveying anything so bulky as the S.P.C.K. library from London to Glamorgan at that time; the Bishop of Llandaff said that the books should be sent to Bristol by wagon, thence by boat to Aberthaw, and the final five miles by another wagon. Wyndham's instructions, however, were that the books should be sent by the carrier to Mr Sandamore, a woollen draper in Wine Street, Bristol, by whom they would be forwarded by boat to Mr Morgan at Cardiff, where one of the trustees of the library would receive them. The contents of the library over the hundred and thirty years of its existence in the church at Cowbridge were largely, if not exclusively, theological. Nothing in it would have come under the heading of 'light reading'.

Several attempts were made to provide more palatable fare for the clergy and gentry to read, through book societies, though here again there was nothing like the romantic novels stocked by the circulating libraries satirised by Sheridan in *The Rivals* (1775). The Cowbridge Book Society, founded in 1736 and revived in 1764, was closely connected with the S.P.C.K. library and the grammar school. There were, however, not enough learned men hereabouts to support such an institution once the initial enthusiasm had waned, despite the attraction of the annual dinner at the *Bear*. Another effort of a similar kind, the Cowbridge Clerical Book Club, lasted for rather longer, from 1817 to 1834.

One of the most interesting and important men who was connected with the S.P.C.K. library was the Rev. John Walters, Rector of Llandough, already mentioned as the father of John and Daniel Walters. He deserves to be mentioned again in an account of eighteenth-century Cowbridge because it was he who was responsible for one of the most remarkable developments in the history of the town. In 1769 the Rector's life's work, his *English-Welsh dictionary*, was sufficiently well advanced for him to begin to think of

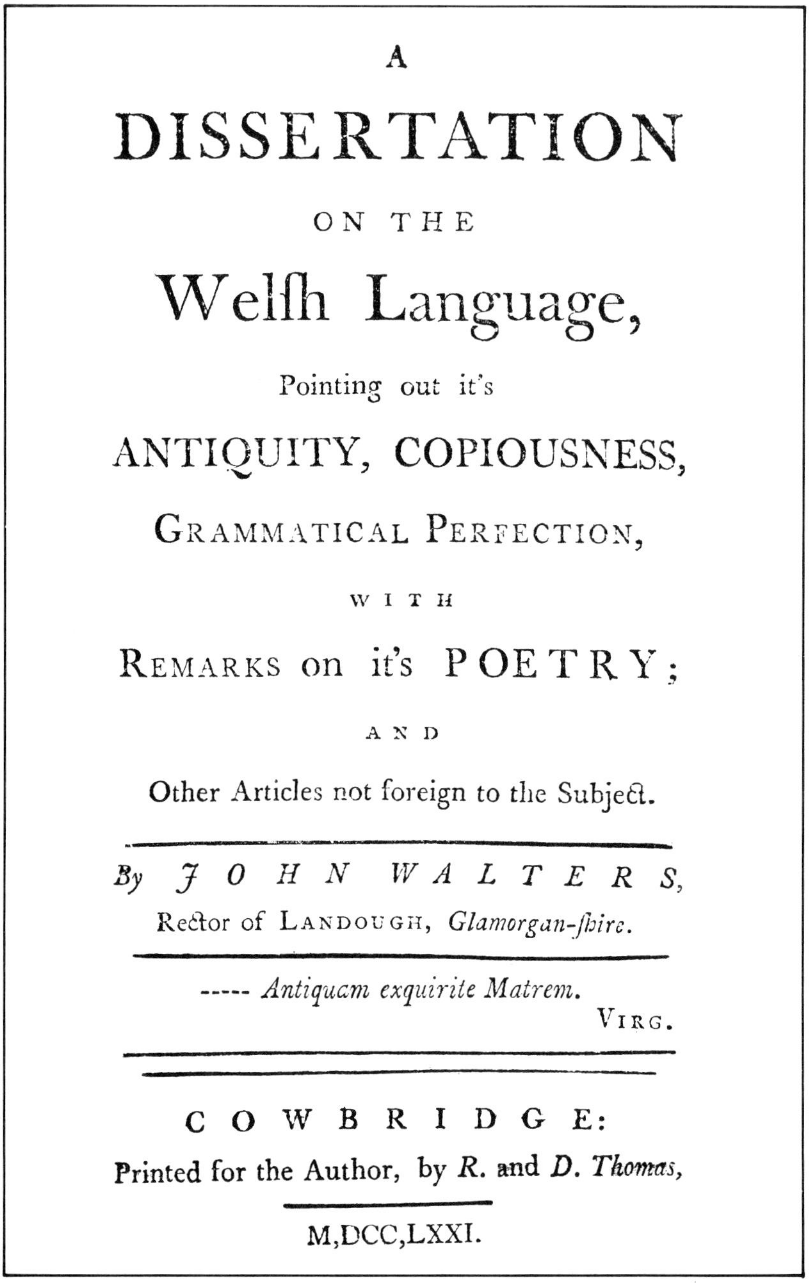

A

DISSERTATION

ON THE

Welſh Language,

Pointing out it's

ANTIQUITY, COPIOUSNESS,

GRAMMATICAL PERFECTION,

WITH

REMARKS on it's POETRY;

AND

Other Articles not foreign to the Subject.

By JOHN WALTERS,
Rector of LANDOUGH, *Glamorgan-ſbire.*

----- *Antiquam exquirite Matrem.*
VIRG.

C O W B R I D G E:
Printed for the Author, by *R.* and *D. Thomas,*

M,DCC,LXXI.

18. *A Dissertation on the Welsh Language*, by the Rev. John Walters, printed at Cowbridge by Rhys Thomas in 1771. This was one of the first, and the most elegant, products of the Cowbridge printing press

publication. He had exacting standards and there were few Welsh printers capable of taking on such an enormous and complex task. Walters was about to take his manuscript to Bristol when he received an offer from Rhys Thomas of Llandovery; within a few months Rhys Thomas had set up a printing office in Cowbridge[29]. He was the first printer ever to exercise his craft in the county of Glamorgan; he was among the best Welsh printers of his day.

The first instalment of Walters's *Dictionary* was published at Cowbridge on 5 April 1770, priced at two shillings. The fourteenth part of the *Dictionary*, bringing the great work down to the word 'stain', was printed and published in the town in 1783. The business of the printing office proceeded smoothly and efficiently for the first three or four years. By 1773 Rhys Thomas had printed seven parts of the *Dictionary* together with an impressive range of other works, of which John Walters's *A dissertation on the Welsh language* (a sort of preface or introduction to his *Dictionary*) and Iolo Morganwg's elegy on the death of Lewis Hopkin the bard of Llandyfodwg, *Dagrau yr awen*, are the most noteworthy. From 1774 onwards clouds gathered over the printing office and the essentially unreliable character of the printer became more and more obvious to the exasperated Rector of Llandough. Publication of the *Dictionary* slowed down to one instalment in each of the years 1774, 1775 and 1776, and then one in each alternate year 1778, 1780 and 1782. From a series of letters written by the Rev. John Walters we can follow some of the difficulties and frustrations. In November 1774 he wrote:

> The 9th Number would have been published ere this but that the ink at the Office hath run short, and I am amazed that Thomas, the Printer, who is either now in London, or on his journey homewards has not sent down some, as he promised to do immediately upon his arrival in Town.

Rhys Thomas was involved in some lawsuit which dragged on in the courts at Westminster for years and was still the subject of rueful comment by the Rector in 1778 and 1779. What the business was about we have no knowledge since it could hardly have arisen from a disgraceful incident in Cowbridge in 1774, as a result of which 'certain printers . . . to wit Daniel Thomas, Rees Thomas and Gamaliel Davies', were charged with assaulting one of the sergeants at mace (the bailiffs' officers) who had come to arrest Daniel, Rhys's brother. The outcome of this episode is unknown, but it may be significant that 1774 was the year in which the affairs of the printing office in Cowbridge began to go awry. The next crisis in the printer's career came in 1777. Daniel Walters noted the following in his diary under date of the 14th of May:

---

[29] Probably at 70 Eastgate. See 'The Cowbridge Printers', in *Glamorgan Historian*, vol.IV (1967), for a more detailed account.

Courtliness Dillynder moesau, &c. See Civility, and Complaisance.

Courtly, Boneddigaidd ei ymadrodd a'i ymddygiad, moesawg, moesawl, da ei foes, llawn moesau da, tebyg (yn) ei foes i ŵr llŷs, llysawl. See Courteous, &c.

Courtly [elegant; flattering] Dillyn-foes, dillyn, destlus; gwenhieithus, gwenieithgar, &c.

Courtship [the making love to a woman, &c.] Carwriaeth, caru; ymgaru: ymerlyniad am fodd gŵr mawr, &c.

To cousen. See to Cozen.

Cousin [a title of relation] Câr (fem. cares), cytgar, câr o waed, cŷd-waed, câr-ŵr; undràs.

Cousin by marriage, Cyfathrachwr, cyfathrachddyn, cystlynol o herwydd priodas.

Cousin-german, or first cousin, Cefnderw, cefnder; pl. cefnderwedd, cefnderwydd, cefnderoedd, and cefndyr: fem. eyfnither, cyfnitherw, cyfnithderw, cefnither, &c.

The grand-children of cousin-germans, Ceifnaint (fing. ceifn).

A cousin-german removed, or second cousin, Cyfyrder (pl. cyfyrdyr), vulgò cyferdder.

Cow, Buwch (pl. buchod, ¶ gwartheg), buw, bu, buch, ¶ henfon (See Cowbridge), biw. ¶ Curst cows have short horns [Prov.] Da gwaith Duw, roi cyrn byrrion i'r fuwch a hwylio (ar fuwch weinad).

A little [young] cow, Buchan, buwchan, buchig, anneir-fuwch, treisiad-fuwch, ¶ cyn-flith.

A barren [dry] cow, Buwch hesp. See Barren.

A cow with [vulgò in] calf, Buwch gyflo.

A farrow-cow, Mysfwynog.

A milch-cow, Buwch flith; pl. ¶ gwartheg (da) blithion.

A hard cow [that with-holds her milk] Buwch gronnedig.

A cow desiring the bull [vulgò a tufty cow] Buwch wasod (derfenydd).

A cow's desire of the bull [vulgò the tuftiness of a cow] Gwasodrwydd (terfenydd) buwch.

A cow that draws near her time of calving [vulgò a leech-cow] Buwch ddowydd (Verb—Dowyddu: Subst.- -Dowyddiad).

A cow that hath a calf, Buwch mam llo.

A cow-herd, Bugail (heusor) gwartheg.

A cow-house, Beu-dy, cawty, glow-ty.

Cow-dung, or cow-turd, Biswail, tail (tom) gwartheg.

Dried cow-dung [in some places used for fuel, and called Cow-blake] Glaiad (fing. glaiaden); clêd (fing. cleden).

Having many, or abounding with cows, Gwarthegog.

Cow-wheat [in Botany] Glinogai.

A cow-yard [where cows are milked] Buches, buarth.

To cow [dishearten, keep under, &c.] Digalonni, gwan-galonni, ofni, torri yspryd (càlon, awch) un, hurtio, llyfrhàu.

Coward [a poltroon, or one who wants courage] Dŷn llwrf (llwfr, digàlon, gwan-gàlon, annewr, anfilwraidd, anwraidd, di-yspryd, ofnog, ofnus, anhy, llegach, cachad, llegys, lleferthin); anwr, llyrf-was: vulgò cil-gi, cach-gi.

Cowardice, or cowardliness [excessive timidity] Annewredd, llyrfder, llyrfdra, &c. See lack, or want of Courage above.

Cowardly, Llwrf, llwfr, digàlon, &c. See under Coward.

Cowbridge [a town in Glamorgan-shire] Y Bont faen.- - N. B. Pont faen (i. e. Stone-bridge) seems to be nothing but a corruption of Pont-y-fôn (i. e. Cowbridge); nor will the transition be thought at all unaccountable by such as are conversant in etymological enquiries.—— That Bôn signifies- -a Cow- - and Y Fôn - -the Cow - - is clear from the following Proverbs, viz. - -Y sawl a biau'r hen fon ym'aeled yn ei chynffon;-- i. e. Let him, whose the old cow is, lay hold of it's tail (in order to assist it to rise): quasi dicas, Let him, who is interested in the affair, take the toil upon him. Newydd bennyg yn hen fon; i. e. New (young) tripe in an old cow : - - a Proverb used to express one's disbelief of an improbable story; as if one should say - -I as much believe it as I do that there is young tripe in an old cow. —It may serve to corroborate what hath been here offer-ed, to mention, that the Arms of the Town are, A Cow : - - that an ancient Chorographer, sirnamed Ravennas, writes it Pontuobice, as it should seem, for Pont-y-buch, Pont-y-fuch, alias Pont-y-fôn, - -and that there is at this day, at the west-end of the Town, a little bridge called Pont-y-fuwch.—It must not here be disguised that Dr. Davies (in his Dictionary) hath Henfon, Vacca; i. e. A Cow simply. But the Proverb quoted above affords more than a Presumption that he was herein not sufficiently attentive ; for Newydd and Hén are evidently contrasted with, and opposed to, each other,

Cowcumber. See Cucumber.

Covered [unskimmed] Heb dynnu ei hufen, â'i hufen arno.

Covered-milk-cheese [i.e. made of unskimmed milk] Caws llefrith, caws drwy hufen, caws llaeth o dan ei fam.

Cowl [a monk's hood] Cwfl (hŵf, cwccwll, penguwch, pen-wisg) mynach, &c.

Cowl [a two-eared tub, where-in water is carried on a pole between two] Mydd, mit, ystondir, ystondart.

Cowl-staff,

19. John Walters's *English-Welsh Dictionary*, printed at Cowbridge between 1770 and 1783. This page shows Walters's account of Cowbridge itself

To the Printer's office to seize the Goods. Mrs Thomas after sending C. [i.e. Caleb, her son] backwards and forwards many times came with tears in her eyes to entreat my Father to come to Cowbridge. He went, and the goods being appraised, bought them.

The printer's business affairs were evidently in a mess, but the Rector's generous purchase of 'the goods', which probably included the printing press itself, made no great difference to Rhys Thomas's conduct. Walters's letters to his London friend Owen Jones (Owain Myfyr) become more bitter as he complains of the indolence of both printer and compositor. He recognises his correspondent's readiness to sympathise with him in his trouble 'under the burden of my unyielding task'. In January 1779 the Rector again wrote to his friend in London:

I am vexed to tell you how slowly the Press goes on with the work which the Printer suffers every insignificant job to break in upon mine for no other reason that I can assign but that he is ungrateful and thinks I must now continue with him, though he use me ever so ill.

The final crisis in the tangled affairs of the first of the Cowbridge printers came in 1783. In a letter dated from Cardiff gaol on 22 November in that year, Rhys Thomas humbly addressed his reverend patron to inform him that he had been unable to find a substitute for himself who could both compose and handle the press. The printer was evidently in gaol for debt as we may learn from a poem written on the occasion by his assistant, Siôn Morgan, who had not been paid his wages:

> Diar ddeddf yn hir ddihangodd,
> O'r diwedd hi a'i daliodd,
> Ac a'i rhoes yn Siael Caer Dydd,
> Er maint ei ffydd am nefoedd.
>
> — — —
>
> Ag yno boed ei drigfa
> Nes talo'r ffyrling eitha . . .

(From the law he long escaped, at last it caught up with him, and put him in Cardiff gaol, despite his great faith in heaven. And there let his dwelling place be till be pays the last farthing.)

Siôn Morgan's mocking verses brought forth a reply from John Williams of St Athan rebuking him for being a drunkard and for rejoicing in an old friend's misfortune. We hear no more of the unfortunate Rhys Thomas after this, and in 1790 John Walters officiated at his burial in the churchyard at Llandough.

The Rector's solution to the problem of keeping the printing press working while the master printer was in gaol was to bring home his son, Henry, then aged seventeen who had been since the beginning of 1783 learning the printing trade under Robert Raikes, publisher of the *Glocester Journal*. He could not have learnt his craft very thoroughly in that short time. In the following March Henry Walters printed a handbill respectfully informing 'the gentlemen of this county, &c. . . that Printing in general is executed with neatness, care, and dispatch, at the Printing-Office, in this Town, on the most reasonable Terms, by their most humble Servant . . .'

However, Henry Walters was not equal, either by training or by temperament, to the task of running a business. He moved his premises in 1784 or 1785 to Ballard's Court, more or less opposite the *Bear*, and there he lived for the rest of his life, growing gradually more eccentric. The Rev. William Williams of Swansea saw him once and left this description (the original is in Welsh) of the man who was known as the 'Cowbridge hermit':

> His face had not felt the razor for ten years at least; and it did not appear that there had been much acquaintance between him and soap and water for some time. His unkempt hair hung to his waist, and his body was covered by a single loose, grey garment from his neck to his heels. The house clearly showed either that there was no broom or that it was unused. Henry was always in the house, amidst the dust and the dirt, the ashes and the books. Yes, books; he could manage those splendidly. It was said that he used to go out secretly at night to gaze at the stars. If small children went to the door to satisfy their curiosity by taking a look at him, a piece of wood, or something worse which was within reach, would probably address their shins . . . but he allowed friends to come inside and sit down; and it was no little edification to sit an hour with Henry Walters. He would speak of the worlds which revolve in the sky above, the hidden treasures of the earth beneath, of languages and nations beyond the seas, and of mountains and birds, and fishes, and everything.

The hermit died in 1829 and his books and manuscripts were carted up to the Stalling Down and burnt.

The printing press had been sold in 1791 to John Bird of Cardiff 'for the trifling sum of Seventeen Guineas'. The Rev. John Walters lived on until 1797, though now much broken by the deaths as young men of his elder sons, John and Daniel, of whom so much had been expected. His one joy was the completion of his *Dictionary*. Anyone looking at this very substantial book will see nothing there to tell him of the long struggle of its author to print it in Cowbridge, for the title-page merely mentions the date 1794 and the fact of its having been printed for the author in London.

Iolo Morganwg

'Iolo Morganwg', the bardic name of Edward Williams of Flemingston, is mentioned so frequently in this history of Cowbridge that it seems appropriate, if not actually necessary, to draw together scattered references to this the strangest man to have been born and bred in the Vale of

Glamorgan. Some account of Iolo's career and personality is made doubly necessary by the misleading impression of him which readers of older works of local history may have gained.

Edward Williams was born at Pennon, near Llancarfan, in 1747 the eldest son of Edward Williams, a stone-mason, and his wife Ann Matthews. The family was not especially poor by the standards of the time but it was certainly the case that Ann Matthews had married beneath her, since she had been brought up at Boverton Place with her distant relatives, the Seyses. Clearly his mother was the great influence in Iolo's life and character; he was her favourite son and she taught him to read in her small collection of English books. English was the language of their home. As a young man Iolo began to meet local poets and educated men of the district who encouraged him in his early steps on the road to literature and scholarship. He had no formal schooling but was apprenticed to his father's trade; on one occasion he claimed to have learnt to read by watching his father cut letters on tombstones.

Despite his lack of a proper education, Iolo Morganwg grew into a man of extensive learning, wide reading and astonishing range of interests. He became, in particular, the great authority of his day on the literature and history of Wales; his familiarity with the manuscripts wherein the treasures of the Welsh language were preserved was profound; he spent much of his time travelling on foot between the Welsh country houses and the English libraries in which these manuscripts were kept. His special interest was in the traditions of his own county of Glamorgan—its dialect, its poets, its history, its folklore, everything. Only a little of his great store of knowledge was published during his lifetime; he was one of a group of scholars who published an edition of Dafydd ap Gwilym in 1789 and a massive collection of Welsh poetry and prose—the *Myvyrian Archaiology*—in 1801-7. In 1794 he published two volumes of his own English verses entitled *Poems, lyric and pastoral*. But his knowledge and his theories were widely disseminated in occasional articles in such periodicals as the *Gentleman's Magazine*, and in endless conversations with admirers who clustered around him in his later years when his reputation as the great Welsh scholar, the sage, the eccentric but ever honest countryman, was secure and unquestioned.

All this is true; Iolo Morganwg *was* the most learned Welshman of his day; his knowledge of the manuscripts *was* unrivalled. But his was a dual personality. A romantic by nature, a dreamer, a drug addict (he took laudanum to relieve his asthma), he became unable to distinguish truth from fiction. His undisciplined imagination led him to embrace strange theories, especially about the fashionable 'druidism' of eighteenth-century antiquarians, and it was but a step from the theory to the fabrication of the documents necessary to prove the theory. Iolo Morganwg was, of course, the originator of the Gorsedd of the Bards which he managed to associate with an eisteddfod held at Carmarthen in 1819—since when the eisteddfod (a genuinely ancient institution) and the gorsedd (a complete fake) have been

inseparable. The essential premise of the theory was that the Welsh bardic
order had originated in the ancient Celtic order of druids—the priests of the
ancient Britons; Iolo claimed to be the only surviving inheritor of the
mysteries of the bards; he was therefore also the only surviving druid.

The fictions of Iolo Morganwg and the documents and chronicles, poetry
and even vocabulary and an alphabet, which he wrote or invented, bedevill-
ed the study of Welsh literature and history for more than a century after his
death, and even gained strength with the posthumous publication of
Cyfrinach Beirdd Ynys Prydain in 1829, the *Iolo M.S.S.* in 1848, and
Barddas in 1862-74. Iolo's works had great authority among nineteenth-
century students of the Welsh past, and even when some of his ideas and
documents came to be suspected no one doubted Iolo himself, especially
since his reputation for simple, unbending honesty had been so completely
established by Elijah Waring's biography, *Recollections and anecdotes of
Edward Williams, the bard of Glamorgan*, published in 1850. Perhaps no
one has ever been more thoroughly taken in than honest, naive Elijah
Waring. It was not until Iolo's immense collection of notebooks and papers
was deposited in the National Library of Wales in 1916 and the late Professor G. J. Williams began his lifetime's research into them that the real
character—and indeed the real scholarly achievement—of Iolo Morganwg
began to be appreciated. The rogue was found out because he had carefully
preserved every scrap of paper that he had ever written on; the evidence for
the forgeries was overwhelming. It took many years for this new assessment
of Iolo to become generally accepted; the Rev. Dr Hopkin-James of
Cowbridge was perhaps one of the last scholars of repute to cling to the old
view. Alas, even now writers of local history sometimes rely upon documents
which were composed by that brilliant but perverted mind. Nor are
professional scholars immune from such mistakes. For example, the entry
from *Brut Aberpergwm* quoted on p. 23 has been used to date the founding
of the borough of Cowbridge in fairly recent books by two eminent
authorities, M. W. Beresford and Harold Carter. Ironically, Carter's book
was actually printed in Cowbridge!

The Cowbridge connections of Edward Williams the stone-mason and
businessman and of Iolo Morganwg the bard, scholar, visionary and literary
forger were very important and interesting. For a man whose home was at
Flemingston, Cowbridge was inevitably the local centre to which he would
go more or less frequently. He was the intimate friend of the Walters family
of Llandough and in 1772 Iolo's first booklet, *Dagrau yr awen*, was printed
by another friend Rhys Thomas. A much less happy event occurred in
August 1786 when Iolo was taken to court in Cowbridge by two of his many
creditors, Evan Griffith of Penllyn and Dr John Walton of the town. He was
unable to pay and was promptly committed to Cardiff gaol where he remained until set free at the great sessions of August 1787. After a period in
London when he had tried to set himself up as a literary figure much as
Robert Burns had (successfully) done in the *salons* of Edinburgh, Iolo

Morganwg returned to Glamorgan in 1795 and soon afterwards set up as bookseller in the High Street at Cowbridge, traditionally where Bird's shop is now. (In 1926 the site was marked by a plaque with a Welsh inscription.) In fact he sold books, stationery and grocery and attempted to start a small circulating library. Many stories (doubtless quite untrue) were later related by the Bard about his shopkeeping experiences. He claimed to have been the first person in Wales to sell East Indian sugar. Since this commodity was produced by free labourers not slaves, he advertised it in his shop window as 'East India Sweets, uncontaminated with human gore'. Elijah Waring retold several other stories about the bookshop and Hopkin-James printed a list of books which Iolo claimed he had ordered from London from time to time,

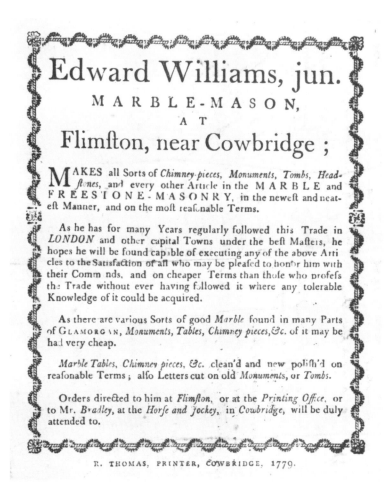

20. A handbill printed in 1779 by Rhys Thomas for his friend Iolo Morganwg, here referred to by his real name, Edward Williams, marble-mason

21. The plaque placed on the wall of R. S. Bird's shop in 1926, the centenary of Iolo Morganwg's death. He is thought to have kept a bookshop here in 1795-6

(Photo: Haydn Baynham)

but we need not take this satire on the unbookish neighbourhood too seriously[30]. About this time of his unsuccessful and soon abandoned bookshop Iolo also wrote his libellous poem on the 'Cowbridge Topers', to which reference was made on p. 50. Another product of his vitriolic pen is that other well-known poem on the Cowbridge sexton. Dr Hopkin-James demurred from quoting this in full but it may be of sufficient interest to be reproduced here:

> Here lies interr'd upon his back,
> The carcase of old surly Jack,
> Fe dyngwys lawer tra fu fyw
> Myn crog, myn Cythraul, a myn Duw,
> With many a curse and many a damn,
> Da gwyddai'r Diawl ag yntau pam,
> But now he struts, a blustering blade,
> Lle mae'r iaith honno'n iaith y wlad.

It is hardly worth learning Welsh just to find out what it means!

---

[30] *Old Cowbridge*, pp. 89-91.

Iolo Morganwg, the bard of Glamorgan, died peacefully in his fireside chair in the cottage at Flemingston where he had lived most of his life. That was in December 1826 when he was in his eightieth year. A monument to him and to his son Taliesin was placed in the church there at the time of its restoration in 1855, but their graves are unmarked.

Cowbridge and Llanblethian in Victorian Times

The heyday of Cowbridge lasted perhaps until about 1830, or at the very latest 1850. C. F. Cliffe, author of *The book of South Wales* published in 1847, commented:

> Cowbridge is an old-fashioned town, chiefly consisting of one long street, which is likely to bear a crop of grass, as soon as the South Wales Railway is in operation.

The bustling market town, social centre of the county gentry, one of the four chief towns in Glamorgan, had become by the middle of the nineteenth century 'old-fashioned'. David Jones of Wallington, the talented local historian born in Llanblethian, has three vivid sentences which show the almost catastrophic decline in the importance of the town by the 1860s:

> Tuesday is the Market day and hither come from the 'Vale' on one side and the scanty Villages on the other all who have farming stock and produce to sell or who require to buy household necessaries. On the remaining six days of the week the long single street of the town might be used as a ground for Rifle practice with but small danger to any of her Majesty's subjects. It will thus be seen that the sole trade of the town is only that derived from its being the centre of an agricultural district.

What had happened to bring about this decline?

The basic reason was that Cowbridge could no longer compete on equal terms with the other towns of Glamorgan. It had never been the largest of them, yet none of the other places had been very much bigger; but by 1831 Cowbridge had only 1,097 inhabitants compared with Cardiff's 6,187, Swansea's 13,256 and Neath's 4,043, while the rise of new industrial communities such as Merthyr and Aberdare had shifted the county's centre of gravity away from the Vale and into the hills of Blaenau Morgannwg. Cowbridge did not become involved in the industrial development of the county. Another important reason for the decline of the town's importance was, perhaps unexpectedly, the improvements to the main road which passed through the town. As we have already mentioned, the town hall at Cowbridge was removed to widen the street, and several realignments of the road — to avoid the steep ascent of the Stalling Down, for instance — were made. One such realignment had a much greater significance; the main road was diverted through Bridgend instead of passing from Brocastle

through Corntown, over Ewenny Bridge and so on to Laleston Cross.
Opened in 1832, the new stretch of road gave a fillip to the growth of
Bridgend as the main urban centre and market of Mid Glamorgan.
Bridgend had never previously been a rival to Cowbridge but by the mid
nineteenth century it was a busy and growing town with 2,000 inhabitants,
serving the rural area of the western part of the Vale and the expanding industrial settlements of the Llynfi Valley.

The final blow to the importance of Cowbridge was, as C. F. Cliffe had
predicted, the opening of the railway between Cardiff and Swansea in 1850.
The original intention of the promoters of the railway was to route it
through Cowbridge, but the leading property-owners and members of the
Corporation, fearful that the coming of a railway would undermine their
control of the town, successfully opposed this scheme. Bridgend was confirmed in its new prosperity. In 1850 the mail coach ceased to run through
Cowbridge and in the same year the quarter sessions for the county were
held in the town for the last time. Markets and fairs remained important,
for there was no lack of prosperity among the farmers of the Vale, but the
wider functions which had made Cowbridge for so long one of the 'county
towns' of Glamorgan ceased and the valuable casual trade from travellers
along the road likewise vanished, for after 1850 everyone went by rail. In
1853 a correspondent of the *Cardiff and Merthyr Guardian*, reporting on
that year's Cowbridge show, remarked:

> The want of railway accommodation reduces Cowbridge and its
> delightful environs to a state of hopeless isolation, and cuts them off
> from the rest of the world . . . The absence of the greatest improve-
> ment of the age confines Cowbridge to the humble position of a small
> country market town, and there is not at present any hope of its
> advancement.

The stagnation of the town in the middle decades of the nineteenth century is brought out very clearly by population figures. The figure of 1,107
reached by 1821 remained very little changed for the next fifty years, for in
1871 there were 1,134 inhabitants in the borough. The population of
Llanblethian fluctuated rather more but even there the 703 inhabitants of
1821 had only become 756 by 1871. One might suppose therefore that
Cowbridge was more inward-looking, a less interesting and less lively place
in 1850 than it had been in 1750; and so it probably was. On the other
hand, it is possible to find out far more about the town as it was in 1850 than
in 1750 for the simple reason that the sources of information available to us
are richer and more detailed and varied. For example, it is possible to
discover who owned and occupied each house and each piece of land from
the Tithe Plan and Apportionment of 1841-44; the name, age, occupation
and birthplace of each resident can be found in the unpublished records of
the Censuses of 1851, 1861 and 1871; much interesting information may be
gleaned from a number of directories, the earliest published in 1835, which

include Cowbridge. And there are many other sources which, taken together with those already mentioned, enable the historian to reconstruct a much more complete and rounded picture of the town as it was in Victorian times than at any earlier period in its seven-hundred-year history.

Tradesmen, Craftsmen and Publicans

Perhaps we might begin by attempting to sketch the trades and occupations of the inhabitants of the town around about 1850. It has proved surprisingly difficult to discover precisely what trades were followed in Cowbridge in earlier centuries; obviously there were innkeepers, carpenters, shoemakers, and the like, but in what numbers and in what proportions it is impossible to say. Of the more unusual trades and crafts we have only the occasional glimpse; for instance, there were apothecaries, printers and clockmakers in the eighteenth century—it is interesting to note that the oldest grandfather clock in the Welsh Folk Museum's collection was made by Phillip Walton of Cowbridge about 1710. Perhaps one of the most interesting questions is, when did retail shops make their appearance in Cowbridge? Generally in country towns this was a development of the sixteenth and seventeenth centuries. Traditionally the customer bought either directly from the man who actually made the desired article, or did his or her shopping from stalls set up in the street on market day. By 1850, however, there were many retail shops in Cowbridge, but there was still some reliance upon market stalls (especially for fresh food—there were no butchers' or greengrocers' shops as yet) and on the purchase of goods direct from craftsmen's workshops.

The census of 1851 returned a total of 274 males of twenty years and more resident in the borough of Cowbridge. By occupation these can be divided as follows:

Gentlemen and Professional Men	25
Shopkeepers and Innkeepers	38
Craftsmen	123
Minor Professions, Functionaries etc.	38
Farmers and Farm Labourers	29
Labourers (trade unspecified)	20
Unstated	1

The figures are not so cut-and-dried as this table suggests, for several innkeepers, for example, also had a trade or craft, and a number of craftsmen were also small farmers. But the general idea of the occupations of the inhabitants is clear enough. The range of trades and crafts included the following:

flannel manufacturer	carpenter	stationer
tailor	joiner	grocer
bookbinder	cabinet-maker	druggist
shoemaker	wheelwright	hairdresser

saddler	coach-builder	draper
tanner	cooper	innkeeper
skinner	clock & watchmaker	publican
fellmonger	miller	maltster
chandler	tinplate worker	victualler
currier	(i.e. tinsmith)	hostler
hatter	nailer	groom
builder	puddler	boots
tiler	blacksmith	hawker
plasterer	butcher	farmer
glazier	baker	gardener
painter	ironmonger	farm labourer
paper-hanger	timber merchant	carrier
stone-mason	coal merchant	waggoner
sawyer	bookseller	lodging-house
		keeper

This is a marvellously long and varied list which shows in a particularly telling way how self-sufficient a small country town was in the middle of the nineteenth century. The large number of men following certain of the basic trades is even more surprising; there were 23 shoemakers, 15 stone-masons, 15 tailors and 12 carpenters and joiners.

Although it is not entirely comparable to the complete list of inhabitants and their occupations to be found in the census records, we can gain some impression of the way the commercial life of the town had changed by 1914 by studying the list of names published in Kelly's *Directory* in that year. The following trades and occupations are mentioned:

bootmaker	coach-builder	shoe shopkeeper
shoemaker	tailor	publican
boot repairer	cabinet-maker	beer retailer
printer	shopkeeper	coal merchant
watchmaker	grocer	haulage contractor
baker	greengrocer	hairdresser
builder	fishmonger	chimney-sweep
stone-mason	confectioner	laundress
blacksmith	butcher	garage proprietor
painter	stationer	cycle dealer
plasterer	draper	agricultural
house decorator	chemist	merchant
plumber	earthenware dealer	wine and spirits
cooper	ironmonger	merchant
brewer	newsagent	lodging-house keeper
saddler	fried fish	photographer
harness-maker	shopkeeper	

The main trend shown by these two lists is that between 1851 and 1914 the retail trades attained a much greater prominence in the town, while the handicrafts declined. This means that by 1914 fewer goods were both made and sold in Cowbridge than had formerly been the case; the town had become much less self-sufficient. Photographs of the High Street around 1900 show virtually as many retail shops as exist nowadays.

Another aspect of the town's trade is represented by its numerous public houses. The census, the tithe map, the minute books of the Corporation and various directories provide an answer to the much-canvassed question of how many licensed premises there used to be in Cowbridge. The answer, in the first place, must be that their number fluctuated. Many of the public houses were surprisingly short-lived, and in fact only two of the present inns can be traced back any distance into the past without either a change of location or a change of name. They are the *Bear* and the *Masons' Arms*. The *Duke of Wellington* is probably one of the oldest inn sites in Cowbridge (see note on p. 50), but it has gone through several changes of name, acquiring its present one in the early 1850s probably as a tribute to the Iron Duke at the time of his death and magnificent funeral in 1852. It seems that about the year 1850 the licensed houses listed in the following table were open to those wishing to slake a thirst in the town; undoubtedly they varied quite a bit in their clientele and in the standard of hospitality they offered. (Those marked 'B' were only beer-houses or beer-shops[31].) On the south side of the street, beginning at the west end of the town there were:

Names of Inns (*c*.1850)	Present Site
Bush (B)	private house, 2 Westgate
Masons' Arms	*Masons' Arms*
Black Horse	*Duke of Wellington*
Cowbridge Arms	South Wales Electricity Board's showroom
Royal Oak	Gaskell & Walker
Farmers' Arms (B)	
Butchers' Arms (B)	*Master Brewer*, until recently known as the *Red Dragon*
Blue Bell	Spar Supermarket
Tennis Court	old cinema, 60 Eastgate
Cross Keys (B)	vacant premises, formerly the Wesleyan chapel
Druids (B)	private house, 44 Eastgate
Crown (*Crown & Anchor*) (B)	private house, Cardiff Road

[31] These were not strictly speaking 'licensed premises' since anyone could open a beer-shop, under the Sale of Beer Act of 1830, on payment of a two-guinea excise fee. This Act led to an immediate increase in the number of places in Cowbridge where liquor could be bought; in 1833 there were 15, in 1835 there were 19 and by 1836 21. Beer-houses had to be licensed by the justices after the Wine and Beer-House Act of 1869.

22   The Ancient Druids, Eastgate, Cowbridge, formerly one of the town's many licensed
premises   *(Photo: Haydn Baynham)*

On the north side of the street, beginning at the east end, there were:

Red Lion ⎫ *Edmondes' Arms* (B) ⎬	*Edmondes' Arms*
Horse & Groom	the present inn is on an adjoining site
Three Boars' Heads	Peter Alan, 25 High Street
White Lion	Lois, 27 High Street
Greyhound	*Vale of Glamorgan Inn*
Bear	*Bear*
Pelican	R. Townsend & Co., 7 Westgate
Westgate (B)	private house, Westgate House

The certain total for 1850 is twenty-one, though possibly two more should be included[32]. A few years later the *Globe* (in the Butts), the *Green Dragon*, the *Ship Aground* and the *Nag's Head* were in business. There were further additions to the list in the East Village after the opening of the railway — the *Commercial Hotel*, the *Railway* and the *Bridge* appear in the 1870s — but other public houses closed down, and there were probably never more than 23 licensed premises in the town at any one time. In 1914 the number was down to 21 again.

In earlier times publicans had brewed their own beer from malt supplied by one or other of several maltsters in the town and district, but as the century wore on most did not brew, relying instead upon supplies from a local brewery. The first brewery, owned by Samuel Howells, was in Malt House Lane, opposite Old Hall[33]. He, together with four others, is listed under the heading 'Maltsters' in Pigot's *Directory* (1835). In 1858 he is listed as 'Maltster and Brewer'. One of the leading citizens of Cowbridge in the late nineteenth century was Lewis Jenkins who founded the Vale of Glamorgan Brewery at 51 High Street about 1870. His son started the Cowbridge Brewery, by the river, in the 1890s. There was another brewery at Aberthin for a time around the turn of the century.

The trades and occupations of the rural surroundings of Cowbridge show a considerable contrast to those of the town itself, of course; more than half the population of Llanblethian were in fact employed on the land either as farmers or as labourers of different kinds. There were also several rich

---

[32] The *Nag's Head* in Westgate is named in the 1851 census, but the tenant is described as a 'kitchen gardener'; the same tenant in 1861 states his occupation as 'Victualler and agricultural labourer'. The other problem is the *Ship Aground*, situated between the *Blue Bell* and the *Butchers' Arms*; it was in existence in 1835 and 1841, but is not heard of again until 1861; it is not safe to presume its continuing existence between those two dates.

[33] The Old Brewery was demolished in the summer of 1977. The west wall of the building proved to be that of an early fourteenth-century house, but most of the remainder was of eighteenth-century date.

families living in the village or in mansions scattered about the parish—John Samuel-Gibbon of Newton and Ralph Thurstan Bassett of Crossways were leading members of the fox-hunting landed gentry in Victorian times, but there was no one who could claim to be the 'squire' of Llanblethian. There was also a remarkably diverse and varied range of tradesmen and craftsmen. Among the occupations mentioned in 1851 were:

mason	coal carrier	coachman
painter	lime-burner	huntsman
tailor	roadman	footman
weaver	maltster	general servant
carpenter	miller	gardener
thatcher	chimney-sweep	waggoner
shoemaker	hay dealer	gamekeeper
cooper	grocer	farm labourer
tinman	victualler	farmer
wire worker	schoolmaster	drainer
sieve maker	auctioneer	haulier
broom maker	letter carrier	woodward
butcher		

The parish was well provided with public houses and beer-houses in the middle years of the nineteenth century: the *Cross Inn*, the *General Picton* (by the Church), the *King's Head* (in 'Piccadilly'), the *Royal Oak* and *Hare and Hounds* in Aberthin, and the *New Inn* and *Fox and Hounds* in Trerhingyll. David Jones of Wallington, who was born in Llanblethian in 1834 and whose family subsequently lived at Great House, has left us a lively account of the two public houses in the village, both long since closed.

> Dancing for some years has been discontinued, and the revel has sunk into a mere sottish carousal. Our host John o' the Picton emulates his neighbour Shon-y-Gwaith[34] as to who shall have the best tap and the competition for that honour causes each of them to add an extra bushel of malt to his brewing, to gratify the village topers. The thing [i.e. the revel] is probably finished up with a little fighting, at least it is a portion of the standing annual gossip of the village to enquire after the event 'Has there been any fighting?' The General Picton is by far the best house of the two—close to the Church it derives all the benefit that bell ringing, marriages, and burials can bring it, as well as being the place of meeting for all parish vestries. But 'Shon-y-Gwaith's' is the oldest house, and, down in the village, must be considered the village ale house. Shon-y-Gwaith (John the Weaver)'s[35] name is quite a

[34] Had David Jones been more familiar with written Welsh he would have spelt this name 'Sion y Gwehydd', i.e. John the Weaver. The weaver-innkeeper's real name was John Thomas; he was 71 years old in 1851.

[35] See footnote 34.

23. A view of 'Piccadilly', Llanblethian. One of the cottages shown was formerly the *King's Head*, home of the 19th century character, Sion y Gwehydd

(Photo: Haydn Baynham)

household word at Llanblethian, and popular consent has conferred his name upon the little 'public' instead of the name it bears on the sign. If you wanted the house you might ask 20 people in the village for its whereabouts, not one of them could at a first thought tell you anything of the King's Head, but ask for 'John the Weaver's' and the youngest child that plays at the roadside will tell you. Johnny is a village character. Far advanced in years his physical strength has survived his mental, he presents the sad spectacle of an active old dotard. His delusion—which has been slowly creeping on . . . for many years—is that the whole parish belongs to him, and he goes on acquiring fresh estates year by year. Those who should know better . . . encourage him in his delusions . . . Poor old fellow.

Like most country innkeepers, John also followed a trade. He was one of seven weavers in the parish in 1851, mostly working in their own homes. But there was also something called the 'Factory', the history of which is by no means well documented. 'William Price, woollen cloth manufacturer, Llanblethian' is listed in Pigot's *Directory* of 1835, but it is difficult to establish when the factory was set up as such. On the other hand it is known that it stood on or very near to the site of a tucking mill mentioned in a deed of 1637 and that on one of the maps of the Llanmihangel estate (1782) it is shown as part of a tenement described as 'House, Garden, Felt Mill & Croft' rented from Charles Edwin by Edward Ballard and Son. In Worrall's *Directory* (1875) Evan John is described as a 'Flannel manufacturer & all kinds of woollen goods, stocking yarns, &c'. In Kelly's *Directory* for 1895 the name of Mrs Jane Howell, flannel manufacturer, appears. Miss Maud Gunter wrote the following interesting account of the factory in an article published in *The garden of Wales* in 1961:

> Possibly the oldest inhabited house [in Llanblethian] is the former woollen factory at the extreme western end of the village . . . on which Mr. and Mrs. Rhys Roberts have spent ten years in loving restoration, opening up a very solid medieval stone stairway, exposing the oaken rafters and establishing that the original building was a single storey, for the shoulder of the first roof is visible in the first floor. The detached building on the other side of the brook is (apart from its windows) almost as old as the main building where the wool was washed, carded and spun. It housed at least two looms. The mill pond was west of it, fed by a leat, now overgrown, parallel with the brook. The millwheel and looms are now at St Fagan's. Even sixty years ago many of the older villagers wore the products of this factory both for underwear and outer garments, especially the 'brethyn llwyd' [36] so serviceable for country wear. The women spinners and the weavers lived in the village except in the final phase of its existence when it depended on itinerant weavers. Cloth and flannel were taken into Cowbridge and Bridgend on market days within living memory and among the customers were the cockle-women of the Swansea area for whom a special black flannel with narrow scarlet stripes was woven. The factory ceased to function before the first World War.

Churches and Chapels

By 1850 the great majority of those who attended religious worship in Cowbridge and Llanblethian (and these were, of course, a large majority of the population) were nonconformists. The wealthier and more influential sections of society—the gentry and the professional class—had generally remained faithful to the Established Church of England, and the Vicar (who was the head of the dominant Edmondes family) characterised the social status of the nonconformists in his parish in reply to the bishop's visitation queries of 1848 thus:

> Their rank is that of trades people and of the labouring or menial class.

Nonconformity had its local origins in the Methodist Revival. On 10 July 1742 the Welsh Calvinistic Methodist leader, Howell Harris, preached at a

---

[36] Grey cloth.

house in Aberthin and there was soon a permanent society meeting there, for whom a chapel was built in 1749. The first visit of John Wesley to Cowbridge on 7 May 1743 was, by contrast, a disaster. He described the occasion in his journal:

> We came into the town about eleven, and many people seemed very desirous to hear for themselves concerning the way which is everywhere spoken against. But it could not be. The sons of Belial gathered themselves together, headed by one or two wretches called gentlemen, and continued shouting, cursing, blaspheming and throwing showers of stones, almost without intermission. So that after some time spent in prayer for them, I judged it best to dismiss the congregation.

This stoning of Wesley and his hearers is said to have taken place in front of the town hall. Wesley did not come to Cowbridge again for six years, but on the second occasion and on at least sixteen later visits up to the year 1790, he was invariably well received and listened to by large congregations who packed the assembly room (behind the *Spread Eagle*) or the town hall. In 1780-1 the Wesleyan Methodists of Cowbridge built their own meeting

24. Ramoth Chapel, Cowbridge, the Baptist Chapel built in 1828

(Photo: Haydn Baynham)

house or chapel; it is not certain if this was the building near the bridge and next to the *Blue Bell* where they were meeting in the 1840s[37].

Neither variety of Methodism was strictly speaking nonconformist at this early date, but eventually both became so. The Independent or Congregational church at Maendy was an offshoot of the Methodist society at Aberthin which was riven by a series of disputes towards the end of the eighteenth century; Maendy chapel was built in 1802. In 1806 a group of Baptists registered 'a house called Ramoth lately in the tenure and occupation of Mr. Hunt' as a meeting place; they seem to have been an offshoot from the Baptist church originally at Wick but by 1808 settled at Ruhamah chapel in Bridgend. This first Baptist congregation did not flourish, however, and the revival of the Baptist cause locally resulted from the preaching of the blacksmith, John Roberts, about 1818. The present Ramoth chapel was built in 1828. Many of the Calvinists of Aberthin were in fact Cowbridge people and in 1825 they erected their own chapel, Sion, in the Limes. The religious complexion of nineteenth-century Cowbridge and Llanblethian was thus settled by the 1820s. Apart from the two Anglican churches (still both under the one vicar) there were two congregations of Calvinistic Methodists (Aberthin and the Limes), two congregations of Wesleyan Methodists (one worshipping in English, the other in Welsh), a Baptist congregation (Ramoth) and an Independent congregation at Maendy.

The picture of attendance at church and chapel services revealed to us on a single Sunday, by the census of 30 March 1851, is worth studying since religious observance was a very important part of the way of life in the Victorian age. The Vicar held three services on that Sunday in 1851; in the morning and evening at Cowbridge 193 and 212 were present, while at the afternoon service in Llanblethian there was a congregation of 49. The two Wesleyan chapels, separated by language, each held morning and evening services, with 46 and 49 present at the English chapel and 21 and 94 at the Welsh. There were congregations of 150 and 350 at morning and evening services at the Limes, while the single afternoon service at Aberthin attracted 100. Maendy had 150, 60 and 160 worshippers at its three services (the afternoon one almost certainly a Sunday school); at Ramoth there were 100 at the morning service and 250 at the evening service, though the minister said that 500 was the average size of his evening congregation and claimed that 'I have seen a 1,000 in the chapel in the evening before now'. Since he had declared the seating capacity of Ramoth to be 480 it is difficult to imagine that this is anything other than a considerable exaggeration. Nevertheless, it is true that the Baptists, under the leadership of a succession

---

[37] This was the Welsh Wesleyan chapel, which closed somewhere about 1880. A 'Dissenting Chapel' in the court behind the *Royal Oak* in the 1840s may just as well have been the original Wesleyan meeting house. A chapel for the English Wesleyans was built on the corner of Bethel's Court in 1850, and a new chapel was built across the road in about 1890.

of very active ministers[38] in the 1840s and 1850s, were the most flourishing religious body in Cowbridge.

Taking these figures at their face value, it would appear that there were about 660 worshippers at morning services and 1,115 at evening services in the town and parish. The combined population at that time was 1,833, so at least two thirds of the inhabitants—and most probably more—had gone to church or chapel on that Sunday. The thriving state of the Anglican church in Cowbridge, with its congregation of about 200, is striking. It seems to say something about the nature of the community in the town; there was a substantial English and anglicised population in Cowbridge—all the chapels (apart from the English Wesleyans) worshipped God in the Welsh language, while Church services were in English. Also there were many families of gentry and professional people living in the town, who were mostly Anglican and who rarely had more than a smattering of Welsh.

Some figures are also available for the year 1905 though they are not readily compared with those of 1851. By this date the five nonconformist chapels were claiming 465 members and 476 adherents, a total of 941, while the Anglicans claimed 320 communicants in the parish of Llanblethian with Cowbridge and Welsh St Donat's. The condition of the Established Church had apparently very greatly improved over half a century or so, since in 1848 the average number who took holy communion was only about sixty, with about 75 at Easter. The nonconformists were beginning to face serious difficulties on account of the local decline of the Welsh language. Only 261 (22%) of the inhabitants of Cowbridge admitted that they could speak Welsh at the time of the census of 1901—and the great majority of them were already past middle age. Comparable figures were not published for Llanblethian until 1921, when 176 (22%) were Welsh speaking, though in 1901 one may guess that between 35 and 40% would have spoken Welsh. About the turn of the century the chapels were changing from Welsh to English, but in some cases it was already too late; the Welsh Wesleyan chapel closed about 1880, and Aberthin chapel had only 17 members in 1905. The Anglican Church had benefited from the decline of the speaking of Welsh in the district.

An important feature of church life in the Victorian period was the Sunday school. All the denominations supported Sunday schools by the time of the Education Commissioners' inquiry in 1847, but none seemed particularly thriving at that time. The schools grew in popularity in the second half of the century. In the 1860s the Sunday school treat became one of the great events of the year; waggonloads of children would be taken down to the Leys for a day at the seaside, the longest journey from home any of them would have made.

---

[38] The most famous was Thomas Morris, known as 'Ten Chapel Tom' on account of the number of chapels he had built during his ministry. His daughter married Thomas Miles, a Cowbridge grocer, and some of their descendants still live in the town.

Schools

During the nineteenth century the fortunes of the Grammar School fluctuated greatly under a succession of masters who struggled with greater or
less success against the difficulty of inadequate funds. A dispute rumbled on
for years between successive masters, with their local supporters, and Jesus
College, Oxford, over the school's claim to a larger share of the income from
Sir Leoline Jenkins's estate. The College never conceded the claim, but it
did pay for the rebuilding of the school in 1847-52[39]. Other disputes among
local worthies, divided on political and denominational lines about whether
the school was an Anglican foundation, and about whether it should
become an 'intermediate' school under the Act of 1889, almost brought the
grammar school to ruin. The details of these vexed and tedious questions
can be found in Mr Iolo Davies's book. Perhaps of greater general interest
are the achievements of that lamentably short period in the 1870s when,
under the Rev. J. C. F. Morson, the school came near to being a successful
public school with the number of both staff and pupils[40] increased, the cur-
riculum widened to include 'modern' subjects and—most remarkable of
all—rugby football introduced. The claim is made that the game was first
played in Wales at Cowbridge and it is certainly true that Cardiff Rugby
Club's first away match was played against the school on 21 November 1874.

There was an amazing number of other schools in Victorian Cowbridge.
The Eagle School was very well established and several farmers' and
tradesmen's sons who rose to prominence in later life were educated
there—men such as Judge Gwilym Williams of Miskin (1839-1906), William
Thomas (1832-78) the Welsh poet 'Islwyn', and David Howell 'Llawdden',
Dean of St David's (1831-1903). It evidently provided both an elementary
and a secondary or 'intermediate' type of education, but avoided the grammar school's emphasis upon the Classics. From the 1840s the school was conducted by two William Lewises, father and son. The son was remembered
by one of his pupils of the 1860s, Ebenezer William Miles[41] as a
disciplinarian who administered corporal punishment without mercy. The
following passage occurs in E. W. Miles's memoirs:

> His instrument of punishment we called a ferule; a flat piece of thin
> cigar-box hard wood about a foot in length, oval on the top, with
> which he would slap the open hands of the boys who had to hold them

---

[39] The new building cost nearly £5,000, and the architect was John Prichard who restored Llandaff
Cathedral.

[40] There were about 62 boys (from many parts of South Wales and further afield) at the school in 1875.
26 pupils went on to Oxford University during Morson's time, 1870-75.

[41] E. W. Miles was born in Cowbridge about 1852 the son of Thomas Miles, grocer. He practised as a
solicitor for many years at Taynton House, 23 High Street. In 1931 he wrote down some of his
reminiscences which form the basis of much that is most valuable in *The Cowbridge story*, written by
his greatnephew, Mr John Richards. There is a copy of the reminiscences in the Glamorgan Record
Office.

out. There was a sting in the impact and the recipients winced with pain. The general idea was that the ferule had been soaked in vinegar. Another method was a flogging with a long pliable ash stick as long as a bean stick. The desks across the oblong school room were 12 feet or so long in rows and if there was any transgression at a particular desk, Lewis, who was of medium height with a strong body, would take one of these sticks from the recess in the pedestal by his desk in the top corner, walk down the aisle scowling fiercely and articulating his complaints, and when reaching his objective, would flog the whole row at that desk until they were crying with pain. No doubt some of the transgressors derived permanent impressions — many were the subdued threats of revenge. Lewis did not always escape retaliation from the adult boys. It was common knowledge that one of the older scholars, who had completed his school career a few years before I was admitted . . . , threw a bottle of red ink at him, which fortunately missed, but the bottle smashed against the wall behind his desk. The red ink left its stain there for a very long time.

William Lewis (the younger) committed suicide in 1880 and the Eagle Academy was closed never to reopen.

There were many other private schools and dame schools few of which continued in existence for any length of time and most of which are known only from entries in the directories. Worrall's *Directory* (1875) lists no fewer than seven such schools in the town (including the Eagle), the only one with any claim to particular mention being that of Mrs and the Misses Culverwell at Great House; Mrs Culverwell was the widow of a gentleman farmer who had lived at Llwynhelyg; her school, still listed in a directory for 1895, was an academy for 'young ladies'.

The first real attempt ever made to provide education for the children of the poor resulted in the opening in 1839 of the National (or Church) School on the Cardiff Road; the building still stands, now a private residence. In 1876 the elementary school, managed by an elected school board and partly supported from the rates, was opened on Broadway; a separate infants' school was added in 1891. In 1880 Parliament made attendance at school up to the age of thirteen (with certain exceptions) compulsory. In 1895 an average of 251 children attended the Cowbridge Board Schools which served the town together with part of the parish of Llanblethian; another school had been built at Maendy in 1876 for Ystradowen, Welsh St Donat's and the northern part of Llanblethian parish. The Board Schools spelt the rapid decline of the private schools of the town; indeed, the ending of the Eagle Academy after so distinguished a history is directly attributable to this competition. There remained the need for an intermediate (or secondary) school or for an intermediate department attached to the grammar school. Gradually the grammar school came to provide this type of education for boys. The party in the town that was trying to turn the grammar school into

COWBRIDGE is a parliamentary borough, market and post town in the parish and hundred of its own name, situated in the pleasant, fertile and well-cultivated vale of Glamorgan. It is 172 (by rail 186) miles w. from London, 56 s.w. from Bristol (*via* Bristol and South Wales Railway), 12 w. from Cardiff, 7 E. from Bridgend, and 40 E. from Swanesa. It is in the Bridgend and Cowbridge union and county court district, the Cardiff district Court of Bankruptcy, and in the diocese of Llandaff, and deanery of Gro-Neath (lower division). The town consists chiefly of one long street, stretching from east to west, containing some well-built houses, a Town Hall and convenient Market House. It is a contributory borough, with Cardiff and Llantrissant, in returning one member to Parliament; and is governed by a mayor and two bailiffs, the former appointed by the Marquis of Bute for life, and the latter elected by the burgesses annually. A court of record may be holden under the charter of Charles II. but the Corporation do not avail themselves of the privilege ; the only court is one of common council. held as occasion may require, for transacting the borough business. Petty sessions are held at the Police Station every alternate Tuesday. This place is without manufactures and its trade, which is local and domestic, is chiefly supported by those engaged in agriculture, and by the market and fairs which are numerous and well attended. In the eleventh century the town was encompassed by a wall, by Robert de St. Quinton, one of the Roman adventurers, who afterwards rebuilt and strengthened a castle called Llanblethian, situated near the village, of which only one of the gates now remains standing. The parish church of St. Mary is a handsome building in the Norman style of architecture, with square tower and peal of eight bells, and was restored in 1851 at a cost of £1,400. Dr. Benjamin H. Malkin, the celebrated historian of South Wales, was buried here, and there is a tablet to his memory. There are also chapels for English and Welsh Baptists and Wesleyan and Calvinistic Methodists. The living is a vicarage consolidated with Llanblethian and Welsh St. Donatts, in the gift of the dean and chapter of Gloucester. The Grammar School was founded and endowed by Sir Leoline Jenkins, who was judge of the prerogative court, and Secretary of State in the reign of James II. and had been educated at the school. He not only endowed the school but gave the site of the present building. He founded six monitorships each of the present value of £16 10s. and provided for the admis-

POST OFFICE, COWBRIDGE, Thomas Felton, *Post Master.*—Letters arrive from London, Bristol, Cardiff, Swansea, Gloucester, Bridgend, Carmarthen, and all parts of the kingdom at thirty minutes past seven morning, and from Ireland, Scotland, and North of England at ten minutes past ten morning. Letters are despatched to London, Cardiff, Bristol, Swansea, Gloucester, and all parts of the kingdom at twenty-five minutes past six evening, and to the North of England, Ireland and Scotland at forty minutes past four afternoon.

BOOT & SHOE MAKERS.
David Thomas, Cowbridge
Davies Edmund (dealer), Cowbridge
Gifford Nathaniel, Llanblethian
Giles David, Cowbridge
Jones Daniel, Cowbridge
Lougher Daniel, Penlline
Morgan Morgan, Cowbridge
Reynolds David, Penlline
Samuel Edward, Maindy

BUTCHERS.
Evans Thomas, Cowbridge
Hancock William H. Cowbridge
Howe John, Cowbridge
Morgan William, Cowbridge
Thomas Morgan, Cowbridge
Thomas William, Aburthin

CARPENTERS & JOINERS.
Davies David, Cowbridge
James William A. (& builder), Cowbrige
John Thomas, Cowbridge
Nicholas Thomas, Cowbridge
Price Christopher, Llantrithyd
Thomas Thomas, Colwinstone

CHEMISTS & DRUGGISTS.
Felton Thos. Stamp office, Cowbridge
Llewellyn John, Cowbridge
Thomas John, Cowbridge

CORN MERCHANTS.
Hall Joseph W. Cowbridge
Hall, Reynolds & Co. Cowbridge—
Edward John, agent
Morgan Morgan, Cowbridge
Thomas John R. (& flour), Cowbridge
& Llysworney

GARDENERS & SEEDSMEN.
Lewis Thomas, Cowbridge
Moore William, Cowbridge
Thomas John (seedsman), Cowbridge

GROCERS AND DEALERS IN SUNDRIES.
Butcher Charles, Cowbridge
David Jane, Cowbridge
Evans John D. Cowbridge
Griffiths John, St. Mary Church
Griffiths Philip, Cowbridge
Hall K. Cowbridge
Hopkins Cecilia, Llysworney
Howe John, Cowbridge
James Morgan, Cowbridge
Miles Mary Ann, Cowbridge
Mordecai Edward, Ystradowen
Morgan Ann, Cowbridge
Parsons John, Cowbridge
Samuel Edward, Welsh St. Donatts
Scott Edwin, Cowbridge
Thomas David, Aburthin
Thomas Isaac, Cowbridge
Traherne Mary, Ystradowen
Williams Edward, Cowbridge
Wood George, Penlline

INNS & PUBLIC HOUSES.
Ancient Druid, Joseph May, Cowbridge
Barley Mow, William Thomas, Penlline
Bear Hotel (commercial and posting), Thomas Thomas, Cowbridge
Blue Bell, Wm. Williams, Cowbridge
Bush, Isaac Williams, Cowbridge
Bush, Rebecca Williams, St. Hilary
Carne Arms, John David, Llysworney
City, Ann Sweeten, Llansannor
Commercial, Wm. H. Davies, Cowbridge
Cowbridge Arms, Morgan Thomas, Cowbridge
Crown and Anchor, David Hopkins, Cowbridge
Duke of Wellington (posting), David Thomas, Cowbridge
Edmondes' Arms, Jane Turberville, Cowbridge [thin
Farmers' Arms, David Thomas, Aburthin [blethian
Fox and Hounds, Margaret Williams, Penlline
General Picton, Edwin Thomas, Llan-
Gronow Arms, Wm. Sant, Ystradowen
Hare and Hound, Thomas Morgan, Aburthin
Hare and Hounds, William Jenkins, Colwinstone [bridge
Horse & Groom, Lewis Jenkins, Cow-
Masons' Arms, Joseph Braddick, Cowbridge
Pelican, Thomas Evans, Cowbridge
Railway, William Jones, Cowbridge
Royal Oak, David Williams, Cowbridge
Three Boars' Heads, John Howells, Cowbridge
Three Horse Shoes, Thomas Llewellyn, Welsh St. Donatts
Westgate, Iltyd David, Cowbridge
Wheelwrights' Arms, Richard Aubrey, Cowbridge
White Lion, David Davies, Ystradowen
White Lion, Thos. Evans, Cowbridge

RETAILERS OF BEER.
David Elizabeth, Colwinstone
Horton Mary, Cowbridge
Howell John, Llantrithyd
Morgan Gwenllian, Cowbridge
Phillips Mary, Cowbridge
Thomas Mary, Cowbridge
Warren Solomon, Cowbridge

IRONMONGERS.
Ballard & Co. Cowbridge
Bird Nathaniel, Cowbridge

PAINTERS.

Davies William J. Cowbridge
Hayter Samuel, Cowbridge
Hayter William, Cowbridge
Warren Solomon, Cowbridge

SADDLERS.

John Lewis, Cowbridge
Llewellyn Jane, Cowbridge
Yorwerth William, Cowbridge

SEED & MANURE MERCHANTS.

Hall Joseph W. Cowbridge
Hall, Reynolds & Co. Cowbridge—
Edward John, agent
Morgan Thomas (hay and manure),
Llsyworney
Morgan Morgan, Cowbridge
Price William (Tuesdays), Cowbridge
Thomas John R. Cowbridge, & Llys-
worney

SOLICITORS.

Marked thus * are commissioners for
taking affidavits in the Supreme
Court of Judicature, and thus † for
taking acknowledgments of married
women.

Liles Ebenezer W. Cowbridge
*rd Edward, Cowbridge
Rees Thomas (and clerk to the Cowbridge United District School Board),
Cowbridge
†Stockwood John (& town clerk, and
clerk to the magistrates of the
borough and of the hundred of Cowbridge and division of Pontypridd,
to the commissioners of taxes, and to
the District Highway Board), Cowbridge

SURGEONS.

ates Edward, M.D. Cowbridge
avis Evan T. Cowbridge
dwards Daniel, Ithiel, Cowbridge
hillips & Stanistreet, Cowbridge

TAILORS.

vans John D. Cowbridge
vans Saml. D. (& draper), Cowbridge
illiams Thomas, Cowbridge

WHEELWRIGHTS.

ubrey Richard, Cowbridge
vans John, Llysworney
hn Thomas, Penlline
reece John, Cowbridge
amuel John, Ystradowen
illiams David, Maindy

MILLERS.

raddick Henry, Howe Mill, St. Hilary
ddolls Thomas, Llandough
dmunds William, Llanblethian
vans Evan, St. Mary Church
arding Lydia, Town Mill, Cowbridge

AGRICULTURAL IMPLEMENT MAKERS & DEALERS.

John Edward (dealer), Cowbridge
Morgan William (dealer), Cowbridge
Tilley William, Cowbridge

AUCTIONEERS.

Thomas & Alexander (and valuers),
Cowbridge

BAKERS & CONFECTIONERS.

Butcher Charles, Cowbridge
Hayter William, Cowbridge
Howe John, Cowbridge
Stibbs Elizabeth, Cowbridge
Samuel Edward, Welsh St. Donatts
Williams Mary, Cowbridge

BANKS.

LONDON & PROVINCIAL BANK, LIMITED,
Cowbridge—draws on Glyn, Mills &
Co. London — Thomas Hambly,
manager
NATIONAL PROVINCIAL BANK OF ENGLAND,
Cowbridge—draws on head office.
London—Thomas Payne, manager

BLACKSMITHS.

David Jacob, Ystradowen
Griffiths John, Cowbridge
Griffiths William, Maindy
Hopkins John, Llysworney
Lewis Thomas, Cowbridge
Mordecai Daniel, Llansannor
Preece John, Cowbridge
Tilley William, Cowbridge
Watkins Evan, Colwinstone
Watts George, St. Hilary
Williams David, St. Mary Church

BOOKSELLERS & STATIONERS.

Davis Ann (& newsagent), Cowbridge
Davis Ebenezer (& printer), Cowbridge
Rogers Joseph, Cowbridge

LINEN & WOOLLEN DRAPERS AND OUTFITTERS.

Davies Edmund, Cowbridge
Evans Samuel D. Cowbridge
Price William L. Cowbridge
Rees David, Cowbridge
Thomas David, Cowbridge
Williams John, Cowbridge

PUBLIC BUILDINGS, OFFICES, &c.

PLACES OF WORSHIP

AND THEIR MINISTERS.

CHURCHES OF THE ESTABLISHMENT.

ST. MARY's, Cowbridge—Rev. Thomas
Edmondes M.A. vicar ; Revs. Owen
B. Price and Philip M. Edwards,
curates

DISSENTING CHAPELS.
BAPTIST (English), Cowbridge
BAPTIST (Welsh), Cowbridge and Col-
winstone
CALVINIST, Cowbridge, Llysworney,
Aburthin, Penlline and Colwinstone
INDEPENDENT, Maindy
METHODIST (Wesleyan), Cowbridge

PUBLIC OFFICERS.

*Mayor of Cowbridge & Constable of the
Castle of Llanblethian*—Geo. Whit-
lock Nicholl, Esq.
Deputy Mayor—George Montgomery
Traherne, Esq.
*Bailiffs and Justices of the Peace for
the Borough*—John Samuel Gibbon,
Esq. & Edward Bradley, jun. Esq.
*Magistrates acting for Cowbridge
Division*—William Salmon, Esq.;
John Richards Homfray, Esq.; John
Samuel Gibbon, Esq.; Rev. Frederic
Francis Edwardes ; George Mont-
gomery Traherne, Esq.; Geo. Henry
Jenkins, Esq.; John Blandy Jenkins,
Esq.; Hubert Churchill Gould, Esq.;
George Whitlock Nicholl, Esq.; Rev.
Thomas Edmondes ; Thomas Deere
Salmon, Esq. ; Francis Edmund
Stacey, Esq.; James Simpson Bal-
lard, Esq.; and Ralph Thurston
Bassett, Esq.
*Town Clerk and Clerk to the Magis-
trates of the Borough, and of the
Hundred of Cowbridge and Division
of Pontypridd*—John Stockwood, Esq.
Borough Treasurer—John Thomas
Medical Officer of Health—Edward
Bates, M.D. Cowbridge
*Registrar of Births and Deaths and
Relieving Officer for Cowbridge Dis-
trict*—William H. John

Cowbridge Farmers' Club—George E.
Tutton, secretary
Cowbridge United District School
Board—Thomas Rees, clerk
Gas Works, Cowbridge—J. T. Parsons,
secretary ; John Jenkins, manager
Glamorganshire Agricultural Society,
Cowbridge—Wm. V. Huntley, sec
Police Office, Cowbridge — Frederick
Jennings, sergeant in charge
Stamp Office, Cowbridge — Thomas
Felton, distributor   [keeper
Town Hall, Cowbridge—John Pike,
Young Men's Reading Room, Cow-
bridge—David Tilley, secretary

CONVEYANCE BY RAILWAY,

ON THE TAFF VALE LINE—LLANTRISSANT
AND COWBRIDGE BRANCH.

Station, COWBRIDGE—Oscar Hurford,
station master

CONVEYANCES.

To LLANTWIT MAJOR, Christopher
Punter & John Bowen, from Cowbridge, Tuesday, and daily during
summer

MILLINERS & DRESSMAKERS.

Harman Susannah, Cowbridge
Jones Mrs. —, Llanblethian
Morgan Annie, Cowbridge
Williams Fanny, Cowbridge

an intermediate school succeeded not in that aim but they did get a high school for girls, which opened in 1896 largely owing to the exertions of John Bevan and Alderman Edward John; it was originally known as 'Cowbridge Intermediate School for Girls'.

Reform and Change

Possibly the extension of elementary education to all irrespective of their parents' wealth is one of the most important changes which happened in Victorian times. But there were many other things which tended to bring change to Cowbridge and Llanblethian, and to bring them into closer touch with the world beyond the horizon. For although we have characterised the town as declining in importance at this time, this is by no means to say that there were no signs of 'progress'—to us a word much in vogue at the time. Some changes may seem of small interest (who is likely to be interested in the drains?) and slight importance (the gas works?); others—like the reform of the Corporation—have an obvious significance; but all had a part in shaping the community in which the people of Cowbridge and Llanblethian have lived for the last three or four generations.

In 1835 the first bank was opened in Cowbridge—a branch of the National Provincial Bank of England—at 62 High Street, the premises of Barclays Bank at the present time. By the end of the century there were three branch banks in the town.

The next innovation was the police station, at first only a room in the town hall established in 1842. Law and order had, from time immemorial, been enforced by six constables chosen annually from among the poorer burgesses of the town. From 1842 there was a professional police force in the town—but at the beginning it consisted of a single officer of the Glamorgan Constabulary who was provided with reinforcements on fair days, for at other times the ancient borough was well-conducted and law-abiding. In 1862 the police station was built and gradually the complement was increased, so that by 1914 there was a sergeant and three constables.

In the early 1850s the Cowbridge Gas and Coke Company was formed and its works were erected in the Limes in 1853. It was very much a local affair, owned and directed by prominent tradesmen and solicitors. The streets of the town were lit by gas from about 1855, the Corporation paying for about twenty lamp posts to be erected.

In the 1840s the Corporation had successfully opposed the routing of the South Wales Railway through the town. By 1860 the consequences of this shortsighted policy were clear to all, and in that year the mayor presided over a well-attended meeting of gentlemen, tradesmen and farmers 'to consider the expediency of using means for obtaining railway communication between Cowbridge and the Llantrisant station'. It was estimated that the railway would cost £25,000 to build. A prospectus of the Railway Company, with a share capital of £30,000, was issued in July 1861. The list of provisional committeemen shows members of the Corporation well to the fore, the names of the mayor, the bailiffs and several aldermen appearing, with the ubiquitous John Stockwood, town clerk, as secretary. An Act of Parliament was obtained in 1862 to authorise the construction of the railway. Mr E. W. Miles wrote that he had 'a faint recollection of the cutting of the first sod of the Cowbridge Railway to Pontyclun by Dr Carne of Dimlands... who led a procession through the town dressed as a navvy with a shovel on his shoulder. There was great enthusiasm locally, and many tradesmen ventured to invest £50 in shares and lost the greater part of the investment as the Company worked the line at a loss'. The line opened for goods traffic early in 1865, and for passengers later in the year. The Corporation celebrated the occasion in some style, resolving that 'a Public Breakfast be given . . . on the occasion of the opening of the Cowbridge Railway for Passenger Traffic'. It also conferred the freedom of the borough upon Dr Nicholl-Carne 'as a slight acknowledgement of his indefatigable exertions in obtaining the Cowbridge Railway'. The Corporation also gave £10 towards the cost of 30 tons of coal, the first freight brought to the town on 30 January 1865, for distribution among the labouring class and the poor. An extension of the railway southwards to Aberthaw was opened in 1892 and a new station was erected at Cowbridge. The whole undertaking was absorbed by the Taff Vale Railway Company in 1895. The consequences of the opening of railway communication with the outside world were important for Cowbridge, as Mr Miles comments:

> Great expectations were aroused by tradesmen from this acquisition, but in course of time it proved detrimental to their business by taking people out of the town and district rather than bringing them in. This, with the construction of the Vale of Glamorgan Railway[42] later and stock sales at Llantwit Major, deprived Cowbridge market of its predominance as a centre for livestock sales.

The opening of the railway also meant some housing development in the East Village where Croft Street (formerly Taff Street) and Croft Terrace were built to house railway employees opposite the original terminus. It is no coincidence that the censuses of 1871, 1881 and 1891 showed the population of Cowbridge increasing to the maximum ever recorded — 1,377 in 1891.

E. W. Miles also tells us that in the 1870s travellers to London and Bristol had to leave Cowbridge on the 7.30 a.m. train, wait an hour at Llantrisant Station, and then catch the up train on the main line. The London train went through Gloucester and arrived at Paddington between 5 and 6 p.m. The journey to Bristol entailed crossing the Severn on a steam tug from Portskewett and then catching a train to Bristol on the other side — since the Severn Tunnel was not opened until 1886. Still, with all its discomforts, the journey from Cowbridge to London took about ten hours by rail whereas the stage coach had taken more than twenty-one.

---

[42] This was the line from Barry to Bridgend, through Llantwit Major. It was opened in 1897.

An important aspect of nineteenth-century reform was in the field of public health—which means primarily improved drains and water supply. The sanitary state of Cowbridge was affected by several factors—the stagnant ditches on the northern side of the town, the dirty streets (befouled by cattle and horses at the markets and fairs) and the fact that the contents of what drains there were eventually found their way into the river Thaw. The water supply, obtained from many wells in and around the town and from the three or four massive iron pumps along the main street, was however largely uncontaminated, but there was plenty to complain of in other aspects of the town's health.

In 1853 there was an epidemic of 'gastric fever' (some called it 'Cowbridge fever'; we would say typhoid) in the town and neighbourhood following a particularly glittering hunt ball at the *Bear*. The epidemic was so severe and the public so alarmed that even the Corporation was stirred into action; they appointed an inspector under the Nuisance Removal and Diseases Prevention Act of 1846. Within a few days the inspector had drawn up a horrifying report on the state of the town, paying particular attention to the *Bear* itself. The first item on his list of 'nuisances' was described thus:

> An offensive open gutter, known as the Town Ditch, containing a quantity of putrid matter, from which an effluvia of a very offensive nature arises.

Into this ditch, which had once been part of the moat surrounding the medieval walls of the town, emptied many an 'offensive privy' or 'offensive pig-stye'. (It is remarkable how many pigsties there were in the town as late as the 1850s.) Verity's Court and Ballard's Court were singled out for their lack of proper sanitation. The state of Cowbridge became a public scandal. The local press published numerous letters on the subject, but when the landlord of the *Bear* tried to defend himself and the reputation of his hotel, the editor of the *Cardiff and Merthyr Guardian* firmly pointed out that the evidence of the inspector was against him. Certain improvements were put in hand fairly quickly, the most important being the cleansing of the town ditch. The ditch was filled in and a covered drain replaced it. The line of the ditch then became the back lane which joins Eagle Lane and Town Hall Square.

The state of the town and the ineffectiveness of the Corporation and the local highways board in cleansing and maintaining the streets and pavements were subjects aired by witnesses appearing before the Municipal Corporations Commission in 1877. Markets and fairs were still held in the street (except for the sheep and pig markets which had been provided with a permanent site adjoining the *Masons' Arms*). An effort had been made to persuade householders to clean up opposite their houses after the market, but, as Lewis Jenkins remarked, 'those who do not think that cleanliness is a virtue leave the dirt, and it is dried up by the sun and blown away by the wind'. Edward John told the Commissioners that he had given shelter in his house for nearly a week to a man who had been kicked in the groin by a horse on fair day, and he had seen a woman gored by a cow. One of the first things that the new Corporation did when it came into office was to extend the market site along the town wall by draining the Butts Pool, itself once part of the town moat. The new cattle market came into use in 1888.

But this is to get too far ahead of the story. We must go back now to 1830 to begin to trace the history of the old Corporation of Cowbridge down to the time of its abolition in 1886. First we must be reminded that the town had been governed (if that is the word) since 1681 by a corporation consisting of two bailiffs (chosen annually), ten aldermen and twelve burgesses. It was a self-perpetuating body which never had to submit itself to an election; the bailiffs were appointed by the mayor (a man who was himself appointed for life by the lord of the borough, the Marquess of Bute) from among the aldermen; the aldermen and capital burgesses selected whom they wished to fill vacancies in their ranks. Membership of the Corporation came to be restricted to a few families of professional men and the more substantial tradesmen. Their public functions were few. They admitted no responsibility for the improvement of the town but, from time to time, they paid for the erecting of pumps or lamp posts or for the repair of pavements or the cleaning out of the disgracefully polluted river. They saw their functions as, in the first place, the management of the corporate property, which included the tolls of the market, and in the second place, the admission of burgesses or freemen to their privileges. The latter was a very important matter because burgesses had the right to vote at parliamentary elections. The freedom of the town could be obtained by inheritance, by marriage to a freeman's daughter, by apprenticeship to a freeman, or by gift of the Corporation. Generally the number of burgesses was kept as small as possible, but when a contested election was at hand there was often an unusual increase in the number—as for example when Lord Mountstuart (the future Marquess of Bute) was anxious to get his son elected in 1790, he caused more than a hundred burgesses to be sworn in at Cardiff, and even in Cowbridge where his direct influence over the Corporation was comparatively slight, nineteen new names were added, making an electorate at Cowbridge of 107.

The political importance of the freedom of the borough ceased with the Reform Act of 1832 which, while protecting the rights of the existing resident freemen, conferred the franchise upon the '£10 householders'. There were 55 of these householders in Cowbridge on the electoral register for 1832, side by side with fifty resident freemen. Very few bothered to take up their freedom after 1832 and the number of people qualified to be members of the Corporation dwindled until only a few families, the Edmondeses, Ballards, Llewellyns and Bradleys, entirely controlled it. The number of resident burgesses had fallen to nineteen by 1877, and at the time of Hopkin-James's *Old Cowbridge* (1922) only one, Alderman John Llewellyn, chemist, was a freeman by right as opposed to a freeman by gift (or honorary freeman). As David Jones of Wallington put it:

> Whatever it may have been in the halcyon days preceding the Reform Bill its Corporation has now dwindled down to a snug little family party who look upon the town funds, of about £300 a year, as so much private patrimony.

A full-scale investigation into the affairs of the Corporation was undertaken by the Municipal Corporations Commission in 1877. They questioned John Stockwood, the town clerk, and John Thomas, the treasurer and agent (who both spoke on behalf of the Corporation), Lewis Jenkins, brewer and maltster, and Edward John, calling himself 'an implement agent and seed and manure agent' (two leading critics of the Corporation). It quite clearly emerged that the Corporation was indeed a 'snug little family party', the majority of whom were Conservatives and none of them nonconformists, and many of them lived at great distances from Cowbridge. They did nothing for the advantage of the town. Jenkins and John spoke of the need for an elected town council and of the need for improvements to the town — a cattle market, better drainage and paving, for instance; they complained of the way that leases of the Corporation's property were granted and of how their income was spent[43].

In the fullness of time the Royal Commission reported, recommending the dissolution of the Corporation of the Bailiffs, Aldermen and Burgesses of the Town of Cowbridge. This was enacted by the Municipal Corporations Act of 1883, with effect from 1886. The office of Constable of Llanblethian Castle, or mayor, was also abolished; the last constable was George Whitlock Nicholl of Ham, Llantwit Major. Meanwhile the townspeople petitioned Queen Victoria for a new charter, which was granted on 28 September 1886. This provided for the election by the ratepayers of a municipal corporation or town council consisting of four aldermen and twelve councillors to be presided over by a mayor chosen annually by them. The men elected in November 1887 were of a very different complexion from the members of the old Corporation (in fact only one had been a member of it); they were, with one exception, leading tradesmen and innkeepers, many of them Liberals and nonconformists, and among the new aldermen were Edward John and Lewis Jenkins who had led the attack on the old Corporation in 1877. Thomas Rees, solicitor,[44] was top of the poll with 164 votes. After the declaration of the poll Rees was placed in a chair and carried home by men singing 'See, the Conquering Hero Comes'. He became the first of the new line of annually chosen mayors.

---

[43] David Jones seems to have been wrong in setting the income so high; it was more like £150 a year; the Corporation had been very loath to publish accounts. The Corporation did not levy a rate, its income deriving from property and tolls.

[44] Thomas Rees, a prominent Liberal and Wesleyan Methodist, was founder of the firm of solicitors later known as Gwyn and Gwyn.

Leisure and Social Life

During the course of the reign of Victoria there was a remarkable transformation of the leisure pursuits of the inhabitants of this district. Up to about 1850 the traditional festivals and pastimes continued, at least to some extent, as an elderly lady told Dr Hopkin-James:

> The revels in Cowbridge I can recollect, the fairs also, and in every public house to finish up the fair there was dancing held. As a child I saw the young people dancing. They came from most of the outlying villages. It was much thought of in those days.

David Jones of Wallington described the sinking of the Llanblethian revel into 'a mere annual sottish carousal' by the 1860s, dancing no longer a part of the proceedings. The disapproval of clergy, ministers and churchgoers of all denominations had virtually killed off the old celebrations and the withdrawal of the patronage of the 'respectable' section of society left the revel to the rougher elements. It soon died out completely. One of the few old customs to continue down to the early years of the present century was the *Mari Lwyd* at Christmas time. Hopkin-James and John Richards both give descriptions of this curious wassailing custom[45]; the horse's skull, padded with calico and decorated with ribbons, which had been used by John John of Cowbridge (1846-1937), is now in the Welsh Folk Museum at St Fagan's.

E. W. Miles remembered from his childhood the playing of football, bando (a local form of hockey), cricket and rounders though there were no special grounds[46] for them and the rules were local ones. At the *Tennis Court Inn* in the East Village was a high-walled court in which 'ball tennis' was played with bare hands and a hard ball. It sounds like the game of 'fives'; the grammar school's fives court is, of course, still in existence in Church Street.

The main social event in the gentry's year in the 1850s was the Cowbridge Hunt Week, held in November. This combined hunting (with various packs of foxhounds, especially the Cowbridge harriers—the Glamorgan Hunt itself was not established until 1873), with three days' racing on the Stalling Down and the hunt ball at the *Bear*. It is not clear when the races were given up, but E. W. Miles seems to refer to them as a mere childhood memory. The race course was still more or less visible until the last War when part of the Down was ploughed up.

By the turn of the century the games played in Cowbridge were well-organised in clubs and teams, well-provided with permanent grounds and conducted according to formal rules hitherto known only to the young

---

[45] The best general account of the *Mari Lwyd* is that in T. M. Owen, *Welsh folk customs* (Cardiff, 1959), pp. 49-58.

[46] There had once been a bowling green, mentioned in documents of 1672 and 1748, though it may be remembered that one of the town's ordinances of 1610 had forbidden the playing of 'unlawful games' (see p. 39).

gentlemen of the grammar school. Other entertainments of the late nine-teenth century were provided in the form of 'penny readings', amateur con-certs, amateur dramatics and the occasional eisteddfod. Sometimes a circus or menagerie would come to town.

It is appropriate to enquire at this point to what extent the townspeople had leisure in which to play these games and to enjoy these entertainments. An interesting report in the *Bridgend Chronicle* for 25 June 1859 describes a meeting of shopkeepers, their assistants and apprentices which had been held under the chairmanship of R. C. Nicholl-Carne of Nash, the mayor, at which the shopkeepers had agreed to allow their employees Wednesday evenings 'for the purpose of recreation and mutual improvement'. The con-sequent closing of the shops at 5 p.m. on Wednesdays was the beginning of 'early closing' in the town. E. W. Miles, probably referring to conditions in the 1870s, says that shop assistants had to attend to their duties from 8 a.m. to 8 p.m. He visited the businessmen of the town and persuaded them to close their shops at 3 p.m. on Wednesdays. About 1873 Miles was one of the founders, and the first secretary, of the Young Men's Institution, a society for reading, debating and playing chess which was permitted to meet in the town hall. The Institute at the back of the town hall was erected in 1895 through the generosity of Nathaniel Bird, the ironmonger. Miles seems not to have known (or to have forgotten) that a similar, but short-lived, society, then known as a mechanics' institute, had been in existence around 1852 with Nathaniel Bird and Thomas Miles as its secretaries.

Several other organisations existed in Cowbridge and Llanblethian in Victorian times; they all had a serious as well as a convivial function. The most widely supported were the benefit clubs or friendly societies, especially the Oddfellows lodges which held elaborate processions and feasts on their 'anniversaries' in June; the Cowbridge Oddfellows had their club room at the *Royal Oak*, while the Llanblethian lodge met at the *Picton*. At Cowbridge there was also a lodge of Ivorites.

Another organisation which is often mentioned in connection with Vic-torian Cowbridge is the Volunteer Corps, formed in 1860 under the com-mand of Captain Robert Boteler of Llandough Castle. The Corps, in their impressive red and blue uniforms, received a rigorous training in drill and in the use of bayonet and rifle. The recollections of his time as a volunteer around 1870, written down by Alfred George James (1853-1922)[47], show that there was a great deal of fun to be had while at the same time learning the serious business of being an amateur soldier. One of the most popular features of the Corps so far as the townsfolk were concerned was the brass band which was formed about 1862. Several of the volunteers saw service in South Africa, but the Corps was disbanded in 1908 on the formation of the Territorial Army.

---

[47] I am indebted to his great-granddaughter, Mrs Ceridwen Harris of Ottawa, for a copy of these recollections.

26. The old course of the River Thaw after the bridge was widened in 1911

PART IV

Cowbridge in the Twentieth Century

The last days of old Cowbridge, 1900-1920

The period immediately before the First World War saw the last days of that closely knit, self sufficient and rather smug community that was Victorian Cowbridge. The town was far more class conscious than it is today, but if the doctors and lawyers did not mix too freely with farmers and blacksmiths, everyone certainly knew everyone else. In one sense, life had not changed much for hundreds of years. The countless inns, family businesses and crafts still depended almost entirely on the fairs and markets of the town, and the markets on the local farmers and nearly everybody on the horse. Apart from the railways, the horse had been the only serious form of transport throughout the Victorian Age. For a few more years of the present century, his ten miles an hour continued to determine the pace and pattern of most people's lives and to restrict the extent of the world for the average citizen as it had done for centuries. If the horse was still supreme, his hegemony was soon to be challenged in the early years of the century by the bicycle (first introduced in 1874), the motor cycle, which arrived in 1900, and the occasional motor car. These changes in transport came slowly to Cowbridge however and did not show themselves clearly until the 1920s. Until then everyone's employment was still centred exclusively within the local community. Men toiled, as they had done for centuries from dawn to dusk in the numerous courts and alleyways at a wide range of rural crafts. John Sanders' smithy in Eagle Lane was as busy then as the bus-stop near the Town Hall is today. For recreation, few ventured far outside the borough walls, preferring to find their fun and entertainment in John Warren's brass band or Fred Knapton's Fife and Drummers, the boisterous concerts of the Minstrel Troupe at the Town Hall or just smoking long clay pipes, clog dancing or tippling ale until 'stop tap' at the twenty or so taverns that lined the High Street. Attendance at the March and St. Mary Hill Fairs were the red letter days in most people's lives and the Sunday School outings to Aberthaw were

28. A Proclamation during the mayoralty of David Tilley in 1910—probably announcing
the death of King Edward VII and the accession of King George V. The Duke of
Wellington has not altered much structurally over the years, but the adjacent Cowbridge
Arms Hostelry has entirely disappeared. Mill's Garage has a plentiful supply of bicycles
for sale in its window

talked about from one year to the next. The Church at this time had lost
none of its Victorian self-confidence; the morning and evening services were
still faithfully attended by the town ladies in their sleek silken finery and by
gentlemen in their sober serge. It was the same with the Nonconformist
chapels: each chapel in the town had its choir and every Easter they would
gather at 'Ramoth' to raise their voices in such full-throated singing as to
make the rafters hum. It was this intimate, unquestioning society with its
innate virtues and shortcomings that the Great War of 1914-18 swept away.
The social upheaval of the war and its aftermath, the great improvements in
educational opportunities and transport facilities, in which the horse was
replaced first by the omnibus then the motor car, would lead a new society
to look much further afield.

The Boer War

Although the war was fought in a distant country, the British successes at
Ladysmith and Kimberley in 1900 were greeted with gay abandon in the
streets of Cowbridge. The brighter sparks among the young children, for

instance, descended like scavengers on the town's rubbish dump near the Council School, dug up all the tin cans they could find and formed a victory band. As news of the victories were announced, the 'battle drummers' marched patriotically through the streets beating their tin drums and waving Union Jacks in a blur of colour. When the news of the Relief of Mafeking reached Cowbridge, the whole town went wild with excitement. According to John Richards' book, the citizens were determined to paint the town red, late in the night though it was. Jack Warren's band blazed martial music and some wags rolled a burning barrel of tar through the streets. Later the gay procession wended its way through the fields to Aberthin, looking like a brightly-coloured scarf in the moonlight and they even collected a stray donkey on the journey. At the *Farmer's Arms* that night there were many who had a drop too much, but the donkey made more of an ass of himself than anyone by drinking numerous pints of ale.

The First World War

Soon after war was declared in August 1914, a volunteer force was formed in the town to be trained on the cricket field by ex-Sergeant Major William Brown and the late Mr. Vivian Gwyn, the well-known Cowbridge solicitor. Later the force was disbanded and the men were made to enlist officially.

29. Cowbridge Carnival—July 1913

30. A view of Eastgate Street about 1908. The offices of the goods section of the Taff Vale Railway are on the right and also the entrance to the passenger Railway Station. The water pump on the left-hand pavement is just discernible

Selwyn Davies, as a schoolboy, remembers remonstrating violently with the ex-Sergeant Major for shouting and swearing as he trained the enlisted troops in a field on the site of the new Sheep Market. As the war anxiety grew even the boys of the Grammar School were trained in the use of a rifle—this time by Sergeant Bradbury, whose voice was as stentorian as Brown's. A Food Office was set up and Alderman David Tilley was appointed Food Officer for the town. A depot was then opened at John Pickard's grocery shop (where the Vale of Glamorgan Borough Council offices are now) for the reception of comforts for the troops and it was run voluntarily by the ladies of the town.

Cowbridge was also an important centre for the collection of hay for the feeding of the cavalry and a well-known Cowbridge citizen, Captain T. J. Yorwerth, was made responsible for the purchasing of fodder for the whole of South Wales and Monmouthshire. It was not surprising that the feelings of the local farmers often ran high as both their hay and horses were commandeered without notice by the Army authorities—the last straw occurring when farmers had their horses taken from them on their way to market. Just outside Cowbridge two residences, New Beaupre (St. Hilary) and Ash Hall (Ystradowen), were turned into hospitals for wounded soldiers. At Ash Hall Mrs. Tudor Owen performed such sterling war service as matron that she was later awarded the Order of the Red Cross. On occasions a Grammar School master used to take a small orchestra to entertain the wounded soldiers, though whether the patients improved or deteriorated after the performances is hard to say! There were some food shortages in the district before rationing was introduced in February 1918. Dripping became a popular substitute for butter and the poorer families picked nuts and blackberries while watercress from the River Thaw made quite a useful contribution to the larder at various seasons. Finally, it was even found necessary to plough up part of Stallingdown but the yield from the potato and corn crops was negligible.

As the War dragged on, Cowbridge could no longer look at itself in the mirror with the old smug complacency. The cracks in the looking glass began to split asunder as the death toll from the mud of Flanders increased and cut deep into the insularity of the old town. With twenty eight of its townsmen making the supreme sacrifice for King and Country and many others severely wounded, the old borough could no longer look with bland indifference upon the outside world. The Great War was indeed coming home to people's lives: even the ears of the children buzzed with the wild rumours of German atrocities which the Belgian refugees brought with

31. Cowbridge Cricket Club goes to war (1915)
Top row: J. Foulkes, Frank Dunn*, Charlie Morgan, A. Gibbs*, Harold Moynan,
(seated) I. Pell, B. S. Bird, Lyn Llewellyn, J. C. R. Dunn*

*Killed in action

them to their new homes near the former Iolo Gallery. In some places the Belgians were unpopular, but at Cowbridge the local railwaymen generously assisted the unfortunate victims of war out of their War Distress Fund. Since September 1914 every railwayman in the Cowbridge district had agreed to contribute 3d in the pound towards the War effort and there were also many prisoners of war who had cause to be grateful for the ten shilling food parcels that arrived from home. The celebration of the National Fete Day of France at Cowbridge Church in July 1917 was a final moving testimony that the Great War was sounding the death knell of local provincialism. On that occasion the Mayor, Captain T. J. Yorwerth and members of the Town Council gathered to honour the grave of Mon. Jules Auguste Simonet, a Frenchman who had long resided in the town. Tributes were paid to France, where the death toll had been twice that of the United Kingdom, and a letter from the Mayor of Chaumont was read. Later, as J. P. Marks drew from the organ eloquent strains of accompaniment to 'La Marseillaise', there were many in the crowded congregation who saw the occasion as an act of farewell to a departing age.

It is appropriate to end this section by listing the names of the men of the borough who gave their lives for King and Country in the Great War 1914-18:

Lieut. T. E. H. Torney, 3rd Welsh Reg.
2nd. Lieut. M. J. Marsden. M.G.C.
2nd. Lieut. W. H. O. Moynan. S.W.B.
2nd. Lieut. W. D. Owen. 4th Welsh Reg.
2nd. Lieut. Joshua W. Payne. D.L.l.
Sergt. Cecil Chard. 4th South Staffs.
Sergt. David Fitzgerald. S.W.B.
Sergt. Fred C. Lord. Gren. Guards.
Sergt. Arthur Stockwood. Rif. Brig.
Corp. William Burley. 15th Welsh Reg.
Corp. Owen Evans. Royal Sussex Reg.
Lanc. Corp. A. W. Jones. 5th Welsh Reg.
Lanc. Corp. Ronald Wall. Nthbd. Fus.

PRIVATES

William Archer, R.W.F.
David Robert Bond. R.F.A.
Bassett J. Davies. 10th Welsh Reg.
Albert Gibbs. 16th Welsh Reg.
Arthur Gibbs. Loyal North Lancs.
Ralph S. Goulden. R.G.A.
William Eton Lane. S.W.B.
Charles Lewis. Tank. Corps.

Arthur Miles. 1st Mon. Reg
Richard Morgan. Austn. I.F.
Alexander Pates. 2nd Welsh Reg.
David R. Spencer. Mer. Mar.
William Trew. 1st Leicester Reg.
William Willment. Royal Sussex.
Herbert Williams. 12th Glos. Reg.

The High Street: Crafts, Shops and Businesses

The scene in the High Street before the advent of the motor car was very different from today. The surface of the road, which resounded with the clatter of horses' hoofs, was far from smooth, being flanked by gutters on either side and liable most winters to heavy flooding near the Town Hall. The road had to be tarred regularly with a horse-drawn machine and on these occasions Old Trott's cry of 'Coal, fine sand' was more than welcome. Trott sold sand by the ton at 1d a bucket and people gladly purchased it to stop the tarry mess being trampled into their houses. Mr. Trott, incidentally, kept the lodging house in Eagle Lane. Here swarmed dusty-faced tramps from Cardiff—colourful tatterdemalians out of joint with their times—who did odd jobs about the house to earn a welcome meal and a night's sleep. A more eerie figure of the highway, especially to the younger children, was 'Davey the lamp lighter'. He was employed by the Cowbridge Gas Company, and armed with his staff and pilot light at dusk, he looked like a sceptred monarch of the mists as he lit up the town. Of the countless hawkers who peddled their wares through Cowbridge none stands out more clearly from this period than 'Old Usher' a fruiterer and fishmonger. He would start off from Cardiff on Friday afternoon selling oranges at four for a penny on his four-wheeler cart from St. Nicholas, all the way to the Westgate. He did not complete his round until midnight.

One of the great changes in the commercial life of the town had been the rapid decline throughout the nineteenth century of the traditional crafts. However, one or two were to linger on well into the modern age. Within living memory Harry Collings was to make watches with infinite care and precision: David Tilley to supplement his income by coach building: Nelson Andrews to nail his boots and shoes as if he were slaying demons: John Sanders and Harry Webb to manufacture gate hinges, repair agricultural machinery as well as shoe horses at their forges in Eagle Lane: whilst Jim Lewis continued to make buckets and barrels that lasted a lifetime in his workplace on the very site of the 1978 Roman excavation opposite Old Hall. 'Jim the Cooper' was a larger-than-life character as well as being a skilled craftsman. Whenever he visited the *Masons Arms* he would order a pint and a half—one for himself and a half for his dog. John Ryan, an irrepressible Irish saddler was about the last craftsman to practise in Cowbridge. His shop on the site of the *Three Boars Head* was until the mid 1950s, an open house to all his fellow countrymen and his customary greeting 'If you're Irish, come into the parlour' was a byword for hospitality throughout the whole Irish community in Glamorgan. His leather goods—especially satchels and brief cases—were a byword in quality too! The predominance of the retail trade and the small family business in the High Street can be evinced from an interesting list of shops of the Edwardian period published recently in the Parish Magazine. It seems that Cowbridge was losing its role of self sufficiency and was now clearly bent on providing professional services (legal and medical) and shopping facilities for a wide rural area — a role it continues so successfully to this day. There were nearly as many shops as there are today. But what sort of shops were they? Some were little more than parlour shops selling sweets and ice cream, such as Mrs. Alice Griffiths' at the Westgate and Mrs. Edwin Lewis' at Ramoth Cottage. Then there were high-class family grocers like Mr. Philip Griffiths whose shop stood on the corner of High Street and Verity's Court. Shopping for groceries was very different then. You bought your tea and sugar loose and they were picked for you by the assistant. Nothing was labelled as it is today. Then there were several tailors in Cowbridge. Mr. David Thomas owned a drapery and millinery Emporium with a dressmaking department at Cross House, now 'Fine Fare'. Mr. S. D. Evans' Emporium, where 'Walters' and 'Bay Tree' are today, was another hive of industry. There five dressmakers and a milliner sewed away with nimble fingers as people brought them Brethyn Llwyd (grey cloth) from the factory in Llanblethian to make into suits and jackets. Other town drapers included Mr. Watkins, Mr. John Williams and Mr. William Evans of Church Street. Sad to say, by the late 1920s the days of the local drapery business were numbered. The omnibus killed them off for it enabled customers to shop in the larger stores in Cardiff and Bridgend.

The Woollen Factory at Llanblethian, situated on part of the Dunraven estate, sadly did not survive long into the present century: in fact it ceased production just before the outbreak of the First World War. For over a hundred years, the wool had been provided by the tenant-farmers of the Estate and such was the quality of the woollen products of the Llanblethian factory that quantities of cloth and old Welsh flannel of high quality were still being sold in the markets of South Wales at the turn of the century. Even the cockle-women from West Wales continued to purchase a special black flannel for their working attire. The fourteen or so weavers and spinners had lived in and around the village of Llanblethian; indeed, the last of the weavers, Mr. D. Williams, died within a stone's throw of the factory where he had spent most of his working life. The last manageress before the business was forced to close down in face of stiff competition from modern factories was Mrs. Howells, who in September 1888, had the honour of entertaining Princess May of Teck (later Queen Mary) to tea at Factory House. The Princess, accompanied by her parents the Duke and Duchess of Teck, were visiting the county as guests of the Earl of Dunraven and were presented with several samples of the best quality Welsh flannel.

It is quite a surprise to learn that there were as many as five bakers in Cowbridge and each boasted his own speciality. Mr. and Mrs. John Edmunds made their own seed cake at 7d a lb. at a bakery near the traffic lights. Morgan Thomas had a bakery where Derek Sanders has his shoe shop now. Mrs. Williams, the grandmother of Councillor Selwyn Davies, had hers nearby and Miss Stibbs' premises stood where the Ogmore Bakery is still trading. Miss Stibbs' baker was Mr. Charles Davies, who was Mayor of Cowbridge on several occasions. He was affectionately known as 'Charlie

Buns' (to distinguish him from Charles Davies, the hairdresser) and his speciality was a puff pastry turnover. Finally, Mrs. Hayter kept a bakery near the bridge. Delivery to the outlying districts was left to the Llanblethian bakers, John Thomas and David Spencer, 'Johnny the Bakehouse' used to heat his ovens with firewood and the branches of trees and, in an act of piety to the trade he loved, always wore a bowler hat when working. His daughters, Mabel and Edith, delivered bread to the north of the town as far as Penllyn. By contrast, David Spencer concentrated on the villages to the south of Cowbridge with the pungent smells of the brown crusty loaves trailing deliciously behind his big, open cart all the way to Llancarfan.

Of the remaining shops of the period mention can be made of the four butchers W. G. Morgan, Evan Edwards, William Morgan, and Mr. Escott. Whereas many of the family businesses over the past fifty years have been swallowed up by the larger concerns, the first two mentioned are still in the hands of their descendants. Messrs. Birds and Arthur John and Company are likewise still run by the same families. On the whole though, as might be expected, the commercial face of Cowbridge has lost much of its original colour. However, with Scandinavian type shops, jewellers, florists, off-licences, modern outfitters, a variety of super-markets, a top class Garden Centre and two well-stocked book shops, Cowbridge still maintains its links with the past and provides high class shopping facilities for a wide rural area.

Until recently printing was synonymous with Cowbridge. It started in 1895 when Joseph Gibbs, the printer of the *Glamorgan Gazette*, became involved in a dispute with his newspaper. He and his assistant David Brown left Bridgend and moved to Cowbridge to set up a successful printing business of their own at 43 High Street.

Later Gibbs and Brown moved to a new site at Town Hall Square where they carried on for twenty years. In 1929 the firm became D. Brown and Sons, when David's twin sons Neil and Alan joined their father after completing their education. In 1973 the firm re-established their original links with Bridgend by leaving the site in Eastgate and building a large ultra-modern factory on the Industrial Estate at North Road.

The introduction, by Browns, of mechanical type-setting, automatic processes and specialised finishing equipment by the last war ushered in work of a more complex nature such as catalogues, electoral registers, time-tables and guide books. As a matter of interest a large number of town guides produced in the United Kingdom were at one time printed in Cowbridge. Later the firm became involved in the world of book production and the highly successful *Vale* and *Glamorgan Historian* series, which did so much to popularise local history in the last two decades, were printed by Browns. The University of Wales Press Board and the Church in Wales have made substantial use of the firm's services to print academic books and prayer books. At one time over thirty people were employed at the Eastgate plant

32. An old photograph taken in the early 1900s shows the wide variety of articles for sale on the street: straw baskets, pig troughs, chicken wire, galvanised baths, hay rakes, pots and pans, copper boilers, etc. The group standing outside include Dena Bird and on extreme right apprentice Arthur John, who later set up his own business as Arthur John & Co.

but, since the removal of the firm to Bridgend, all that remains in Cowbridge is a busy sales office and bookshop. Neil and Alan Brown still run the company at Bridgend, and have jointly over a hundred years of printing experience behind them. They are very popular figures in the High Street of Cowbridge, not the least reason being that they are identical twins. This causes much merry confusion, and even Brian Johnston did not know which twin he was interviewing when they appeared on 'Down your Way' some years ago. The third generation of the family became involved in the firm in 1958 in the person of Keith Brown, but not before a practical grounding on the shop floor and then graduating as the top student of the year at the London College of Printing. Finally, much of the continuing success of the firm is also due to another member of the family, Robert Whitaker. Mr. Whitaker, a Cambridge Honours graduate, acquired a wealth of experience in printing and publishing at the Pitman Press, Bath, before he joined the company in 1970.

It may surprise the many customers of R. S. Bird Ltd. that this well-established horticultural business has an earlier association with the town than the printing works. In fact, the company has flourished in Cowbridge for nearly two hundred years. It was founded in 1796 when Edward Bird of Cardiff purchased the property now known as 14 High Street together with a meadow nearby called Waun-y-gaer. It is still known by that name. The needs of the farming community were catered for by a succession of brothers and descendants. Nathaniel Young Bird (1827-1893) expanded the business and it was through his generosity that the Cowbridge Institute was built and furnished shortly after his death. The well known bard Iolo Morganwg lived for many years at 14 High Street presumably as a friend of the family. The early part of the 20th century saw much progress in farm and horticultural machinery but the First World War was a great set-back to business. In 1926 the brothers Bruce and Ralph Bird decided to confine their efforts to the sale and servicing of grass-cutting machinery and garden cultivators. Good progress was made and branches were opened in Carmarthen and Hereford. In 1977 an old-established business in Bristol was also acquired. The joint managing directors are Roger and Rodney Bird whose father Ralph is the company Chairman. There are 70 employees.

For 105 years the Thomas family have been recognised builders in the Vale of Glamorgan and some of their finest buildings are now famous landmarks in the area.

One of their greatest achievements was The Orangery at Margam, which was opened by the Queen in her Silver Jubilee Year.

It was on 10th November, 1874 that 14-year-old Isaac Thomas, one of seven sons from The Bakehouse, Llanblethian, started his four-year apprenticeship as a cabinet maker and joiner. His erudite father, Robert, a travelling weaver, was accustomed to holding daily public readings from the newspaper for his less knowledgeable fellow villagers.

Isaac's hard-working mother, Mary, was of yeoman stock, her family (the Llewellyns) having farmed in Llanblethian for decades. Isaac was educated at the Cowbridge rival to the grammar school — the Eagle Academy, whose past pupils include the famous essayist John Sterling (son to the original Thunderer of the Times).

Isaac's apprenticeship indentures make amusing reading in these days of wage inflation and trade union power. His earnings for the first year, if any, were unspecified, but in the second year he received the princely sum of one shilling per week. This doubled to two shillings in the third year and rose to five shillings in his fourth year. He also had to agree to numerous restrictions which included not playing cards, dice or any other unlawful game, not to go to taverns and not to get married during his apprenticeship.

Evidently he was a diligent pupil, as he eventually became the general foreman of W. James and Sons, Fonmon, where his only son, Robert followed an apprenticeship at the beginning of this century. Robert prospered, building a church, country house, fire station and farm. He took a prominent part in public life and was three times Mayor of Cowbridge during long service with the Borough Council. Two of Robert's sons followed him into the family business and carried on the good name after his death in 1965.

The building group R. T. Contractors Ltd., is managed by Robert's son Gethin and grandson Robert Thomas Junior. Contracts completed in recent years by this prominent family include the restoration of Old Hall, Cowbridge, the Shelter Scheme in Cowbridge and Southways Old People's home at Southgate, also Llantwit Major Sports Centre.

The 400 year old building where Isaac Thomas was educated, successively a hotel, school and corn stores, is now owned by the family and is presently being renovated in an attempt to retain its character. A fitting task for a family so closely involved in the history of the Vale of Glamorgan and its buildings.

Inns and Innkeepers

The acrid smell of hops, tar, hay and manure drifted down the main street from a remarkable number of inns at the turn of the century. With more than twenty taverns to choose from, it is hardly surprising that there was a lot of drunkenness in Cowbridge, especially on market day, and Iolo Morganwg's humorous skit about the drinkers of the town was still not entirely out of place seventy odd years ago.

> For Cowbridge hath no sober man,
> Or none of milk sop thinkers,
> And no philosophical fools,
> But great and glorious drinkers.

According to the late Miss Maud Gunter the situation during her youth was so bad that many wives had to go out to work to keep the family together. She also recalled the 'rubicund noses' of the Vale farmers as they hiccoughed their way out of the *Mason's Arms* after striking a good bargain at the weekly market. The inns had always attracted the young and adventurous from the outlying districts for a 'night on the town' — the aim being to have a pint in every pub — an aim which invariably failed. In his youth, John Evans, better known to older *Glamorgan Gazette* readers as Silurian, used to visit the Cowbridge pubs for such a spree and would call in at Sam Howells' brewery for some brewer's barm which was then in great demand. 'Sam', he informs us in a lively account, 'was one of the biggest men he had ever seen and he could easily hit a hole through the pine end of a house with his fist. He had been a well-known pugilist in his day and had large cauliflower ears and as many scars on his face as the map of England'. In his 'Notes and Paragraphs' Silurian also included a poem illustrating the ease of slaking one's thirst in Edwardian Cowbridge. In it a dozen characters appear, who by their very exuberance had made even sleepy Cowbridge sit up and take notice at times:

> O'er Stallingdown I tramped to town and to a *Rose and Crown* I came,
> Then I briskly crossed the road unto the *Edmondes Arms* by name;
> And after some hard drinking to the *Railway* got at last,
> There met an old *Commercial,* a *Druid* in the past.
> He placed me in a *Wheelwright's Arms* among some carts and gigs,
> Then into the *Bridge* we went where I had a few more swigs.
> And there I met a *Horse and Groom;* the groom had leggings on his legs,
> He rang a bell saying *Butchers* come and chopped off *Three Boars Heads:*
> Just then a *Lion* came in sight; to me this was no joke,
> But he toddled back into his den inside some *Royal Oak:*
> And there I met *Lord Raglan* full up with wit and yarns,
> And he led me to a cosy place they called the *Cowbridge Arms.*
> And further on I met a *Duke* who was gazing at a *Bear,*
> It had devoured some *Masons* who happened to be there;
> This did not frighten me a bit, I gave the *Bear* a push,
> And off he trotted round the *Globe* to hide inside a *Bush.*
> When I tried to hook him out the beggar began to squeak,
> So a *Pelican* came to help me with his long and powerful beak.
> And when I got him going again a *Greyhound* that was thin,
> Chastised the blighter up the road right to the *Westgate Inn.*

33. The Duke of Wellington Hotel   *(Photo: Haydn Baynham)*

It was no surprise then that Cowbridge folk at the turn of the century used to boast that they had a pub for every lamp-post standing in the High Street.

It is amazing that a town the size of Cowbridge could support such a large number of public houses. Mrs. Catherine Labdon, the popular licensee of *The Cowbridge Arms*, used to tell passers-by that 'the inns of Cowbridge laugh and grow fat not by catering to the thousand men and women of the borough, but by slaking the thirst of the many visitors that make Cowbridge their Mecca on Fair days'. This making of hay while the sun shone was more likely to have been true of the country inns like *The Morning Star* of Pentremeyrick, *The Crack Inn*, and particularly *The Bell* of St. Mary Hill, where on the day of the great horse fair the takings were so large as to see them through the rest of the year. Of the Cowbridge inns in the pre-1914 period a truer picture is that the landlords were fully employed in other occupations unrelated to the beer trade. A public house was simply a side line, the only exceptions being in the case of widows. In passing it is interesting to note that in former times one seldom came across a village inn, to which a smithy, a carpenter's shop, tailor, or other craftman's shop was not attached. As far as Cowbridge was concerned the *Bear* and the *Duke* were the only self-supporting pubs.

The families who kept the numerous pubs in the town at this time are a picture gallery of fascinating characters. Space, however, allows but a brief mention of some of them. One of the most interesting was Richard Aubrey the noted Cowbridge wheelwright. In the 1900s he was an old man but previously he had kept the *Wheelwright's Arms*. The Rev. J. J. Morgan, the minister of the Limes chapel, mentioned him in his memoirs. He described him as 'Crefftwr diguro', an unsurpassed craftsman. One of his well-known inventions was a three-wheel velocipede, an early form of bicycle propelled by thrusting the feet against the ground. Sad to narrate, when Mr. Aubrey demonstrated his machine in front of huge, cheering crowds on the Stalling-down, the occasion ended in a complete fiasco. The machine, after plunging headlong down the slopes, crashed because of faulty brakes; the velocipede was a complete write-off, and the inventor was lucky to escape serious injury. Thomas John Pugh, the landlord of the *Commercial*, was another popular figure. Pugh was a water diviner of remarkable skill known locally as 'the wizard with the rod', and his twisting twigs were in constant demand throughout the world. He had visited California after the terrible earthquake in 1906 and finally emigrated to Australia in the 1920s, where his successful demonstrations of water divining won much praise from the Director of Agriculture for the state of Victoria. There was certainly the lustre of unique character about Samuel Hayter the landlord of the *Horse and Groom* for many years. Sam, it seems, was well versed in the lore of amateur weather forecasting. In later years he would listen patiently to young Colin Adams as he fidgeted and worried about the heavy Vale mists that used to shroud the cricket ground on Saturday mornings. His voice always boomed with a ring of prophetic zeal: 'Lads, it's all for heat' — thus predicting a glorious summer day.

All the farmers of the Cowbridge district were in fact weather prophets of one kind or another, in the days when the 'Met Office' was unheard of, and Sam — who incidentally was the last lob or underhand bowler in the Cowbridge cricket team — would hear some very strange weather predictions over the bar of the *Horse and Groom*. The movement of sheep and cattle for instance to higher altitude predicted fine weather, whereas their return to lower and more sheltered pastures meant bad weather was imminent. Swallows and martins were supposed to swoop low over the ground before early rain, whereas partridges and pheasants would approach farm houses when stormy weather was at hand. Spiders' webs across narrow lanes would indicate a glorious summer to come, whilst a mist enveloping Garth Maelwg Mountain near Llanharan predicted a heavy downpour.

The Market and Vale of Glamorgan Agricultural Society Show

Before the First World War, Cowbridge was one of a number of small country town markets in Glamorgan and faced stiff competition from Peterston-Super-Ely, Wenvoe, Llantwit Major and Bridgend. During the Great War the market was used for the grading of fatstock under Government Control and business began to increase. The cattle in those days had to be held in the main street for weighing on the town weighbridge opposite the Eagle Stores. Councillor Eddie John helped the auctioneers with the weighing for many years and it was quite a performance starting from seven o'clock in the morning. The controls were eventually removed and in due course the auction sales reverted to a Monday. There were many fluctuations in the market between the wars, but in 1939 stock was once again graded and sold direct to the Ministry. The war years and especially the closing of the markets at Llantwit Major, Peterston and Wenvoe after decontrol in 1954 greatly enhanced the importance of Cowbridge as a county mart. By this time the buildings had become rather dilapidated and, as a result, the auctioneers built a newly covered cattle market in 1958. During the 1960s, the Borough Council found it necessary to acquire the old sheep market for use as a car park and a new covered sheep market was built and officially opened by the Mayor of Cowbridge, Councillor John Roberts, on 19 May, 1969. Also present at the ceremony was Alderman Eddie John, the chairman of the market committee, whose grandfather Alderman Edward John had played such a significant role in the rebuilding of the old market in 1889. Other recent improvements have included the reconstruction of the cattle pens and sale ring, the extension of the sheep pens and a new calf-selling shed and pig market — all of which are a tribute to the modern approach of the auctioneers and the local council. When Messrs. John David, Watts and Morgan decided to close the Bridgend market in 1977, it was a further boost for Cowbridge. Arrangements were made to operate the amalgamated markets at Cowbridge under the name of Glamorgan Marts. It is still run by Messrs. David, Watts and Morgan and Herbert R. Thomas, Son and Edwards, whose joint enterprise has made it into the leading livestock centre of South Wales.

Of the two firms of autioneers, Messrs. David, Watts and Morgan have the earliest connections with the market. John David, who established the firm in 1857, is said to have started the first modern livestock market as a fair. In the early years of the present century the firm was joined by D. C. Watts and Hopkin D. Morgan. Alderman David Watts was a most respected citizen of Cowbridge as well as being a familiar face at the market for over fifty years. He served as Mayor in 1936-37 and was given the freedom of the Borough. Neither John David nor Alderman Watts had any successors in the company. But G. Morgan Joseph joined the firm in the 1950s and the present senior partner is Hopkin Morgan's son, Robert. Subsequently, the concern has expanded into a leading firm of auctioneers, land and estate agents in the Vale of Glamorgan.

Herbert R. Thomas, the head of the rival firm of auctioneers, is a household name to much of the farming community of Mid and South Glamorgan. Since the first batch of fatstock came under his hammer at the tender age of seventeen, Herbert Thomas has graduated by the sheer force of his ability and personality to become the doyen of Glamorgan auctioneers. Much of the success of the Cowbridge market stems from this immensely genial man always brimming over with energy. With words tumbling from his lips like marbles on to a playground, he has for the last fifty years never been happier than in 'the thick of things' directing the sales with a deft and masterly touch. His career has been studded with honours from the world of auctioneering and agriculture. He was elected a Fellow of the Auctioneers and Estate Agents Institute in 1928, and served as a member of the South Wales and Monmouthshire Agricultural Valuers Association as well as President of the branch from 1944 to 1946. During the War he was appointed by the Ministry of Food to the responsible post of County Chairman of Auctioneers for Glamorgan in connection with the control of the marketing of all the fatstock in the country. He was joined in partnership by Mr. Collwyn Edwards, F.R.I.C.S. in 1950 and by his son Mr. Robert Thomas, M.A., (Cantab.), F.R.I.C.S. in 1952. Finally he became a Commissioner of Taxes from 1952 until his retirement in 1977.

The first show organised by the Vale of Glamorgan Society was held in the Cowbridge market and adjoining fields on 22 September, 1892. At the

34. Opening of the new Sheep Market at Cowbridge, 19th May, 1969 (left to right) Robert Thomas, Councillor John Roberts (Mayor), Herbert R. Thomas, Haydn Lewis and Alan Fairfax

outset the Show was a comparatively small affair with gates of less than £20. About the turn of the century T. J. Yorwerth was appointed Secretary and Robert Thomas, father of Mr. Herbert R. Thomas and Manager of the Midland Bank, Treasurer. Mr. Yorwerth continued in office until 1945 during which time he was Mayor of Cowbridge six times. He was the principal figure behind the success of the Show in the 1920s when it was described as the foremost one-day event in the county. At that time a great deal of interest was taken in the Show by prominent men in the world of agriculture, industry and journalism and the Show owed much to the patronage and support of men like Henry G. Lewis, Dan Radcliffe and Robert Webber of the *Western Mail*. King George V exhibited Hereford cattle at Cowbridge Show on several occasions, and in 1929 was awarded the cup for the best animal in the Cattle Classes. As it grew, the Show moved to the Bear Field, where a great stand was erected. It continued there until 1953 when it was moved to its present site near Penllyn Castle by kind permission of the late Capt. H. C. R. Homfray and Mr. A. H. Llewellyn, the tenant of the land. The move was immediately vindicated by a record attendance of 14,000 people.

Since the War no one has played a greater role in ensuring the success of the Show than Herbert R. Thomas, the Secretary from 1945 until 1966. Mr. Thomas, ably assisted by the late Mr. J. Lloyd Jones, was able to raise membership to about a thousand. In 1965 Mr. Jones was succeeded by John Jenkins and Mr. Thomas by Clive Neathey. Under its hard working Chairman, John Cory, J.P. of Peterston, the Show has continued to prosper, although the recent cancellation of the main Show Luncheon has been a distinct loss to the social side of the event. Nevertheless, the Cattle and Sheep Section, the Dog Show and the trade stands have more than held their own in latter years and the Horticultural Show is still regarded as one of the best in the three counties of Glamorgan.

Vanishing fairs and local customs

Until about forty or fifty years ago, the horse was an essential link in the agricultural economy. Even the smallest farmer in the neighbourhood of Cowbridge kept a horse to do a variety of jobs about his farm. Until the 1920s horses were also an important part of the transport system, and schoolboys still rode from outlying villages to the Grammar School by horse as did their fathers to chapel. So it is not surprising that the hiring and pleasure fairs at Cowbridge and St. Mary Hill were well patronised, not only by the local farmers but by the local tradesmen and the general public as the best places to strike a bargain.

In the early years of this century five hiring and pleasure fairs continued to visit the town, but the highlight of the year for old and young alike was the March Fair. On every Tuesday preceding 25 March Cowbridge became a colourful canvas town of noise, gaiety and excitement. As most of the dealing was still done in the roadway, the High Street was choked with the carts of the farmers parked tightly on the forecourts of the inns and resounded with the clatter of horses' hoofs as they jog-trotted to and fro in front of prospective buyers. Above the animated cries of the vendors as they sold tallow candles, glass beads, china ornaments, gingerbread and exquisite brandy snaps made specially by 'Charlie Buns' the local baker, rose a greater tumult from Studt's pleasure fairground on the Bear Inn Field. Here vociferous and well-oiled Tom Cobleys from the Vale, all immaculately dressed in holiday garb, were bent upon committing as many of the Seven Deadly Sins as their purses would allow. The most popular feature of the afternoon's entertainment was the grand Horse Parade. The magnificent horses, manes and tails gaily plaited with coloured ribbons, paraded up and down the High Street and everybody applauded the genteel cadences of the trotting matches.

After the horse parade, pleasure seekers tried their luck on the Bear Field, and if a child had sixpence to spend in those days he was fortunate. If you failed to shy shillelaghs at Aunt Sally's head or knock down a Jumping Jack as resilient as a boomerang with your fists, you could always grin like a satyr through a horse's collar and collect a prize for making the ugliest face. Occasionally a circus visited the town and a man with a dancing bear attracted large crowds on the Aberthin Road. The circus used to pitch its tent behind one of the many inns and a much-loved story of one of the oldest inhabitants is that the elephants would be taken down to the River Thaw to drink. On his way one of the beasts put his trunk into a tailor's shop and the tailor rather stupidly stuck a needle into it. On his return from the river, the elephant again thrust his trunk in through the window of the shop, but this time to everyone's amusement he avenged himself by drenching the tailor. This little tale, if true, proves that old people as well as elephants never forget!

A far more important horse fair in the Cowbridge district was, of course, held at St. Mary Hill, three miles outside the town. Tradition has it that the fair was held originally at Ogmore-by-Sea. Traders from all parts of England used to visit the site and often outwitted the Welsh by putting the horses on board ship prior to paying for them. To avoid this the Welsh farmers moved the fair further inland, first to Pencoed and then to St. Mary Hill so that all bargains could be safely made. The fair in Medieval times was held in August on the Feast of the Assumption of the Virgin Mary and has always had a reputation for lurid happenings since Good Queen Bess's reign, when it was regarded as one of the most dangerous spots in the county. A popular belief persisted into our fathers' days that it always rained on 26 August to wash the blood away. It was one of the most famous fairs in Wales, second only to the Dallas Fair in Cardigan. At the turn of the century it was still in its heyday and all the inns of Cowbridge and Bridgend would be fully booked up with visitors from England. A chronicler in the

Glamorgan Gazette in 1906 wrote that all the brakes within a radius of ten miles of Bridgend were brought out to ply for hire at the foot of Station Hill, such was the rush to attend the fair. Pickpocketing and even bare-faced robbery were still rife on 'The Hill', but the most common malpractice was shady dealings in horses.

One such victim, according to Silurian, was a Llanhari character called Wil Ty Draw. Wil had keen ambitions to become a haulier in the fast-developing collieries of Gilfach Goch. He already had a ramshackle cart and all he needed was a horse. Siân, his wife, gave him the necessary money to buy one at the fair, but Wil was easily deceived among the diversions of the fairground and squandered most of his money. He look on trust a short-winded, decrepid old creature, which had been gingered up for the sale. In no time, Wil's lofty ambitions and the horse came a mighty cropper on Llantrisant Hill for the wretched nag dropped dead at the South Gate on its very first journey to Gilfach.

The fair had its literary side too. Mrs. Elizabeth Evans, the landlady of the *Fox and Hounds*, Llanhari, was a genial patron of the arts. She always set up a marquee for the annual meeting of the literary men of the district. In what was the only waterproof tent on the fairground 'Ap Ieuan', the local archdruid, and his attendant bards were always able to read their poems and discuss the events of the day, while all lesser mortals on the field were more often than not, soaked to the skin. By the beginning of the Second World War, the Cowbridge and St. Mary Hill fairs were only shadows of their former importance. The tractor and the motor car had taken over so completely that the number of horses employed on the farms and highways began to diminish rapidly. After the War the fairs died out.

Many of the traditional customs of the Borough had died out long before the hiring fairs. Dr. Hopkin James in his book *Old Cowbridge* tells us that the last Mari Lwyd in the town had been Mr. John John, who lived opposite the Church gates, but the custom had died out before the First World War.

An interesting funeral custom lingered on into the twentieth century. All funeral processions used to approach Cowbridge Church along the north side of the main street, never along the south—until they reached the entrance to Church Street. Here they wheeled left across the street because they were unconsciously following an ancient custom of presenting the body at the Town Cross which stood in the middle of the roadway in Medieval times. Even in modern times a departure from this age-old custom would have caused considerable annoyance to the mourners. About 70 years ago, 'Thomas the *Bear*' provided hearses for most of the Cowbridge funerals. The hearse was always driven by an immaculately dressed horseman with a cockade in his hat, and as the magnificent jet black Irish steeds proceeded sedately along the High Street, the cortege presented an aura of grim pageantry.

St. Valentine's Day as a lover's festival, was held in greater esteem than it is today. Indeed during the week preceding 14 February the flood of

Valentines brought as great a rush on the post as the Christmas mail does today. Most of the newsagents of the town displayed a wide range of cards in their windows, varying from the amorous sort to the humorous and even the plain vindictive. Some that were posted were almost libellous, prompted no doubt by ill will, jealousy or jilted love, and they were not at all popular with the local postmen. While on the topic of postmen, it is worth considering the enormous distances they covered in the days when delivery was all on foot. Miss Freda Evans has written a fascinating account in the Church Magazine of how she used to meet Rowsell and Perry, the Cowbridge postmen, on her journey to and from the Intermediate High School many years ago. She would catch the 6 a.m. train at St. Athan Road Station and it would pick up the postmen at Llanbethery Halt and St. Mary Church. By 8 a.m. the two had walked from Cowbridge delivering the morning mail to the surrounding villages and outlying farms and had cleared the pillar boxes en route. On the train back to Cowbridge they would sort out the remaining mail: 'Old Perry' had lost his left hand and wore a steel hook, but undeterred by this deformity, he would put a small bundle on his knee, steady it with his hook and tie it with his right hand. When Miss Evans returned on the afternoon train the two postmen would be in it again with the afternoon mail on their way to a second delivery and collection. They must have walked thousands of miles in their time, their springy steps devouring the winding trail between Cowbridge and Rhoose unwearyingly, and yet they still found time to cultivate their garden plots and the allotments at the side of the railway line. 'Old Perry' and Rowsell were not the only long range walkers of the age before public transport. A more picturesque sight than the plodding postmen was the gaily dressed procession of Cardiff girls, all with large baskets on their heads mincing their way as delicately as ostriches across Stallingdown for water cress. They must have walked nearly thirty miles a day.

The local quarries, ponds and main street were the natural playground for the children of Cowbridge in the early years of the century. A favourite pastime was to play 'Red Indians' among the foxes' holes and tangled brambles of Ianto Frank's cave, the ghoulish hideout of a seventeenth-century highwayman near St. Hilary. And in severe weather the marble sur-faces of Megan Felin and Pysgodlyn Mawr fish ponds near Welsh St. Donats became a feast of pleasure as young skaters from the town swirled in the air like Catherine wheels while bird watchers eagerly waited the arrival of the saw-toothed merganser. Finally in the High Street, as yet unspoiled by the smell of petrol fumes, the children played their seasonal games. Almost by instinct the kiddies seemed to know exactly when to commence each new game. Marbles were started immediately after Ash Wednesday and the children knew the very day when to begin kite-flying on Stallingdown, tops, battledore and shuttlecock, skipping and duckstones on the pavements, Twm Jawl bach on the window panes and hoops on the deserted thoroughfare.

Church, Chapel and the Welsh Language

In the early years before the 1914 War, religion was still a powerful force in people's lives. Not only was attendance at morning and evening service a cardinal feature of one's upbringing, but three or four evenings a week would also be devoted to activities connected with Church or Chapel such as prayer meetings, Band of Hope, the Temperance Movement, choir practice, preparations for cymanfaoedd ganu, eisteddfodau and even impromptu speech making and public debate. The picture of attendance at the various denominations at the beginning of the present century as seen in the figures below clearly shows that Nonconformity was still very much in the ascendancy, although the figures are to be treated with some caution.

Numbers of Church Members in Cowbridge and Llanblethian in 1905 (from evidence collected by the Welsh Church Commission).

	Communicants	Sunday scholars	Adherents
Parish Churches*	320	284	
Ramoth (Baptist)	180	160	100
Sion, The Limes (C.M.)	68	94	100
Aberthin (C.M.)	17		55
Maendy (Cong.)	129		141
Wesleyan	71	55	80
	785	593	476

* In 1905 there were three parish churches in the united parish of Llanblethian with Cowbridge and Welsh St. Donats. The total population of the three civil parishes was 1,885 in 1901.

N.B. It is fairly clear that the three categories of communicants, Sunday scholars and adherents were not mutually exclusive.

The Church of the Holy Cross was attended by the well-to-do gentry and the majority of the professional people of the town. There was still a distinct social barrier between the Anglicans and the Nonconformists and several older people still recall with a mixture of admiration and envy the Easter Parade of the ladies of Holy Cross as they displayed their finery through the High Street after church. The Church always possessed a fine choir and an enthusiastic team of bell ringers. Tom Rees of Darren Farm in particular is recalled to this very day ladling out jugfuls of milk as if his very life depended on it, so that he could go bell ringing later that morning. Ramoth was undoubtedly the spiritual home of the majority of Nonconformists. The morning services were still held in Welsh which was spoken by the older inhabitants of the Border Vale and Llanblethian village. The chapel possessed a fine choir and its silk-hatted and frock-coated conductor, William Evans, made the choir the envy of every chapel in the Vale. William, known everywhere as Ioan Mere, had been one of the four tailors of Cowbridge. Music was the abiding passion of this tailor with the Toscanini touch; it was in his every gesture and movement as, dressed always in his short sleeves with a coil of grey wool over his shoulders, he worked from dawn to dusk on his table in Church Street. Silurian used to visit him there with his youthful companions and they always 'did a spot of singing and squatting around the tailors' platform, where Ioan and Ebenezer would be sewing away for their very lives. But if ever the youths dropped a wrong note Ioan would drop a long sleeve board on the culprit's head that would make him see stars'. Soon his two pretty daughters would be brought out to join in the choruses and in no time the maestro, flailing the air with his huge tailor's scissors, would unite all the voices in such melodious harmony as to make the roof rattle. In the days before the motor car, Ioan and his merry troupe of choristers—all carrying candles in jam jars to lighten the darkness of the country lanes—would be seen on many a winter evening trudging the whole length of the Border Vale from Penllyn to Llantrisant to earn hundreds of pounds for charitable purposes. He was an all-round working man, a type rarely seen today and was as well versed in theology, politics and philosophy as in the plying of his trade.

'The Limes' chapel was also well attended at this time with the downstairs completely full and half a dozen or so in the galleries. The Rev. Emrys Davies ministered to his flock of Calvinistic Methodists for about thirty-nine years and he made certain that Cowbridge was well represented at the annual Festival of Vale Presbyterian Chapels held alternatively at Barry, Llantwit Major and Cowbridge. The Wesleyan Methodists had their chapel where Louis Fisher's shop formerly stood and was attended largely by the sons and daughters of the Somerset farm labourers who came into the district in the nineteenth century.

Sunday was the only full day's leisure in most people's lives but in some ways was far more stringent than the other six. All shops in the High Street were closed. Work, apart from the feeding of animals, was looked upon with disapproval and the reading of Sunday newspapers with abhorrence. Boots were polished, vegetables cleaned and even the drinking water from the street pumps was collected on the night before. Attendance at Sunday School as well as morning and evening service seems to us moderns to have been rather hard on the children of that time, but according to Mrs. V. J. Russell's recent account in the Parish Magazine, it was a mixture of discipline and delight. She attended the Church Sunday School on the Cardiff Road (now converted into 'School House'). There were six classes of girls and about the same number of boys. Miss Knapton was the Superintendent and her brother Fred accompanied the children on the harmonium. The senior girls' class was taken by Mrs. Jenkins, whose husband, a country postman, encouraged the children to take a keen interest in Botany. He used to tell them where the rare plants and flowers grew and Mrs. Russell recalls her intense delight in finding herb Paris as well as bee and butterfly orchids. The discipline of learning the Collect off by heart, was more than compensated for, it seems, by gazing in wonder at the Rev. Isaiah Roberts' lantern shows, giggling hilariously in the old Schoolroom at Charlie Gwyn's comic songs and above all the once-a-year, never-to-be-forgotten trip to the ends of the earth—the Sunday School outing to the Leys at Aberthaw.

The earliest outings were jostling jaunts along the boneshaking roads of the Vale in a wagonette driven by Mrs. Foster of the *Druids* hotel. There would be a couple of accompanying traps to take the food, which consisted of home-made bread and butter, home-cured ham and Welsh cakes by the ton. Later the Church and chapels used the railway to St. Athan Road station and walked to the beach. One such outing has been aptly described in the Parish Magazine for 1909:

> 'Scholars of three Sunday Schools took part. About 250 children and their teachers left Cowbridge at 9.20 a.m. for the Leys on Wednesday, August 4th. At noon the children were served with sand-wiches and lemonade in true picnic style, with the green grass as the table cloth and at 4 p.m. they were again regaled with an excellent tea. During the day the usual sports and bathing were indulged in and the children with their teachers when they reached Cowbridge in the evening were delighted with their outing by the sea. Miss Culverwell had kindly arranged the catering for the children and she was assisted by the teachers of the Sunday School. Mr. Elias of the Ship Hotel produced the hot water etc. We are very grateful to Mr. Williams the station-master, for facilitating the children to and from the Leys and also to Alderman L. Jenkins for his kindness in placing at our disposal one of his wagons with horse and driver for the cartage of the eatables from Cowbridge to the Leys and the small children to and from the station and the sea.'

The loosening of the hold of organised religion, especially Nonconformity, upon the community after the Second World War is clearly illustrated by the closure of the Wesleyan and Limes chapels. The former cause folded up in the 1960s but the Limes put a brave face on it until lately. The Baptists at this time were having poor morning and the Presbyterians poor evening at-tendances. So a union was mooted between the churches in which everybody attended morning service at 'The Limes' and evening service at Ramoth. Eventually it was decided to close the Limes and all Nonconformists would attend Ramoth which had become the United Free Church. To conclude our section on religion, may we recommend visitors to Cowbridge to make a short tour of Holy Cross parish church the next time they visit the town. It is surprising how many leave without even noticing this interesting medieval building half hidden as it is between the *Duke of Wellington* and the old Grammar School. Yet when one turns into Church Street one is immediately impressed by the massive octagonal tower of the church with its decidedly military appearance. It is claimed by some that the recesses in the ringing tower were built to house the arrows of the defenders. Long ago the tower housed a spire too, but this has long since disappeared. We have already referred to the magnificent peal of bells, all cast in 1722.

The bells are inscribed by the names of certain benefactors, all of whom were among the famous of Town and County at that time: Daniel Durel, Thomas Wilkins, Mrs. Hesther Wilkins, Edward Carne, Francis Gwyn and Edward Stradling. In addition there is an ancient Sanctus bell. It was known to everyone as the Mary Rose in days gone by and was re-hung in 1937. It had been used as a fire bell. The original chancel was extended eastwards in the fourteenth century in a secondary phase of building, which also saw the completion of the Chantry Chapel, now used as the Choir Vestry. This chapel was founded by William the Prior for the perpetual use of a single priest, whose duties were to offer Masses for the Dead and in all probability to teach the children of the town. He may have lived on the premises—in the small room attached to the rear of the Chantry Chapel which is still in use as the clergy vestry.

An unusual feature of the nave is the south aisle. It was added to the nave—the last stage in fact of the building of the medieval church—in 1473, exclusively for the Llanquian worshippers because their church near Aberthin had fallen down and was not rebuilt. The late Rev. Ewart Lewis, Vicar of Cowbridge, maintained that the Llanquian aisle with its striking barrel roof and abundance of light is what architects would admire most in his church.

Of the numerous monuments in the church only two catch the eye from an artistic point of view. The most outstanding is the Carne monument in the Llanquian aisle. Once beautifully coloured, it depicts the parents and weepers presumably weeping for their six offspring. It is dated 1626. The other impressive monument is that to Judge David Jenkins of Hensol. This redoubtable Border Vale squire was such a redoubtable champion of Charles I's cause that he declared himself quite willing to die on the scaffold with the Bible under his one arm and the Magna Carta under the other. He spent several years in the Tower of London for his opposition to Cromwell and narrowly escaped death on several occasions until his release in 1656. His family motto FE DAL AM DARO (It pays to strike), and his emblem (Three Cocks) are also displayed on the monument. There is also the monument to the well-known topographer and historian Benjamin Heath Malkin. He once lived at Old Hall and is buried in the graveyard. Holy Cross is also the final resting place of the poet Lewis Morganwg and the genealogist Rice Meyrick of Cottrell, the author of *Glamorgan Antiquities*. The floor of the church is dotted with burial slabs and I wonder how many Grammar School pupils ever realized that they were walking over the graves of three head-masters of their school—Daniel Walters, Thomas Williams and William Williams—as they traversed the chancel floor?

In its plate, the church is richly endowed. There is an Elizabethan chalice dated 1576. The seventeenth century is well represented by an impressive silver gilt cup, two patens, one of which was donated by the family of Judge Jenkins of Hensol, and by an exquisite silver flagon given by the Seys family in 1680. Further nineteenth century and modern gifts of beauty have greatly added to the treasures of the church.

Holy Cross Church, Cowbridge had been extremely fortunate in having as its rector Canon Stanley H. Mogford. Many improvements have been carried out during his benefice such as the renovation of the roof and the removal of the chancel screen and its positioning near the organ. With financial aid from the South Glamorgan County Council and the Grammar School Old Boys' Association, two stained-glass windows have been removed from the old Grammar School and re-fitted into the Llanquian Aisle and the Vestry. The Old Boys' Association also carried out the in-filling between the chancel and the Vestry as a memorial to Richard Williams, Headmaster from 1919-1938 and to the memory of Old Boys who were killed during the war. The church is now more flourishing than it has been for very many years and this is mainly due to the active interest that Canon Mogford and his colleagues have taken in the activities of the Church.

The suddenness of the decline of the Welsh language in the Cowbridge district during the early years of the twentieth century is underlined by a note in *Iolo Morganwg* by Professor G. J. Williams in which he stated that he met an elderly woman in Ystradowen in 1920 who was for all practical purposes monoglot Welsh. Later he learned from the Rev. T. T. Jones of Maendy chapel that when he first came there in 1890 the same could have been said of many of his congregation. It is probable that G. J. Williams exaggerated the Welshness of the Vale of Glamorgan, but it is interesting to note that as late as 1901 64 per cent of those over 65 in the borough of Cowbridge were Welsh speaking. Other figures from the 1901 Census emphatically prove that the language was rapidly on the decline: only 2.9 per cent of those under 15 years could converse in their native tongue, thus illustrating the crippling effect of the 1870 Education Act which made education available only through the English language. Soon the chapels dropped the language in their morning service and one author tells us that the town was well-known for the quality of its spoken English. It is also significant that Welsh was not included on the syllabus at the Grammar School until the appointment of Tudor Hughes in 1928. By 1961 the figures were down to a negligible 6 per cent, but of late there has been a remarkable revival in the fortunes of the language, although most of the fluent speakers are newcomers to the borough whose roots are in other parts of the principality. Who would have thought even ten years ago that Cowbridge would boast not only a flourishing Ysgol Feithrin (Welsh Nursery School) but also a Welsh primary school preparing young pupils for a totally bi-lingual secondary education at Ysgol Gyfun Glantâf in Cardiff?

35. Cowbridge Borough Council — 1928

Back row: J. G. H. Bird (Surveyor); Councillors W. H. John, Evan Thomas, L.S. Rowsell;
G. Millman and C. Davies (Auditors); D. C. Watts (Borough Agent)
Middle row: E. Villis (Mace Bearer); Councillors Ed. Williams, W. Davies, W. Pickard,
A. T. Mills, Evan Hopkins, C. M. Davies, Wybert Thomas; S. Oakley (Mace Bearer)
Front row: Alderman John Williams, Lewis Jenkins; W. T. Gwyn (Town Clerk);
Councillor W. A. L. Phillips (Mayor); Aldermen John Llewellyn and David Thomas

The Borough and District Councils (1900-1974)

To some of its critics the Borough of Cowbridge has appeared throughout much of the present century as a dodo in ceremonial chains, giving itself airs of pomp and circumstance which were never quite suited to its size and importance. When Mr. Richard Williams arrived at Cowbridge in 1919 to take up his appointment as headmaster he found the town 'medieval — or at any rate early Victorian', with the trains running late, no electric light or water supply and only one bath in the Grammar School itself. As regards the installation of a public sewerage scheme, the town had to wait until 1953. It was not surprising that some caustic jokes were occasionally bandied around about the Rip Van Winkleness of the Borough, the classic being Lord Tredegar's wry comment that half of Cowbridge slept, while the other half went about on tip toes lest they woke the sleepers. But to lay all the blame at the feet of the Borough authorities is grossly unfair. First and foremost it should be realised that as well as being one of the oldest in Wales, the Borough was one of the smallest. It had a population of little more than a thousand, comprised only about eighty acres, and consisted mainly of only one main thoroughfare with the borough boundaries touching the back fences of the properties alongside it. Yet under successive Mayors and their Councils Cowbridge not only maintained the proud traditions of the borough but provided such essential amenities of modern life as the limited financial resources allowed. The chief functions of the Borough Council in the final years before the local government re-organisation were responsibility for cleaning the streets, leasing the markets to the auctioneers, public health, collection of refuse, the letting of Council houses, the maintenance of the cemetery, the care of the children's playing field at the Poplars and the running of the Town Hall. Here the nitty-gritty of Borough affairs were seen to by a town agent working on a part-time basis for a very modest salary. The agent is not to be confused with the Town Clerk who also worked for a nominal fee. It was not surprising that in such a small borough they were faced with some strange anomalies from time to time. The Main Street, for instance, was a trunk road administered by the County Council

36. A meeting of the Town Council during 1934 shows Alderman T. J. Yorwerth, Alderman John Williams, Councillor Bob Thomas (Mayor), Mrs Thomas, Alderman C. M. Davies and A. W. Gwyn (Town Clerk)

37. Proclamation at the South Gate of the 25th anniversary of King George V accession to the throne. Those present include: A. S. Evans, W. Morgan, Morgan Thomas, Rev. D. P. David, L. S. Rowsell, W. Davies, C. M. Davies, A. W. Gwyn (Town Clerk), Johnson Miles (Mayor), Sgt. Burston, W. Batchelor and T. J. Yorwerth

and would be regularly cleaned by a mechanical sweeper, but the Borough had to send its own roadman to tidy up the numerous courts and sidestreets that led off the main road.

Lord Tredegar's remarks about the sleepiness of Cowbridge did not apply in any way to the politics of the borough, especially in the early years of the century. Elections were hotly contested and at that time there was a strong Liberal element in the borough determined that Cowbridge would never have the reputation of being a 'true blue' town. One of the staunchest Liberals of this period was Alderman Edward John. He had been one of the original councillors elected in 1887, a leading official in the District of Odd-fellows and a strong 'Limes Chapel' man. He was especially proud of his close friendship with David Lloyd George the Liberal statesman, and the Rev. Emrys Davies of the above mentioned chapel used to tell how he first met his hero at Caernarfon Castle on the occasion of the Investiture of the Prince of Wales in 1911. On that day of great national celebrations, Alderman John felt like a grain of sand in the vast sea of faces watching the ceremony, but after a while he spotted Lloyd George engaged in deep conversation with a group of admirers. He was determined to meet his hero face to face and notwithstanding the vast crowds he waited his turn. Patience however was not one of the virtues of the Cowbridge councillor and unwilling to wait any longer, he edged forward, pushing and jostling until he was able to prod his hero on the arm. There were pickpockets around that day, so it was not surprising that Lloyd George suspected that he was an object of their attention. Pouncing like a leopard on Alderman John he demanded what on earth he was up to. With security men scurrying to and fro, the poor alderman felt like a fly in a spider's web. He soon recovered his poise however, his explanation was accepted and he struck up a friendship with the great man which lasted until the Alderman's death.

A curious anachronism of the borough which survived well into the twentieth century was the appointment of a Town Crier. One of the best known criers of the Victorian period had been Christopher Norton, who being a tailor was given cloth by the Borough authorities with which to make a uniform. Unfortunately, his poor eyesight prevented him making the clothes and the Corporation was forced to hire another tailor to make the suit for him. In the Edwardian period Richard John and Robert Newman used their large handbells to announce concerts, sales and other important civic events. It is pleasant to note that the deep, stentorian voice of a Town Crier still echoes through the streets of Cowbridge — at least for one week during the year. For throughout the past decade, John Malcolm Davies has been announcing the various festivities and entertainments of 'Cowbridge Week' as well as bringing a lot of good natured fun to the occasion.

The Borough has always succeeded in cutting a dash as far as pomp and ceremony are concerned. On all formal occasions the four Aldermen were attired in scarlet robes, the twelve councillors in blue, and all wore tricorn hats. Our photograph shows Councillor D. C. Watts accepting a Coronation

38. The Town Crier (Malcolm Davies) announcing 'Cowbridge Week'

(Photo: Haydn Baynham)

Year Gift of the robes of office for the councillors from an anonymous donor in 1937. At the same time the first woman councillor, Mrs. Gwenllian Tilley, was presented with a three-cornered hat to wear on civic occasions. Other trappings of office included a pair of silver maces dating from 1606. The Mayor's gold chain dated back to the end of the last century and had been presented to the town in 1887 by Alderman Thomas Rees after topping the poll in that memorable first election of the reformed Borough. Until recently the Mayor took office in November, and in the celebration of the Mayor's Sunday on the first Sunday after 9 November Cowbridge needed no hints from the 'Mansion House' in London about the formation of its mayoral procession. At eleven o'clock in the morning a contingent of stalwart, smartly dressed officers of the Glamorgan County Constabulary assembled at the Town Hall to lead the procession to a chosen place of worship. They were followed by the Cowbridge Fire Brigade (under the command in those days of Chief Officer Brown), a detachment of ex-Servicemen, members of the Red Cross, Boy Scouts and Girl Guides, then the aldermen, councillors and officials of the Borough. The Mayor himself, preceded by two top-hatted, white-gloved mace bearers and supported by the Town Clerk—for many years a member of the Gwyn family—and the Mayor's Chaplain occupied the central part of the parade and these were followed by the county magistrates and public representatives from all walks of life.

The Mayor was the official head of the town for a year and until the last few years he was paid only £100 for his services with an extra £45 for expenses. The Mayors since 1900 have been of a totally different social complexion from those of the old Corporation and have been drawn from all walks of life and shades of political opinion, including even a firebrand Socialist in the person of the late Alderman Johnson Miles. Certain families have achieved the unique distinction of producing several mayors of the town. In the John family, father, son and grandson have held the office, Alderman E. John, 1900 and 1919, Coun. W. H. John 1926 and Ald. Edward John 1951 and 1964, and in 1969 Coun. D. F. Tilley also made history as the first mayor of Cowbridge whose mother and father had also been mayors before him. Mrs. Mary Hall, the mayor in 1971, had the unique distinction of presenting two honorary Freedoms, one to Sir Cennydd Traherne, the Lord Lieutenant of the County, and the other to Mrs. Gwenllian Tilley, known popularly as 'the grandmother of Cowbridge'. The visit of Royalty to the borough in 1973 was the first since Richard II passed through on his expedition to Ireland in May 1399 and it required a great deal of effort on the part of Mayor W. V. B. 'Sandy' Greenwood. Prince Philip stopped at Cowbridge Town hall for forty minutes on his way to Rhoose Airport for the official opening of the £1 million passenger terminal and after signing the Visitors' Book in the Mayor's Parlour attended a reception party and chatted to local people.

The last Mayor of the Borough was William Selwyn Davies, whose term of office ended in 1974—the year of reorganisation of Local Government.

39. Presentation of New Robes to members of the Cowbridge Town Council during
Coronation Year 1937
Left to right: W. E. Jones (High Street Garage); Fred Williams (Bear Hotel); L. S. Rowsell
(Westgate); Johnson Miles (Westgate); Mrs David Tilley (Ivy House); W. J. David
(Butcher); David C. Watts, Mayor (Auctioneer); Bob Thomas (Bus Inspector); Jack
Morgan (Garage); Bert Griffiths (Horse & Groom Hotel)

Many years previously Selwyn had been most impressed when he attended
his first Borough Council meeting and he had felt at the time that he would
sooner have been made Mayor of Cowbridge than Lord Mayor of London.
At his inauguration ceremony he took the opportunity to voice in public
what everybody connected with public life was feeling in private 'Change is
inevitable, but I regret that our town is being swallowed up by a vast, imper-
sonal monster'. The final year ended with a flurry of activity, which included the building of self-contained flatlets for the elderly at Meadow Court, a
children's adventure playground and a new car park. The coup-de-grace of
the six-hundred-year old borough came on 29 March 1974 and was marked
by a ceremonial laying up of robes at the Town Hall. Though the occasion
was accompanied by the clinking of champagne glasses, the eyes of the
many participants were veiled with a sudden melancholy. From that day,
Cowbridge became part of a much larger District Council, but has managed

to salvage some of its civic pride by becoming a Town Council with its chairman given the title of Mayor. The first Town Mayor was Mr. Norman Williams. To many, the new authority is the cake without the cream on top, but it will no doubt do its best to see that Cowbridge retains a degree of independence and that its ancient traditions are fully maintained.

Mayors since 1900

1900	Ald. E. John	1901	Ald. L. Jenkins
1902	Cllr. J. Williams	1903	Cllr. J. W. Hall
1904	Cllr. W. L. Jenkins	1905	Cllr. J. Pickard
1906	Cllr. C. M. Davies	1907	Cllr. T. J. Yorwerth
1908	Cllr. R. E. Watkins	1909	Cllr. D. Tilley
1910	Cllr. D. Tilley	1911	Ald. L. Jenkins
1912	Cllr. C. M. Davies	1913	Ald. J. Llewellyn
1914	Ald. W. A. James	1915	Cllr. D. Thomas
1916	Cllr. T. J. Yorwerth	1917	Cllr. W. L. Jenkins
1918	Cllr. W. L. Jenkins	1919	Ald. E. John
1920	Cllr. A. T. Mills	1921	Cllr. W. Thomas
1922	Cllr. W. Thomas	1923	Cllr. E. T. Hopkins
1924	Cllr. E. Thomas	1925	Cllr. W. Davies
1926	Cllr. W. H. John	1927	Cllr. W. A. L. Phillips
1928	Cllr. W. A. L. Phillips	1929	Ald. T. J. Yorwerth
1930	Ald. C. M. Davies	1931	Ald. A. T. Mills
1932	Ald. A. T. Mills	1933	Ald. T. J. Yorwerth
1933	Cllr. W. A. L. Phillips	1934	Cllr. R. W. Thomas
1935	Cllr. J. Miles	1936	Cllr. D. C. Watts
1937	Ald. C. M. Davies	1938	Col. H. R. Homfray
1939	Col. H. R. Homfray	1940	Ald. T. J. Yorwerth
1941	Ald. T. J. Yorwerth	1942	Ald. T. J. Yorwerth
1943	Ald. L. S. Rowsell	1944	Cllr. Mrs. G. Tilley
1945	Cllr. Rev. B. T. Roberts	1946	Cllr. Dr. (Mrs.) E. M. Meller
1947	Cllr. W. J. David	1948	Cllr. Robert Thomas
1949	Cllr. Robert Thomas	1950	Cllr. Mansel Edwards
1951	Cllr. Edward John	1952	Cllr. Mrs. F. E. Hinton
1953	Cllr. W. F. Batt	1954	Cllr. R. H. Williams
1955	Cllr. Geo. Caines	1956	Cllr. James James
1957	Cllr. Albert Morgan	1958	Cllr. Trevor Williams
1959	Cllr. Glyn McNeil	1960	Cllr. Ken Hutchings
1961	Cllr. Tony Cooksley	1962	Ald. Robert Thomas
1963	Ald. Mrs. G. Tilley	1964	Ald. Edward John
1965	Cllr. R. H. Williams	1966	Cllr. Glyn McNeil
1967	Cllr. R. R. W. Edwards (Roy)	1968	Cllr. K. A. George

1969	Cllr. D. F. Tilley	1970	Cllr. John Roberts
1971	Cllr. Mary D. V. Hall	1972	Cllr. David Jones
1973	Cllr. W. V. B. Greenwood	1974	Cllr. W. S. Davies
1975	Cllr. N. E. Williams	1976	Cllr. N. E. Williams
1977	Cllr. H. Bevan	1978	Cllr. Margaret Weston

The Cowbridge Rural District Council

The Cowbridge Rural District Council was established by the Local Government Act of 1894, and the first meeting was held at the Police Station, Cowbridge, on 1 October, 1895. Mr. J. Blandy Jenkins, squire of Llanharan House, was elected Chairman and Mr. Rees Thomas of Llantwit Major, Vice Chairman. The district administered by the Council was based upon the boundaries of the ancient Hundred of Cowbridge with small modifications. The boundaries of the district used to stretch from the coast of the Bristol Channel to the mountain slopes of Mynydd Meiros, and within this area the Authority administered twenty-eight civil parishes between Thomastown (Tonyrefail) in the north and Llantwit Major in the south. These varied in size from Llantwit Major (with approximately 7,000 people) to Stembridge, near Colwinston, which comprised only 38 acres and one half of a dwelling house. The population grew from 10,000 in 1895 to over 23,000 in 1974. The badge of office illustrated the chief industries of the area, namely the agriculture of the Vale, coal production at Llanharan, iron mining at Llanhari, the two Royal Air Force bases at St. Athan and Llandow and the historical nature of the area is depicted by the Celtic cross. The badge of office can now be seen in Cowbridge library. On 5 November 1895, the Council transferred its meeting place to the Town Hall, Cowbridge, and on 6 October, 1896 to the Institute close by. In 1923, a new Council Chamber and offices were acquired at 79 Eastgate for a mere £2,500 and these were officially opened by Councillor Richard Morgan of St. Hilary on 23 March. This property was transferred to the Vale of Glamorgan Borough Council in 1974 after the reorganisation of local government and is now one of their divisional offices.

The main function of the authority in the early days were those of sanitary authority, highway authority and rating authority. Various functions were added, particularly housing, and at the time of reorganisation the Council transferred to the new authorities some 2,800 houses. The Council became a constituent authority of the Mid-Glamorgan Water Board in 1920 and the latter body was responsible for the provision of a piped water supply to all but a small number of isolated homes. The Council assumed additional powers during the two World Wars, including food control, fuel control, reception of evacuees and air raid precautions. The Grant of Arms and Chain of Office were provided by public subscription and were presented in 1957 to the Chairman of the Council, Councillor Joseph Aaron David, J.P. of Llanharan by Major C. G. Traherne T.D., J.P., Lord Lieutenant of the County of Glamorgan and the late Captain H. C. R. Homfray of Penllyn Castle.

40. Members of the Cowbridge Rural District Council 1957
Front row: Councillors Henry R. Thomas, George Johnson, P. C. Thomas, L. G. Grey,
J. Hughes, J. A. David (Chairman), N. T. Roderick (Clerk), D. L. Jenkins,
Mrs M. Turnbull, Miss D. Ackland Allen, Mrs C Reed
Second row: Councillors Clifford H. Thomas, A. J. Vincent, Godfrey Lewis, J. T. Taylor,
E. Light, Terry Williams, D. J. Battrick, C. A. Mace, H. S. Morgan, W. Thomas Ivor
Llewellyn, T. C. Lewis
Back row: Councillors Evan Meatyard, Cyril David, A. J. Charles (Deputy Clerk),
W. R. Hawkins (Surveyor), Hubert Thomas (Public Health Inspector), W. Hoare,
G. McKim Thomas (Medical Officer), D. C. Hopkins (Treasurer)

Leading Citizens and Memorable Characters

It is difficult to disentangle the wefts from the warps in the class structure of twentieth-century Cowbridge. The late Maud Gunter was in no doubt that it was a very class-conscious town in her youth and this was manifested particularly in people's dress. The well-to-do always had expert dressmakers to make their clothes, whereas the less fortunate had to make do with home-made, amateur work. She recalled the after-church parades when the doctors', solicitors', and drapers' ladies used to parade up to Eastgate in their

summer finery. Even as late as the 1930s Leslie Illingworth, the political car-
toonist, found Cowbridge very English compared with Llantwit Major and
felt that Cowbridge people generally considered themselves a cut above the
rest of the Vale.

At the top of the social scale a few rich people still managed to live in
style; but apart from the Edmondes of Old Hall they resided in mansions
well outside the town. They included the Homfrays of Penllyn, the Owens of
Ash Hall, the Watsons and Leighs of Llansannor, the Byass family of Llandough and earlier in this century the Bassetts of Crossways. Crossways was in
fact the nearest thing to the 'Big House' of Llanblethian. It is a magnificent
building mostly of the nineteenth century, but parts of it date back to Tudor
times and include a fine arched doorway on the ground floor. In the early
1920s it was owned by Mr. Owen Williams the Cardiff ship owner and also
suited the exotic, oriental life style of His Highness Sir Ranjitsinhji Vibbaji,
Maharajah of Nawangar, a close relation of 'Ranji' the immortal Test
cricketer. Apart from the gentry, it was the doctors and solicitors of the
town, together with the headmaster of the Grammar School, who were
thought to be 'out of the top drawer'. Two of the best known Cowbridge
doctors were Irishmen—Dr. Richard M. Moynan and Dr. A. E. Gallaher.
Dr. Moynan loved riding and travelled thousands of miles by horse and
brake at any time of day or night to visit patients in outlandish places. He
was held in great awe by the children because he extracted teeth without
anaesthetic before the arrival of the first dentist. He dealt tactfully with
patients who pestered him with trifles, his catchword being: 'Well Alfred,
my boy, are you eating well, are you sleeping well. If so, I'll see you
tomorrow.' Ralph Bird records in his memoirs: 'Dr. Moynan was a good
cricketer, but disliked fielding. He had an extraordinary understanding
with his maid-servant, who, wearing a white apron and with ribbons flying
from her bonnet, would come across from the back of Woodstock House to
the Bear Field hedge and then wave to the Doctor. This, however, never
occurred before the Doctor had had his innings. The message was always the
same—"sick patient getting worse, immediate attention needed" and off the
Doctor would go!' Dr. Gallaher never failed to receive one of his patients at
his surgeries and had a reputation of treating the poorer ones at the expense
of the rich. He was also mentor to a young Cowbridge medical student,
Evan Thomas, who later became Medical Officer of Health for the County
and Honorary Physician to the Queen. Dr. Hastings Torney will always be
remembered as a medico with a mission for his work among the wounded on
the Western Front during the Great War, but the most celebrated
Cowbridge doctor must surely be Dr. Charles Booth Meller. Such was his
medical skill and great popularity that he was said to have more patients on
his register than any rural doctor in the whole of the Principality. His
appearance, especially in his latter days, was most striking; he wore a
massive beard down to his middle and dressed in his top hat and frock coat
he always retained the tailored look of the doctor. It was a strange sequence

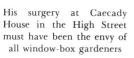

His surgery at Caecady
House in the High Street
must have been the envy of
all window-box gardeners

41. Dr. Charles Booth Meller

of events that brought the good doctor to Cowbridge in the first place. In 1881 the Vale of Glamorgan experienced a snowstorm of exceptional severity. At the height of the blizzard a young physician, Dr. Stannestreet was returning home from an inquest at the *Colliers' Arms*, Llanhari. At Llanhari station he was mistakenly informed that the train had left, so the intrepid doctor decided to trudge his way to Llantrisant surgery along the railway track as best he could. The whirlwind of snow howled with such a ferocity that it drowned the sound of the approaching train and the poor doctor was killed only a hundred yards along the line. Every cloud has a silver lining, which in this case was the arrival of Dr. Meller from Ecclesfield in Yorkshire to establish a highly successful practice in Cowbridge. His skill in medicine, his equal treatment of rich and poor alike and his kindness to all clergymen whom he considered grossly underpaid were such that his name was to become proverbial throughout the whole of the Vale for over fifty years. Mr. Bird recalls that Dr. Meller's first mode of transport was by gig and stallion and that he was always accompanied by his groom. He had several stallions and his stables were located next to his house where High Street Garage is to-day. With the introduction of the motor car, Dr. Meller used Mr. Bird's small 8 h.p. car for visiting his patients with Mr. Bird as chauffeur. There was one incident when his car failed to negotiate Lake Hill and he was forced to reverse down the portion he had climbed and then turning into the road leading to Llandough. There he turned round and climbed the hill in the reverse gear which had a very much lower ratio than the first forward gear. To be ascending Lake Hill backwards in an open car with the ample figure of the Doctor facing the rear was an hilarious situation, but it was either that or go by another route.

Solicitors were regarded as no less men of distinction than the town doctors, and no Cowbridge practice has earned more respect than that of Gwyn and Gwyn, not least because it provided the Borough with two of its most distinguished Town Clerks. The firm was founded in 1867 by Thomas Rees, who later became the first mayor under the new charter. In 1883 he was joined by his nephew W. T. Gwyn and in 1888 by Charles Jackson Gwyn. After the death of Thomas Rees on 25 May 1900 the firm became known as Gwyn and Gwyn. The Gwyns themselves came from good Vale of Glamorgan farming stock from the vicinity of St. Mary Church, but they always claimed a prouder ancestry in being decended from Francis Gwyn of Llansannor Court, the Secretary of War to Queen Anne. When Mr. W. T. Gwyn succeeded Mr. John Stockwood[48] as Town Clerk of Cowbridge in 1892 he found the role of playing Horatio to successive Hamlets to his liking for he was to serve no less than twenty-one mayors with dignity and distinction. Mr. Gwyn was a stickler for ceremonial and he always regarded the customs and institutions of the old borough with the sort of awe that a sherpa reserves for the majestic heights of Everest. When he retired in 1931, he was

[48] He belonged to the same family as Mervyn Stockwood, Bishop of Southwark.

succeeded as Town Clerk by his son, Arthur William Gwyn, whose loyalty to the traditions and experience in the administration of the borough were soon to emulate that of his father. Although Arthur Gwyn enrolled as a solicitor in 1913, his legal career was interrupted by four years of distinguished war service in the Cardiff Battalion of the Welch Regiment. He was wounded and suffered shell shock at Mametz Woods, but was nevertheless able to rejoin his father and brother V. S. Gwyn in the family firm of solicitors. As well as Town Clerk he was for many years Clerk to the Magistrates, Clerk and later an active governor of Cowbridge Grammar School and President of the Bridgend and District Law Society.

Arthur Gwyn's latter days were unfortunately veiled in sadness by the tragic death of his only son John David Gwyn, who was killed in action on

42. John Gwyn

the Italian front on 2 December 1943, aged 21 years. John was one of the most brilliant pupils of his day at Cowbridge Grammar School and would have made a great reputation for himself in the legal profession and in the world of letters. At Cambridge he gained a First Class (Division 1) in the Law Tripos, was elected Scholar of St. John's College and was awarded the post graduate McMahon Studentship in Law. John Gwyn achieved further intellectual stature at Cambridge by capturing the St. John's English Essay Prize and was at that time the only undergraduate outside the English faculty ever to do so. It is fitting that his parents created the John David Gwyn Memorial Prize to foster a love of English among the pupils of Cowbridge Grammar School. They could have chosen no better way of keeping their gifted son's name and ideals alive in the town of his birth.

In the closely-knit intimate community that was pre-war Cowbridge, a host of colourful characters continued to enrich the lives of ordinary people. Perhaps they are the true descendants of the pilgrims and pedlars, minstrels, scribes, contortionists and clowns of long ago, who by their antics, endless chatter and eccentric behaviour signalled a last farewell to a passing age. They stood out from the rest of their fellow-men as clearly as the monolith on Stallingdown and their wry or witty sayings were laughed at with the same gusto as the catch phrases of today's comedians. Who will forget Ernie Wilcox's quip as with his cart and donkey he carried brewers' grain from Brynsadler brewery home to Aberthin to remove the blemishes from his potatoes? He used to encourage his donkey up Brynsadler Hill by picking up the bag of hops and shouting 'Come on Neddy, I've got all the weight in my hands'. Or which Cowbridge housewife can still recall Jimmy Croome, the Westgate chimney sweep, wistfully placing his index finger under his chin and remarking 'We're a mixed lot, mum?' Harry Collings (watchmaker) is remembered for the prowess of his walking feats, and on many a misty evening as the eighty-year-old tottered across Stallingdown he might so easily have been mistaken for the ghost of a foot-weary pilgrim en route for Pembrokeshire. Other characters stand out by their eccentric behaviour like Ted Surrey of Llanblethian who took a batch of bread and a pot of mustard to Llandough Castle for his lunch. With so slender a diet it was little wonder that Jim was such easy meat for Will the Sawyer in town brawls later that night in the *Cowbridge Arms*. Cowbridge has been the Mecca for pedlars and hawkers since the Middle Ages: their presence in the form of Eder Munden and Ted the Tinker lingered on well into the twentieth century as they sold umbrellas, pins, elastic and light haberdashery as well as passing on the titbits of gossip from the Vale. The last of a long line of hawkers was Tom Bond, who sold everything imaginable from soap to chamber pots from his gaily-coloured horse and trap. During the Second World War soap became as scarce as gold bullion but Tom seemed to conjure it out of the air like manna from heaven to the amazement and delight of all.

I am sure that little Billy Arnott would have felt very much at home among the troupes of jesters and wandering minstrels that thronged the Medieval inns of Cowbridge. Billy ran his own dance band, and on account of his virtuosity on the drums, his concerts at the local dance halls would be a sell-out well before the event. But he was also a one-man band. His rendering of 'Burlington Bertie' before excited crowds waiting for the Borough election results in the Town Hall became part of the folk heritage of pre-war Cowbridge. So were his Eddie Cantor like rolling eyes, his racy monologues his cavorting cartwheels and the continual bobbing up and down like a witch doctor trying to stir up a tribe of natives. Most 'funny men' are said to be serious in private life, but Billy joked and wisecracked to the end of his days. He was very short of stature, yet when you entered his shop a seven-foot grinning genie loomed up in front of you from behind the counter, causing not a little consternation. Billy had stood upon a box — just for a laugh! Reg Tucker, the Cowbridge coal merchant, was another comic character who quick-witted his way out of difficult situations. If his customers complained that the coal was too small, Reg would think nothing of delivering lumps as big as boulders the next time he came round. In an intimate society, where everybody knew everyone else, it was not surprising that nicknames played an important role. There were three Robert Thomases — all of whom were prominent citizens of Cowbridge. But they were known to everyone only as 'Bob the Bank', 'Bob the Builder' and 'Bob the Bus'. Dr. Moynan was everywhere called 'The Physics' and Willie Davies the clerk to Gwyn and Gwyn was known as 'Willie the Scribe' because all the illiterate people of the town used to go to him to have their letters written.

Fame came to three further Cowbridge characters almost without effort: they were Charles Davies the hairdresser, Reg Sanders the bee keeper and Tom David the thatcher. Charles Davies was one of the first in Glamorgan to do ladies' hairdressing. His reputation grew to such an extent that when Randolph Hearst the American newspaper millionaire brought famous film actresses over to St. Donats Castle, he would send a Rolls Royce to fetch Mr. Davies to do the honours. All the youth of Cowbridge waited with bated breath for his return and news of Hollywood glamour. One piece of advice Charles Davies always gave his customers: no girl under 16 years should have her hair permed as it had not had enough time to mature. The buzzing of a few homecoming bees swarming sluggishly among Reg Sanders' neatly ar-ranged hives always welcomed your evening walk along Town Mill Road in the 1920s. Reg, who now lives in happy retirement in Bridgend, entered his honey at many shows throughout Glamorgan and took first prize at the British Empire Show at the Greyfriars Hall in 1935. Reg was doubly pleased for he had pipped at the post none other than David Lloyd George, who was the runner-up. That year he sold a ton and a half of honey. Four years earlier in 1931, Thomas David, who came from a thatching family of great renown, had the unique honour of thatching the little doll's house that was given, by the people of Wales, to Her Majesty the Queen (then Princess

Elizabeth), when she was six-years-old. The thatch had caught fire on the way up to London and Tom was sent to re-thatch it. He was proud to narrate how the two princesses used to watch him at work every morning in the grounds of the Royal Lodge, Windsor, and when he left they gave him a photograph each. The house, which has become popularly known as 'Y Bwthyn Bach', was presented to the Duke and Duchess of York (later George VI and Queen Elizabeth) on their visit to Cardiff on 16 March, 1932.

Into the Modern Age

The upheavals resulting from the Great War, the growth of motor transport, the extensions of public amenities, the development of popular education, the conditioning of people's lives by the new-fangled wireless and film industry and the loosening of the bonds of social etiquette and behaviour, saw Cowbridge emerge well and truly into the modern age. Yet the changes came slowly and did not show themselves clearly until well into the 1920s. It is difficult for us today to realise how primitive Cowbridge really was in the immediate post-war period. For instance there was no electric light or water supply in the town. In Iolo Davies' book *A Certaine Schoole* we learn that the boarders still carried a candle upstairs at bedtime and the teachers had quite literally to see 'lights out' by collecting the candles before retiring themselves. For water, the town was still entirely dependent on the public pumps which were erected strategically along the length of Main Street. Residents continued to pay boys 2/6d. a week to carry water from these wells. During periods of drought many of the pumps ran dry so the townsfolk used to queue up with pails, jars and vessels of all descriptions at the Town Hall well, which, like the Fairy Godmother, never failed to oblige. Bathrooms moreover were few and far between, and at the Grammar School every pupil had to wait his turn to bath in a single tub. In the early 1920s there were few motor cars in the streets and fewer buses. It would have mattered less if the railway had been efficient, but the trains often ran late and there were interminable delays at Pontyclun waiting for the connection to Cardiff. Little wonder then that Richard Williams, when he took up the headship of Cowbridge Grammar School in 1919, condemned the town as being 'late Medieval' in outlook.

Yet change, when at last it did appear, was perhaps greater than in any preceding period of the town's history. None was more significant than the appearance of motor transport in the 1920s. This together with the decline of the railways, was to re-establish the important role of the highway until it became the main artery of traffic in the county. Ever since, the commercial prosperity of Cowbridge and its growth as a dormitory town has been almost entirely dependent on the motor car. The first motor cars had arrived before the 1920s but they were considered something of a novelty and were owned exclusively by the well-to-do. The motor cycle had arrived as early as 1900 and was far more popular. One could get a motor cycle licence at the age of fourteen years in those days and such was the vogue that motor cycle races were run from the Town Hall to the top of Primrose Hill with stewards stopping all traffic at the cross roads where the traffic lights now stand. The first car to appear in the Cowbridge district was bought in 1905 by Col. Homfray of Penllyn Castle. It was a blue Daimler Limousine L.6. — the sixth car to be registered in the county. It used to be said that the old carriage driver when he became a chauffeur continued to say 'Whoa Mare' as he stopped his car in town. It is generally agreed that Dr. Moynan owned the first motor car in Cowbridge itself; it was a six horse-power Humber and it was bought from Arthur Evans' garage in Bear Lane. As the motor car came into its own in the late 1920s and 1930s garages became one of the symbols of the new age. In Cowbridge there was fierce rivalry between the Bridge Garage owned by Arthur Evans, W. E. Jones' opposite the *Bear Hotel* and A. T. Mills' on the site of the present Co-op. By the late 1930s the volume of motor traffic passing through the town was such that the idea of building a by-pass was already being discussed — an idea that was to become an absolute necessity thirty years later.

With the post-war generation demanding greater mobility, the motor 'bus no less than the car, revolutionised the social life of the people. It so happens that one of the first to grasp the full potential of the 'buses was a Cowbridge man, Mr. Albert Maddox, who became a pioneer in public transport in South Wales. He had started his business with a horse-drawn wagonette driving parties to the local race-courses or the seaside; but after about 1912 he was constantly experimenting with new forms of public transport and he kept abreast of every invention. By 1914 he was running a weekly service to Cardiff, and by 1919 he had replaced his wagonette with a Napier charabanc. To improve his bus service to Cardiff, Maddox added next a double-decker bus with solid rubber tyres, which he had bought in London. The top deck was removed and the vehicle was converted into a single decker. About 1920 South Wales Commercial Motors Ltd. also began to put 'buses on the road and quickly established a two-hourly service between Westgate Street, Cardiff, and Bridgend at a cost of three shillings return fare. At first competition between Maddox and his new rival was very fierce with the Cowbridge 'buses leaving the Town Hall a few minutes earlier than the buses from Cardiff. Eventually Maddox's 'bus service was bought out by the larger company, which in 1929 became the Western Welsh Omnibus Company. In passing, it is worth recording that the conductor of the first bus to run between Cowbridge and Bridgend when South Wales Commercial Motors inaugurated the service was Mr. Robert Thomas, the son of a Cowbridge saddler, who was affectionately known as 'Bob the Bus' for many years. He was one of the earliest members of the staff of Bridgend Depot and became Mayor of Cowbridge in 1934.

By bringing the outside world into people's homes, the wireless and in-directly the motion picture—easily the two most popular sources of enter-tainment in the inter-war period—played no small part in the break up of the intimate society, in which social activity at the churches, chapels and clubs had been so intense. The early wireless sets were crude and enthusiasts usually built their own; to meet the demand for components Mr. W. G. Miles about 1923 opened a wireless department at his grocery shop on the site of the present 'Spar' supermarket. Thanks to the initiative of Alderman A. T. Mills the town was provided with a luxury cinema and ballroom in 1924. Known as the Pavilion, it was built on the site of the old Tally Court and *Wheelwright's Arms*. Two of Mills' garage employees ran the cinema in the early days of silent films. Mr. 'Ollie' Jones would operate the projector while his wife strummed tunes on the piano. Upstairs was a ballroom with reputedly one of the best dance floors in South Wales. A couple of nights a week, under the watchful eye of compère L. S. Rowsell, the 'flappers' of the Vale were able to dance away their inhibitions to the jazzy accompaniment of Ken Symmon's band; but as the fox-trot, the one-step and the Charleston followed each other in bewildering succession, it seemed to the older inhabitants that the barbarians were breaking in.

The glittering Hunt Balls were far more lavish affairs and throughout the 1920s were graced by all the leading county families, including the Butes of Cardiff Castle and such prominent socialites as Nancy Mitford. Many important civic functions were held in the Pavilion ballroom as well, none more so than the official luncheon given to David Lloyd George when in 1930 he was granted the Freedom of the Borough. It was a sad blow therefore to the people of Cowbridge when their fine ballroom was destroyed by the fire on 16 April, 1942. The cinema was, however, restored and was run as a successful venture by Mr. Philip Phillips of Pontyclun until the late 1950s when television forced its closure.

The latter years of the 1920s witnessed two much-needed improvements in public services, namely the provision of piped water and electricity. In 1926, under a scheme initiated by the Mid Glamorgan Water Board, the water supply for Cowbridge was pumped from Newton Moors to a service reservoir near Llanhari. This was soon connected to a Llanharan source and in 1931 to Cefn Hirgoed reservoir. Later supplies of water for the Borough came almost exclusively from Newton Moors. In 1927 electric power was ex-tended from Pontyclun to Cowbridge and the current was switched on for the first installations—the street lights and about a score of houses. It is worth noting that electricity had been used for illumination for the first time in Glamorgan at Llansannor House in the 1880s—about forty years before the streets of Cowbridge were lit up. Many years were still to elapse before a sewerage scheme could be introduced to bring the Borough up to modern urban standards of sanitation. Surprisingly this did not commence until 9 February 1953 after financial assistance had been obtained from the Government and the Glamorgan County Council. Only after the 13,000

43. Harnessed to go! This photograph shows the old horse-drawn Fire Brigade Engine. Seated in the front row are W. T. Gwyn (Town Clerk), Edward John (Eagle Stores), R. E. Watkins (Mayor), W. James (Builder) and John David (Founder of John David Watts & Morgan). Standing: E. H. Ebsworth (Llandough Castle), David Tilley, Bill Bond, Sgt. Bradbury, Edward Crowley, Evan Warren, W. James (Jun.). Amongst others seated on the Engine are Bill Brown (Town Hall), Reg Tucker, Arthur Spencer and John Bond

yards of public sewer had been laid could it be truly said that Cowbridge no longer lived in the past.

No service has a prouder record than that given to the town by the local Fire Brigade. Prior to 1902 fire-fighting was in the hands of the County Police, but in that year a Volunteer Brigade of 15 men was formed by Alderman David Tilley, who with the help of public subscription managed to buy a horse-drawn manual fire engine. At first the only way of calling the Brigade was by word of mouth, but later a bell on the Town Hall was used. In 1911 a horse-drawn steam fire engine was obtained — again by means of public subscription — for £1,000. It was used quite effectively until 1929, but there was more often than not a problem of finding a horse to pull it. Walter Carswell, an elderly citizen, can actually recall funerals having to be delayed because it was considered more important to use the horse for the fire-engine than for the hearse. Well before World War II an internal combustion motor fire-engine was put into service and sensibly the Borough and District Councils were amalgamated. During the War all fire services were nationalised and as part of the National Fire Service, the Cowbridge brigade attended several aircraft fires and the Cardiff blitz. During the N.F.S. period two major fires occurred in Cowbridge itself; the cinema fire already referred to and that which completely destroyed Frank Sanders' Bridge Garage. After the War there was a return to local authority control and Cowbridge became a 'nucleus' fire station belonging to the County of Glamorgan B division and employing full and part-time men. The brigade has been involved in many serious fire situations and tragic accidents in the post-war period, none worse than the Llandow air disaster. When in 1950 a Welsh rugby supporters' plane crashed with great loss of life, the Cowbridge brigade was first on the scene. Another illustration of the diversity of tasks that a modern fireman has to face occurred in 1954 at Llanhari quarries. Late at night Divisional Officer Lewis and his team had to arrange for a surgeon to perform an amputation on a man trapped 20 feet below ground level. Since reorganisation of local government in 1974, Cowbridge has become a South Glamorgan fire station and it now has an all-professional staff.

Few people before 1914 would have believed that a Socialist would ever be made mayor of Cowbridge. However, the unbelievable happened in 1935 when the late Alderman Johnson Miles was elected to that august office; Cowbridge indeed seemed to be marching with the times. Alderman Miles had spent his younger days as a miner in the Carmarthenshire coalfield championing the causes of the working classes. When chairman of the local Miners' Lodge he was victimised throughout the coalfield and was forced to seek employment in the Cowbridge district after the First World War. He

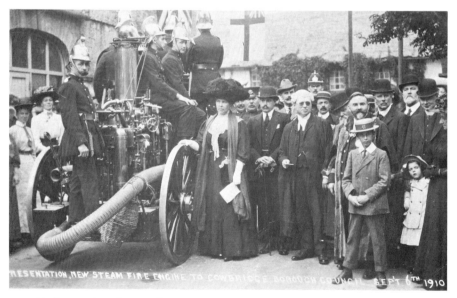

44. Presentation of a new Fire Engine to Cowbridge Borough Council, 6th September, 1910. The photograph shows: Bill Brown, Mrs E. H. Ebsworth, Lord Ninian Crichton-Stuart, Col. B. Prichard (Pwllywrach), W. T. Gwyn, Edward John, David Tilley, John Williams (Draper), A. W. James (Upholsterer), A. T. Mills (Garage)

became chairman of the Llanelay lodge, at Pontyclun, and with Ted Williams, the M.P. for Ogmore and later High Commissioner of Australia, he successfully fought a case in London on behalf of his work force after the colliery had closed following the Depression. On coming to live in Cowbridge he was much resented at first on account of his abrasive speeches on the political platforms and was introduced to David Lloyd George in 1930 as 'the stormy petrel' of Cowbridge politics. For years he found it impossible to get elected to the Borough Council despite having a solid base among the railway element in the town. When finding himself bottom of the poll he once declared in Robert Bruce vein 'That greasy poll I failed to hold, but some day Cowbridge will place me on top'. At the sixth attempt the walls of Jericho fell with a flourish when the burgesses of the town elected him top of the poll and carried the new 'Joshua' shoulder high from the Town Hall to his home near West Gate, confident that a new era was about to dawn.

The Second World War

For Cowbridge, the Second World War sounded the death knell of the inward looking society and the town was swept once and for all into the twentieth century. It was above all a People's War, in which even the troops were much more a part of the community than they had been in 1914. Early on in the War, soldiers were billeted for a month or so in the Pavilion Cinema and later, as the Allies prepared for the invasion of Europe, American soldiers were stationed in large numbers at St. Mary Hill and Llansannor, a few miles outside the town. The presence of the Americans particularly brought the war home to the author as a boy; to us children it was fought only by the Yanks 'up there in Penllyn Woods or on the Downs'. They brought our first childhood glimpses of coffee, candy, citrus fruits and colour prejudice — as whites and negroes, locked in mortal combat, tumbled out of the village dance halls into pools of blood.

The civilian population, whether in Civil Defence, the Home Guard, the War Weapons Week campaign or simply being bombed by the enemy, felt more closely involved in this war than the previous one. There was a strong Home Guard under Captain R. H. Williams, the Cowbridge chemist. Unlike a rival unit from a nearby Border Vale village, which wasted valuable ammunition by 'shooting the moon' as it rose over Ruthin Down, the 'A' Company of the 10th Welsh Battalion H. G. was a by-word for efficiency. At the sand-bagged fortress of the Town Hall, A.R.P., National Fire Service and Ambulance depots were in operation and the Food Office was centred at Woodstock House. The 'blackout' was the worst hazard to be faced in the town: a ghastly blue paint was smeared all over the windows of the boarders' dining room at the Grammar School, whilst the stentorian yells of W. G. Miles, the Chief Air Raid Warden to 'put out the lights' were feared almost as much as Hitler's bombs. As to the bombing, a few fell in the vicinity of the town but none within the boundary of the borough. One that dropped on Stallingdown blew the sundial off the front of Great House, Aberthin, two miles away; a direct hit was made on a farm house at St. Mary Church and some incendiary bombs fell behind the High School. Fortunately, the only fatality in the whole series of raids was that of a cow. Finally, in such schemes as 'War Weapons Week' the ordinary people of Cowbridge and district showed emphatically that they, too, were very much a part of the War effort by raising such a remarkably large sum of money that they earned a telegram of congratulation from Sir Kingsley Wood, the Chancellor of the Exchequer at the time.

The following is a list of names of the men of the borough who gave their lives in the Second World War:-

ROYAL NAVY

PETTY OFFICER DAVID MORGAN JOHN

HIS MAJESTY'S ARMY

LIEUT. JOHN DAVID GWYN,   WELSH REG.
LIEUT. GEORGE THOMAS J. PRATT,   ROYAL FUS.
PTE. PERCIVAL MERVYN SERVIOUR,   WELSH REG.
PTE. EMLYN WILLIAMS,   R.AOC.

ROYAL AIR FORCE

PILOT OFFICER DAVID ROY WATTS
SERGT. MAYNARD H. BURSTON
SERGT. GERALD V. PAYNE

MERCHANT NAVY

CHIEF ENGINEER THOMAS J. RICHARDS

The Railway

The decline of branch railways has been one of the saddest features of the modern age. As already indicated, the pattern of public transport was changing by the early thirties in favour of the car and motor 'bus so it was no surprise when the Cowbridge—Aberthaw line was closed to passengers in 1930. To get to the Leys or Barry many a Sunday school outing had travelled through Beaupre Woods, St. Hilary Halt, St. Mary Church Road Station and eventually Aberthaw Low Level. The passengers would then proceed up a hill and under a bridge, carrying on to the Barry/Bridgend line and into the Aberthaw High Level to catch a train for Barry. One great drawback on this line was that the stations between Cowbridge and Aberthaw were a great distance from the villages they served. The Llantrisant — Cowbridge line struggled for another twenty years and never fails to evoke nostalgic memories among the many who travelled in the diminutive 'Emma' with her single carriages on either side of the engine. It took five minutes to get to Llanhari station, which had its own stationmaster and two slip-offs to the lime kilns and iron works. Across Ystradowen Moors with its down gradient, where John John John of Ystradowen had used his enormous strength to rescue the stranded trains of long ago; and with a rollicking 40 miles an hour into Ystradowen station to be greeted by a friendly wave from stationmaster Billy Lewis. On past Maendy and Trerhyngyll until the little train slowed up for the staff to be handed in at Cowbridge station. It was a friendly service even if the time-tables were not always strictly adhered to. Mr. Gwyn 'Dusty' John of Llanhari would be picked up from his farm work on the middle of Ystradowen Moors; while Billy Lewis, the genial Ystradowen stationmaster, would hold up the 10 o'clock night train sufficiently long for the Llanhari drinkers to down their last pints at the *White Lion* before returning home. Little wonder the last train was known as 'The Rodney'! By 1951 the British Railway Executive finally decided that the Cowbridge to Llantrisant line was uneconomical to run and the line was closed on 30 November in a blaze of glory. Among the passengers on the last train, which was carrying a large wreath of laurel leaves, were the Mayor of Cowbridge, Mrs. F. C. Hinton, Aldermen and Councillors of the Borough and a host of railway enthusiasts.

Education

The Grammar School

We make no apologies for such a brief account of Cowbridge Grammar School in the twentieth century. This period has been amply covered in an admirable full-length history entitled *A Certaine Schoole* by Iolo Davies, which grew out of the 350th anniversary celebrations in 1958. Instead, the following reminiscences of his early teaching years at the school by deputy headmaster Bryn Edwards will provide an evocative description of the quaint, almost Dickensian atmosphere of school life fifty or so years ago when the school boasted fewer than a hundred pupils and every boarder had to bath in a single, small tub with a meagre supply of hot water. Mr. Edwards writes:

Some years ago I was sitting next to a clergyman at a dinner at the *Bear Hotel*, Cowbridge. When I told him that I was on the staff of the Grammar School, he said, 'I had an uncle there once. He ran away'.

'When was that?' I asked.

'About 1925'.

'I remember him — Jones minimus'.

'That's right,' and laughingly he added, 'He's now a prosperous sheep farmer in New Zealand'.

Jones minimus was my first contact with the boys of the Grammar School, or the College, as it was called in those days.

I had arrived on a cold, dreary, January night in 1925 to take up the post of French Master and Boarding master. It was a bleak beginning. On my walk from the station I saw no one. The street was unlit, with only an occasional glimmer from a pub doorway. I had dinner with the Headmaster, Mr. Richard Williams, and Mrs. Williams and then retired to the study to await my colleague Eric Reid who was on his way from Belfast.

There was a timid tap on the door, and a small boy entered. He asked if he could go out to post a letter at the end of Church St. This was a problem. I was inexperienced and ignorant of the rules. So I thought that the safest answer at that time was 'No!'. But Jones minimus slipped out to post his letter and was caught on the way back.

Thinking it was time I familiarised myself with my surroundings, I walked through to the main school room. It was lit by paraffin lamps hanging from the ceiling. It was then I realised that there was no electricity, and later that evening I found that there was no mains water, no heating system and no sewerage. My bedroom was damp and cold, and it became often necessary to dry my clothes before the study fire. It was three years before these drawbacks were remedied. It was a spartan existence, but I must add, I never caught a cold.

That evening I met Eric Reid—a rich and rare personality who had a tremendous influence on my life. He was utterly unselfish, but he would condemn what he considered bad with a puritanical fierceness. He had a delicate Irish humour, and would recount his own *faux pas* with glee. Once, when addressing an audience on the League of Nations, he opened his attaché case on the rostrum to get out his notes, and brought out a dirty football jersey and a pair of muddy boots some boy had left in the study. He had picked up the wrong case. I shall always remember him with affection and thankfulness. That same evening I met my other colleagues—W. R. McAdam and J. D. Owen.

McAdam and Reid were both from Queen's University, Belfast, but had never met until they came to Cowbridge.

McAdam was a brilliant teacher of Mathematics. A just and effective disciplinarian with flashes of dry Irish humour, he was a great favourite. A delightful after-dinner speaker, he was widely read. Once after reading an article of his in the *Bovian*[49], I asked him how he had acquired such an attractive literary style. He answered 'The Bible and the Shorter Catechism'. After Church, on Sunday evening, he took the Boarders in Choir Practice and would accompany on the harmonium if necessary.

[49] The School magazine

45. The Dining Room

Owen taught mainly Chemistry, but his real interests, I am persuaded, were local history, gardening and motoring. He knew the Vale of Glamorgan from end to end; in his little Morgan runabout he had travelled most of the highways and byways of Wales.

These were the men with whom I was destined to pass the early years of my teaching career. I was very fortunate.

The next day, the first day of Lent term 1925, saw my baptism as a teacher.

I had breakfasted with the boys, sitting at the head of a long table. A subdued Jones minimus sat on my left side. In time I was to come to know him as a delightfully witty boy whose remarks were often pertinent and revealing. Breakfast consisted of tea, porridge, fried bread, and 'doorsteps' — a thick slab of buttered bread. Porridge was a dish I liked normally, but during the next two years I was to come across two other kinds of porridge — one which seemed to be topped with paraffin and the other chlorinated, or so I thought, swimming in a green slime. Eric Reid put it down to some kind of disinfectant as the water was collected from the roof into a large tank in the stable yard, or pumped from wells.

At 9 o'clock the boys assembled in the main classroom for roll-call and prayers. There was a faint hum of light conversation, with an occasional 'Quiet' from a prefect. Suddenly the latch of the door rattled for some seconds before the Headmaster entered. This rattling of latches was quite a feature of school life. It was a means of communication between the staff and boys—a warning that we were on the way. We never entered the school room or dormitory without rattling the latch first. Richard Williams called the roll, a prefect read the lesson and we sang a hymn. A boy played the little harmonium. In later years this instrument was played by a good looking fair-haired boy, who became a top civil servant was knighted and whose decisions on matters of public interest received considerable publicity. I refer to the Ombudsman—Sir Idwal Pugh. After prayers we dismissed to our classes. My first lesson was French with Form II in the main classroom. The Head taught Greek to three boys at the far end of the room. It was McAdam who explained to me that this was a deliberate move so that he could keep his eye on the new master. But he never intruded.

By the end of the morning I had met the rest of the boys. The school numbered about a hundred. The classes were small and discipline was easy. I examined the honours board in the Schoolroom and the stained-glass windows in the Seys and Founders classrooms. These alone gave me the impression of something special connected with this school and that impression has remained with me to this day.

During lunch I noticed that many boys were interested in envelopes which they had brought in surreptitiously. I must confess that during my two years

46. Founders' classroom (the stained glass window has been transferred to Holy Cross Church)

in the Boarding House I failed to find what use they made of them. When I asked Eric Reid he replied with a smile, 'You haven't seen them!' It was an Old Boy who explained to me that they were used as receptacles for bits of gristle and uneatable meat. They were taken out and emptied over the wall into the Church cemetery next door.

After lunch I strolled into the town. It is hard to realise today how Victorian Cowbridge was then. I saw two little old ladies who might have walked out of one of Jane Austen's novels, scurrying past the school, in nodding bonnets and trailing skirts with their umbrellas in the crook of their arms. Farmers on horseback, or driving a pony and trap, were more frequent than buses or cars. Flocks of sheep and herds of cattle would be driven through the street. After tea, which was served in our study, I was told to take the junior boys for a walk. In fact they took me, as I didn't know my way about. We went down to the Old Mill Road, along the river and through Llanblethian to Cross Inn, and back on to the Llantwit road. These walks were enjoyable and valuable to me as I got to know the boys outside the classroom. We talked and argued and settled problems and difficulties. In the case of the younger boys especially these walks helped to relieve some of the stress of the classroom.

At six o'clock I supervised tea. This was a meal where they were allowed to eat almost anything they could get hold of. They were given tea and 'doorsteps' but otherwise it was sardines, H.P. sauce, tomato sauce, cake, and the occasional boiled egg, which they brought from their own tuck boxes.

Prep started at 7 o'clock. At half-past-seven we were relieved by a prefect, when we went in to dinner with the Headmaster and Mrs. Williams. The prefects had their own study and were paid a small sum each term.

The Head took prayers and the juniors went to bed. The seniors were allowed to stay down until a later hour. There was nothing left for me to do apart from seeing that the lights were out in the dorms, and the candles which the boys took up with them, collected, and brought downstairs. To reach my own bedroom I had to go through 'long dorm'. Here and there were faint glimmerings of electric torches under the bed clothes. An inveterate reader in bed, I ignored them. Indeed, Mrs. Williams complained that I was using too many candles, so I bought my own.

The matter of taking a bath now concerned me. I had noticed two bathrooms at the end of the long dorm with geysers, but the boys warned me against using them. It seems that the geysers either sent their flames downward or went out altogether and left you shivering. On the Friday night, however, the problem was solved. As Reid and I were quietly reading in the study, about ten o'clock, there was a loud thump outside the door and a prolonged rattling of handles. Outside were two large cans of hot water. 'Go and find two large boys', said Reid, 'to take them up to your bedroom'. I searched the schoolroom and the classrooms and the prefects' study without success. This would happen every Friday night, and I was never able to find

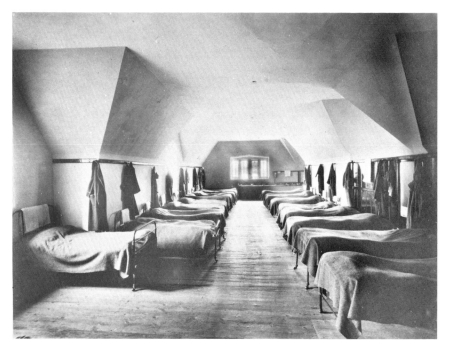

47. 'Long Dorm'

out how some nine or ten boys could hide themselves so successfully. Soon I realised that the thumping and the rattling were the maids' warning signal to the boys. However, the cans were taken up to my bedroom, and when I went up I stumbled against a large tin bath in the middle of the floor. Friday night was obviously the staff bath night. In fact we all had to bath in tin tubs, even the Headmaster.

On Sunday we attended morning and evening service in the church of the Holy Cross. The Headmaster read the lesson in the morning service and McAdam read in the evening service. During the next two terms I found myself teaching a variety of subjects. My degree subjects were French and English, but it was not long before I was teaching Junior Latin, some Junior Maths, some History, Drawing and P.T. I enjoyed most of this work but Drawing and P.T. posed some problems. The previous Drawing Master had his own peculiar method. He drew something on the board and told the class to copy it. Fortunately I had had an excellent Art Master in my old school, and soon the boys were painting, doing designs, and lino cuts, some of the latter reproduced in the *Bovian*. P.T. was another matter. I had been warned that I might have to take the boys in 'Drill'. So I had 'swotted' up the Board of Education Syllabus in Physical Training, and to the boys' disgust put this Syllabus into action. In the past, I learnt, P.T. meant a run in the country. An Inspector who came along a few weeks later made the report,

'Neither the boys nor the Master seemed to enjoy themselves'—a true judgment. Inspections were rare events. In the forty-two years I spent at the Grammar School, I remember only one 'full kit' inspection.

Games, naturally, played an important part in our life. Soccer, Hockey, and Cricket were played—Soccer in the Michaelmas term and Hockey in the Lent term. The juniors played their winter games on Ma Mitch's field, a bumpy piece of ground grazed by a lone cow. Too often the game resolved itself into dribbling the ball between the cow pats. Later the new dining hall and gymnasium were built on this field. I had a fair knowledge of the rules of Soccer, but Hockey was new to me. I had to learn the rules and it was not long before I realised the necessity of two umpires. I had played a great deal of Cricket before coming to Cowbridge, and I had looked forward to the Summer Term. Though my batting was of the lower order, I hoped to make some kind of a show in my first game which was against the Town. I took six wickets for fourteen runs, and so established myself as a member of the team when it played adult games. There were some fine players in Cowbridge in those days—Fred Dunn, Bruce Bird and his brother Ralph, Dr. Evans and many others against whom I enjoyed pitting my wits as a slow spin bowler. In addition to the usual school and club matches there were pleasant games of village cricket against Fred Dunn's team in Pentremeurig, Vicar Thomas' side in Llancarfan and at Llandough Castle.

48. The School Room

Bathing in the 'Town Baths' was extremely popular. These 'Baths' had been excavated out of the River Thaw's bed behind the Town Hall. More than once in the winter after a hard frost I walked the boys up to Mynydd-y-Glew, beyond Welsh St. Donats, to skate on the pond.

The school activity that interested me most was the Dramatic Society. I had done some acting, and producing, and written a short Welsh comedy which had been well received. The school play was put on in the Pavilion Cinema at the end of Summer Term after the Exams. This meant that Eric Reid and I spent most of our spare time that term in rehearsing, costume making and painting scenery. The latter was done in a dilapidated workshop opposite Old Hall, where Lewis the cooper did his work. We worked in the loft where it was impossible to stand upright. Here we painted the backcloths for the Duke's palace, the seashore, Olivia's house etc., and came away with a splitting headache each time. Nearly every boy had some part in the production and there was never a dearth of willing helpers. The Matron and her staff sewed, Mr. Marsden and his woodwork boys did the hammering and nailing. Some of the individual performances still remain in my memory.

The Debating Society varied by 'Mock Trials' was another activity which occupied our winter evenings. During the next two years many alterations and improvements were made. New changing rooms with showers were built at the end of the corridor. The Chemistry lab. was doubled in size and a boiler room and book store were added. The school was wired for electricity and connected to the mains water supply, enabling central heating to be installed.

On the scholastic side Welsh was introduced as a subject and the examination board of the Central Welsh Board took the place of the Oxford Exam, after thirty years.

At the end of 1926, an additional Boarding House was opened by Sir Thomas Mansel Franklen. This house was the gift of Sir Thomas. It opened with seven boys and by the end of 1927 it was 'filled to its limits'. Franklen House was under the care of Mr. Reid and his sister Miss M. B. Reid, a graduate of Belfast University. A hard tennis court was constructed, again through the initiative of Sir Thomas. Miss Reid was an excellent gardener and the place was a blaze of colour in the summer.

In Franklen House I was privileged to meet Helen Waddel the famous writer and scholar, author of *The Wandering Scholars, Peter Abelard etc.* She was a cousin of the Reids. Members of the famous Quaker family—the Hodgkins—were also visitors at the house. Here I remained until 1929 when I left to be married.

During these four years the school was gradually getting back to the standards of the 1850's and 1860's. Names were beginning to be added to the Honours Board, the numbers were increasing rapidly. A time came when the VIth form was greater than the whole school when Richard Williams took over. As I write these words I think of the school as more of a community, with a nucleus in the Boarding House of scholars and athletes. They came from all kinds of homes. There was nothing élitist about the Grammar School.

Along with most old boys of those years, I still think of them as 'Dick's days'. Richard Williams retired in 1938. Twenty years later in 1958 at the Old Boys Dinner, during the three-hundred and fiftieth Anniversary, the ovation he received when he stood up to speak lasted for minutes on end—a striking demonstration of gratitude and affection.

The High School for Girls

We have already briefly mentioned that this school was the brainchild of two Cowbridge men, John Bevan and Edward John. By the provisions of the Welsh Education Act of 1889, new schools were to be established offering an education intermediate between the Board Schools and University and one such school had been allocated to Cowbridge, as the centre for the Vale of Glamorgan. John Bevan, who was then living in Lombardy, had long nurtured ambitions for a girls' school equivalent to the boys' grammar schools, and now took up cudgels on behalf of the new Intermediate School. With assistance from Edward John, he obtained a site and paid for a hostel that

49. Cowbridge High School, Form V in the 1930s with Miss Maud Gunter

accommodated twelve boarders and he did not neglect the minutiae of providing grass plots for flowers and even tennis balls and racquets. The
architect was Robert Williams of Ystradowen, who made a world-wide
reputation for himself first in London and later in Egypt. When the school
opened in 1896 only eighteen girls were admitted: this included seven from
village primary schools and the rest from Great House and Plas Hen private
schools. There were a few scholarships, otherwise the girls had to pay £3 a
year. The subjects taught were English, History, Mathematics, French and
Latin, but no Science as it was considered unsuitable for schoolgirls. The
first head was Miss C. M. Gladish and she was followed by Miss Edith L.
Renaut, B.A. (London), who taught at Cowbridge from 1899 until 1913. She
was paid about £150 a year while her assistants got a mere £90: but she was
an inspired teacher who encouraged her pupils to aim at a university education. Her dream was soon fulfilled because in 1908 five girls, including
Maud Gunter, the Vale historian, went on to university. By now there were
eighty pupils on the books and in 1909 it was found necessary to enlarge the
hostel by the addition of two classrooms, a cookery room, a gymnasium, a
laboratory and a dormitory at a cost of £4,000.

Before uniforms were introduced, it seems the school fashions were as free
and easy as they are today. In an account in the School magazine, Maud
Gunter wrote that the girls wore 'midi skirts', white blouses tucked in neatly
under a leather belt and 'sailor hats' in stiff straw with navy bands. Most of
the girls had hair down to their waists, shining after vigorous brushing morning and night. In class this had to be plaited neatly with a black or navy
bow at the ends. 'I remember when I was thirteen "Alice Bands" were
fashionable, but our headmistress preferred us to draw the hair back to
another bow at the back of the head. She herself was majestic in a black silk
dress with a high collar and a skirt that fell to the floor in heavy folds.'

Uniforms were introduced in 1910 to avoid class distinction and to make
the girls proud of their school; they consisted of navy blue gym tunics, white
blouses and black stockings and shoes and even in the 1920s woe-betide any
girl if she did not wear her gloves in front of Lady Franklen of St. Hilary
when she visited the school as governor. On such visits it always amused the
Cowbridge girls to see the St. Hilary school children still curtseying to the
great lady just as they were accustomed to in their own village. The school
retained its Boarding House well into this century, but there was a gradual
reduction in the numbers of boarders until they ceased in 1939. Although a
few girls came from as far afield as Cheltenham, most of the intake were
from the immediate neighbourhood—Tonyrefail, Pencoed, Llanharan,
Llanhari, Pontyclun and the Vale. They travelled chiefly on the Taff-Vale
railway to school, though Miss Gunter recalled a girl being brought from
Colwinston by pony and trap. It is an interesting observation that of the
Cowbridge parents it was the railway element in the town who had the
greater ambitions for their daughters' education. It was the railwaymen's
children who in the early days sat for the scholarships to the High School

50. A class at Cowbridge High School in 1959

and Grammar School—either because their parents had come from further afield than most Cowbridge folk or because they saw education as a means of improving their status in the town.

'A haven of peace and tranquillity, disturbed only by the ceaseless thud of tennis balls on the court or the coughs and splutters of the new fangled motor-cycles speeding over Stallingdown,' is how Mrs. Muriel Phillips the Science mistress describes the school in the early twenties. Lessons were given in a sphinx-like silence and if the girls dared to chat excitedly in her informal garden classes they would earn looks of mild disapproval from Mrs. Forrester, the headteacher. Putting on plays such as 'Christmas Carol' with Owen Phillips' motor cycle providing the spotlight form no small part of the memory of those halcyon days. Or the excursions into the countryside when the girls learnt the flora of the Vale like the Catechism. Contact with the boys of the Grammar School was strictly frowned upon and after one unfortunate incident a barrier was actually erected to keep them out of the school. Sir Thomas Mansel Franklen was delivering his Speech Day address, when to his horror, he spied a host of hot-blooded Romeos with pocket Byrons in their hands and dreamy looks in their eyes sitting on the school wall seeking evening rendezvous with the girls. He immediately ordered the wall to be rebuilt at least five feet higher! The girls had to wait until 1942 before their love games were officially recognised—when the first tennis match with the Grammar School was arranged. The large number of distinctions gained by the pupils in the C.W.B. Junior examinations and the fact that one of the girls later became a Harley Street surgeon of world-wide repute speak volumes for the academic achievements of this period.

The ensuing years under the headships of Miss Bennett Jones, Miss Enid Walker and Miss E. M. Smith saw a widening of the syllabus at the school to include all the necessary subjects of a modern education, a rapid increase in the number of pupils and an expansion in building. In the 1950s the old Boarding House was converted into extra teaching space and a two-form entry system introduced for the first time. By now the numbers had risen to about 240 and since further development on the old site became impossible on account of the proposed Cowbridge by-pass, it became necessary to build a completely new school. This was constructed by Messrs. Tudor Jenkins and Co. of Pontyclun and officially opened by Councy Councillor D. I. Morgan on 1 December, 1960. Many former pupils will have poignant memories of the headship of Miss Enid Walker who moved to Cowbridge from Treforest Girls' Grammar School in 1950. Few will forget her perfectionist approach whether at school or producing plays for the local dramatic society. Her tragic death in March 1959 was deeply mourned throughout the Vale of Glamorgan. The final years under Miss E. Smith saw a considerable extension of the sixth form, enabling pupils to study almost any normal subject in the Arts and Sciences to Advanced Level. In 1974, however, the 78-year-old school came to an end and was replaced by a Comprehensive School serving a smaller catchment area, with its buildings housing the Upper School. The first headmaster was H. V. Williams, M.A. who retired in July 1979. It is pleasing to report that the spirit of the old Girls' School is still very much alive and thanks to the work of Miss E. Smith, Miss Olwen Rowbotham and Mrs. Gwyneth Shuttleworth an active Old Girls' Association still meets twice a year.

Junior Education

The several hundred pupils of Cowbridge who attend an ultra-modern and well equipped junior school, now under the supervision of Miss Dena Williams, would scarcely comprehend what conditions were like in the early Board School, situated on the Broadway. They were very primitive to say the least in the early days; in winter the children huddled around huge open stoves and it was so hot during one summer that a water can was procured to water the rooms every morning. The Board School was in advance of the numerous Dame and private schools in the district, in fact the early log books are full of criticism of the entrants from these schools. One is told that 'the greater part can read monosyllable fairly, but very few know anything of Arithmetic, Grammar or Geography'. The headmaster at the time was also very critical of the indifference of some Cowbridge parents, accusing them of sending the children to school with dirty hands and faces and neglecting to supervise their homework. The children were surprisingly unruly; on one occasion the headmaster had to attend the Police Court to answer charges of administering punishment to a boy for insolent behaviour and insubordination; on another, Canon Edmondes found it necessary to visit the school to warn the children not to indulge in bad language and warn them of its consequences in another world. Attendances were often alarmingly low, especially during the harvest season and the attendance officer of the day was not noted for his efficiency in 'whipping them in' either. There were a great number of school holidays, especially when the Glamorgan Hunt met on Stallingdown or the numerous fairs visited the town. Things gradually improved, especially under the headmastership of J. H. Harvey who, with his assistant Miss Kate Tutton, was still teaching at the school in the 1920s. Mr. Harvey was a 'pedagogue' of the old school and such was the firmness of his discipline that his pupils made up an amusing rhyme about him.

Tommy Harvey is a very fine man,
He goes to Church on Sunday,
And prays to God to give him strength
To whack the kids on Monday.

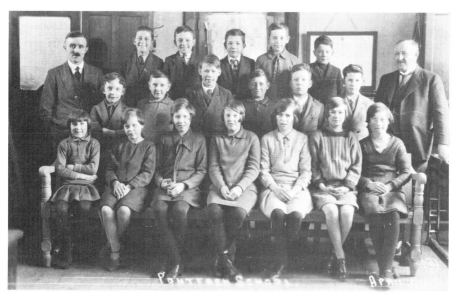

51. Pontfaen School—with schoolmasters H. C. Sloman and J. M. Roberts (1920)

52. Pontfaen School (Standard V, 1922)

Cane in hand, Harvey banged away at tables like Thor with his mythical hammer; his class never disobeyed him, neither did they forget what he taught. Many of his pupils made their way in the world; none thought more of him than one of his first, George Frederick Ackerman, who rose to a high rank in the Metropolitan Police, was for seven years Inspector in Charge of Police at Windsor Castle and was presented with the Royal Victoria Medal by King George V. Harvey was succeeded as Headmaster by H. C. Sloman, later followed by J. M. Roberts and Miss Francis.

In 1973 a new dimension was added to Y Bontfaen School and to junior education in Cowbridge as a whole when, after great parental pressure, a bilingual unit was opened in the original school buildings. Eight young children under the supervision of Mrs. Ann Thomas moved from the temporary accommodation in Maendy County Primary School. The unit enjoyed continuous growth, reflecting the increasing revival of the Welsh language even in the most anglicised part of South Glamorgan, and in September 1979 Ysgol Iolo Morgannwg with over seventy pupils under headmistress, Mrs. Glesni Whettleton, was opened as a school in its own right.

On the borders of Welsh St. Donats and Llanblethian parishes stands Maendy Primary School, which recently celebrated its centenary. It was established by a local school board in 1877 as a result of Forster's Education Act of 1810. As part of the celebrations a religious service of thanksgiving for the establishment of the school was conducted by one of the outstanding ex-pupils, the Rev. W. J. Samuel, Moderator of the United Reformed Church, and a commemorative tree was planted in the school grounds by Councillor Mrs. E. Joy Davies, J.P., Deputy Chairman of South Glamorgan County Council. In passing, it may be noted that another illustrious 'old boy' of Maendy School is Professor E. H. Rhoderick, the distinguished physicist and son of an ex-headmaster of the school.

Sport and Leisure

Throughout the twentieth century sport has become of increasing importance to the men and women of Cowbridge. Shorter working hours and greater all-round affluence has meant that more and more people have sufficient leisure time to enjoy their favourite games in well organised clubs. At the turn of the century, however, one has the impression that sport was little more than a pleasant pastime for the local gentry and well-to-do.

Cricket, in particular, owes much in its early days to patronage from the Big House. In 1895 the Cricket Field, then known as Cae Wyndham, was bought by E. H. Ebsworth of Llandough Castle. Arthur Evans (father of Dr. David Evans) remembered it as an ordinary farm field and recollected

53. Cowbridge Cricket Club in 1904. Rev. Owen Jones is seated centre with W. Russell on his left. Others include F. E. P. Dunn, T. D. Schofield and D. Brown (Umpire)

shooting snipe on it in 1881. A cricket ground was laid out there for Mr. Ebsworth by Alex Hearne, the famous Kent county cricketer. The first run ever scored on the ground was made by the genial squire of Llandough himself in a game between Cowbridge and Bridgend. The old records tell us that Arthur Evans took another twenty off the Bridgend attack in what was a remarkable opening over. Mr. Ebsworth's team continued playing on the ground until 1903, but the following year the Glamorgan Gypsies were founded and played cricket, tennis, croquet and hockey there until about 1911. This was the era of William Russell of Norfolk who was employed as a professional cricketer and groundsman. He was one of the finest batsmen in Glamorgan during the pre-World War I period. In one season he scored 138 not out, 208 not out, 71 and 155 not out in five innings, with only one low score in between. He died in 1908, aged thirty-eight, and his tombstone can be seen in Cowbridge churchyard. His family lived in the old *Westgate Inn* until recent years.

A new club called the Cowbridge Wanderers was formed in 1906. They played all their early fixtures away from home and home matches from August onwards when they used the Grammar School pitch. They were captained by the Rev. Owen Jones, the Rector of Llansannor and Llangan.

54. Cowbridge Cricket Club 1923
F. Fitzgerald, R. S. David, A. C. R. David, Guy Dunn, T. Evans, E. Aubrey, D. Brown
(Umpire), J. C. Baldwin, D. Beith, F. E. P. Dunn, B. S. Bird, I. Pell, Alan and
Neil Brown (scorers)

Owen Jones was a most genial character; he seemed to possess an almost indestructible effervescence which welled up in him like a bubbling mountain spring. On the cricket field he always wore brown shoes, grey trousers and a white cap, and he was a wonderful old type round-arm spin bowler, who bowled many batsmen 'round their legs'. He had the physique of a boxer — indeed he was one. When Rector of Llansannor he had often been called to the *City Inn* by the landlady, Mrs. Barkaway, to sort out with his fists the Saturday night rowdies. He was totally uninhibited and his many young admirers watched him get up to numerous antics with the sort of breathlessness one watches a trapeze artist in full flight. He would bat deliberately low in the order simply to enjoy a wee drop of the elixir of life in the *Duke of Wellington* with his friend Arthur Spencer. One afternoon the customers were challenged to drink a bucketful of beer in a set time. Jones, to everyone's surprise, gleefully accepted the challenge. He left the bar for a few minutes, then returned and proceeded to drink the ale without difficulty. When asked by the landlord why he had gone out, the Rector replied with a wicked grin 'Naturally, Arthur, I tried a pailful of water first to see if I could do it'. When Selwyn Davies played his first game for Cowbridge, Owen Jones was bowling donkey-droppers from the Llwynhelig end. Selwyn greatly admired the clergyman, but things weren't going his way and several catches had been dropped off his bowling. At last a dolly catch came Selwyn's way, but to his utter dismay he dropped it. By now, the Rector was as aggressive as a cock sparrow and he roared down the pitch at the unfortunate youngster: 'For God's sake, buy a bloody bread-basket, boy'. Selwyn was far more horrified hearing a parson swear than dropping a simple catch. Owen Jones was indeed a great club player in terms of character, and his best figures of 9 for 12 runs in 1903 reveal the pure splendour of his aggressive bowling.

In 1912 the Cowbridge Wanderers undertook to take over the ground by arrangement with E. H. Ebsworth at a rent of £25 a year. Three years later the ground was bought for £700. Almost as soon as the ground was acquired, steps were taken to improve the facilities to meet the sporting and social needs of the club with the formation of the Cowbridge and District Club in 1913. There was no cricket played during the First World War. Eight members of the team joined the Army but tragically three out of the five Dunn brothers — the mainstay of the pre-War team — did not survive the slaughter of those murderous years. F. E. P. Dunn, however, continued to serve Cowbridge cricket club for many years as player, secretary and president, and the Memorial Gates at the entrance to the ground are a permanent tribute to his memory. Cricket restarted in 1919 when the professional was Pell (from Yorkshire) and he was followed by Harry Edwards from 1922 to 1927. Edwards was a native of Cobham in Surrey and he used to extol the cricketing abilities of 'Jack 'Obbs' to all and sundry. Edwards was succeeded as pro by Guy Day until 1932 and later by Trevor Preece (Junior).

55. Cowbridge Cricket Club in 1926 contained three England Test Players: M. J. Turnbull (standing top left), J. C. Clay (fourth from the left standing) and C. F. Walters (seated front)

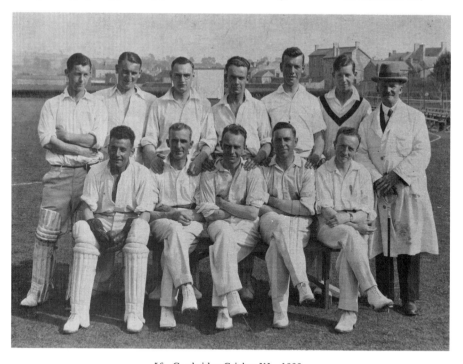

56. Cowbridge Cricket XI — 1933
N. G. Brown, W. E. Thomas, D. G. Williams, V. R. John, E. John, A. T. Brown,
D. Brown (Umpire), C. J. Warren, E. D. Lewis, R. N. Bird, W. Hill and W. E. Whone

57. Cowbridge Cricket Club v. B. L. Muncer's XI on the occasion of W. E. Jones' Benefit Fund, match played at Cowbridge in September 1952. The visiting team included Glamorgan C.C.C. Players: D. J. Shepherd, N. Hever, G. B. Shaw, W. E. Jones, A. J. Watkins, H. Davies, B. L. Muncer, W. G. A. Parkhouse and W. E. Jones and two Australian players. Umpires: J. Lynn Thomas and W. Protheroe-Beynon

Many outstanding cricketers have played on the Cowbridge Ground. Douglas Jardine and Freddy Brown were Test cricketers of the highest order, whilst J. C. Clay played for England as well as being one of Glamorgan's immortals. 'Johnny' Clay was a brilliant bowler who took 1,292 wickets for his county. On one occasion for Cowbridge he played alongside two other Test cricketers Maurice Turnbull and C. F. Walters. Mr. Clay was a past President of the Club, and his sensible advice to all tail-enders to 'give it the willow' has been sadly missed since his recent death. Several Cowbridge players have represented their County. These include L. E. W. Williams, Aubrey M. Edwards, John A. Davies and Howard W. Morgan. Vivian Jenkins, Arthur H. Jones, Graham Jones, Garfield Owen, Barry John and Haydn Davies are some of the rugby internationals who have displayed their all-round talents in playing cavalier cricket on the Cowbridge Ground. Since 1947 three XIs have played on Saturdays, and the Club regularly entertains five or six touring sides from across the Border each year. In 1953 Fazal Mahmood the Pakistani star brought a team called the Eaglets, full of Test players, yet they were unable to beat a Cowbridge and District team.

58. Cowbridge Cricket Club 1971
Back row: W. R. Jones, D. Lewis, R. James, G. L. Leeke, D. J. Bevan, R. Harris,
O. E. Hopkins, W. S. Davies (Umpire)
Sitting: H. W. Morgan, W. E. Lewis (Vice-Chairman), J. A. Davies (Captain), J. C. Clay
(President), E. J. Dew (Vice-Captain), C. H. Adams (Hon. Secretary), J. R. Gabe
In front: C. Dew, M. Bevan

For some years now Cowbridge has participated in the Haig Village National Cricket Competition and organised its own knock-out tournament with Clubs from the surrounding villages taking part.

More than anything over the past forty years the example of hard work and dedication by club secretaries Neil Brown and Colin Adams has greatly helped to forge the links of friendship between the players and public as well as put Cowbridge Cricket Club well and truly on the sporting map. The game has progressed a long way from those halcyon summers at Plas Newydd when Fred Dunn gave hopeful young batsmen from Cowbridge half-a-crown for every six they could clout into his greenhouses.

Rugby was played at Cowbridge three years after the Rugby Football Union was formed in 1871. The following extract from an article published in 1874 gives details of the game in those early days:

> 'The first match played by the Cardiff Rugby Club was against the Cowbridge Grammar School at Cowbridge, on 21st November, 1874, the team journeying to Cowbridge in a coach and four.'

The article continues with some interesting pieces of information about the game as it was then played.

As there were so few teams in existence, play generally consisted of pick-up games against members of the club. Games were either ten a side, or twenty a side, and chiefly depended on individual play. When there were only ten a side, a back would often get a long run with little opposition and with disastrous results to "bellows", particularly as training was unknown. The ball was round, and never picked up off the ground, but had to be "dapped", if only a few inches. The ball when caught on the hop was carried by the player, who made a run for a try, and passing was unknown. A player, when collared, sometimes handed the ball to one of his own side, but never threw it. The usual thing was to put it on the ground and then form a scrum.

When the ball went into touch there was no lineout, but the forwards, twelve of each side, formed a line with their heads down and the ball was thrown into the tunnel by a spectator. The object of the forwards was then to force the ball through, heeling as we know it being unknown.

Punting was considered bad form, but drop-kicking was cultivated. The length of some of the drop-kicks with a round ball was remarkable and both drop-kicking and place-kicking with the round ball were more reliable than appears to be the case with the oval ball.

Tripping was never considered etiquette, but the scientific hacking of a back who was running and could not be reached with the hands was sometimes employed, though not often. Hacking was seldom the cause of an injury, or even a bruise, as it consisted of hooking the instep of the leg which was in the air.

There was no regulation costume, most of the players turning out in ordinary attire, just taking their coats off. One player is said to have played in evening dress. No-one ever discarded his bowler hat.

Scoring was very complicated and varied according to the venue of the match, but it seems fairly certain that the important scoring device was the goal. A goal beat any number of tries. Touchdowns or minors were counted and, where no goals or tries could be scored, became an important factor.

There was no referee, and the only known rules were those in use at Cheltenham College. Each side provided an umpire, and as one umpire had as much power as the other there were constant arguments. During these arguments the game was stopped, and players and spectators joined in the general debate.

The game declined in popularity after the Great War, but one enthusiastic supporter of the club in those days was a character called Bill Batchelor who played for Wales in the Victory International after the war. Since 1945 the popularity of the handling code has gone from strength to strength and today three teams represent the town. The club has become affiliated to the Cowbridge and District Athletic Club and plays an annual match against Llantwit Major for the Hugh Andrews Memorial Cup.

To conclude our section on Rugby Football, it is worthy of mention that a town boy, Haydn Davies, played rugby for Wales at centre in 1959. His

59. Cowbridge R.F.C. Season 1975/76
Back row: K. Paynter, M. Brewer, C. Morris, R. Thomas, L. Thomas, T. Morgan,
B. Thomas, G. Joshua, H. E. Williams, J. Ackroyd, J. D. Cleaver
Sitting: J. Morgan, S. Huish, P. Lathey (Captain), L. Drummond, R. H. B. Thomas

selection brought the total of international caps won by old Bovians to five
in four years, a remarkable school record.

Soccer has never made as much impact at Cowbridge as rugby. In the
early part of the century there were two teams: the Cowbridge Town side
who played on the cricket field and the Albions whose ground was in a field
adjoining the Aberthin road. Of the players 'Sol' Newman stands out in the
memory of local people as one who should have played at a higher level.
During the 1930s there was keen competition for the Francis Hawkins' Cup
between Maendy, Llanblethian, Cowbridge Saturdays and Cowbridge
Wednesdays. The Wednesdays produced one star in Jimmy Blair, junior,
the son of the famous Cardiff City and Scottish International who was
himself a Cowbridge innkeeper at that time. Local football fixtures often
have an element of dottiness about them. Imagine the feelings of the
Wednesdays when on a hard frozen pitch in February 1935 they were
expected to play the same side twice in one day! Their opponents were
Cathays, who after a nightmare of sliding and slithering for 90 minutes to a
2-0 defeat must have thought it a very unpleasant dose of 'double trouble' to
have to face Cowbridge all over again. Determined to win, the visitors used
no fewer than eighteen players: but that afternoon the Wednesdays had

wings on their togs and darted through the Cathays defence like swallows to win by four goals to nil. In more recent times the enthusiasm of Keith 'Nipper' Jewell has done a lot to counter the apathy of a town in which soccer has only rarely captured wholehearted support. On a Sunday morning in November 1964 he arranged a friendly match against a Ministry of Agriculture XI. Such was the interest, especially among members of the Rugby Fifteen, that the idea of playing on Sunday mornings caught on, and the Cowbridge All Stars were formed. Unfortunately, the team has never succeeded in obtaining a pitch so that all games are played away. From 1965 Jeff Thomas lent them a field in Penllyn village and they used to change in the hay barn. Later the team were forced to travel to and from Llandough for 'home' matches. Despite these difficulties the loyalty of the players is truly amazing: Anthony 'Nat' Davies the goalkeeper, for instance, has played in over 350 games for the club since its inception. Anthony 'Tosh' Taylor, the well known Vale of Glamorgan solicitor, has also played many games. His prolific scoring feats seem to suggest that his boots are as eloquent as his oratory.

Today the Cowbridge and District Athletic Club offer a full range of sporting and recreational facilities including squash and hard surface tennis courts. For years badminton used to be played at the gymnasium of the

60. Cowbridge Soccer Team — 1923
Standing: T. Link, M. Edwards, Bert Goulden, W. Chissell, Sol Newman
Seated: W. Hopkins, Owen Phillips, Gwyn Thomas, W. Hopkins, Harry Lewis

former Grammar School, but recently it was decided to discontinue the connection with the Athletic Club and the game is enjoyed by large numbers in
the Upper Comprehensive School. In 1977 the Athletic Club was proud to
erect a new score box in memory of 'Johnny Clay', its President for many
years.

Cowbridge inhabitants who were interested in golf became members of
the Leys Golf Club, near Aberthaw. This was a beautiful course which gave
great pleasure to golfers for more than seventy years. It is interesting to note
that Dai Rees, the Ryder Cup Captain, was born in the Club House at the
Leys. He often stated that the Leys greens were the finest that he had ever
played on. It was a sad day, therefore, when in 1957 the Central Electricity
Generation Board won their case to build a power station on the spot. It was
only a matter of months before the bulldozers arrived to demolish the houses
and bungalows and bury the golf course for all time under the power
station.

Cowbridge Men's Hockey Club was active during the 1920s and 1930s.
The side consisted mainly of Old Boys of the Grammar School. When,
however, the school changed over to rugby its source of supply of players
ceased and the club was not re-started after the Second World War. During
its existence a number of players were called upon to play for the Glamorgan
County Club.

61. The 13th Green at the Leys Golf Club. The Club House was formerly the *Ship Hotel*
and the haunt of smugglers when Aberthaw was a thriving port

62. Cowbridge Hockey Club, 1931
Top row: Jeff Stewart, Vivian John, Guy Day, D. Glyn Williams, J. T. Rees
Seated: Cyril Warren, W. Evan Thomas, Neil Brown, J. C. Ellis, Alan Brown, John
Edwards and Willie Whone

On one occasion, 19 March 1937, sport shared the national headlines with politics as far as Cowbridge was concerned. On that day Evan Williams put the old borough well and truly on the map by winning the Grand National on 'Royal Mail'. Evan was the son of Mr. Fred Williams of the *Bear Hotel*, who was himself a devotee of the sport of kings. Evan had previously ridden the immortal 'Golden Miller' without success in the National. After his great victory he was presented to King George VI and Queen Elizabeth, and on his triumphant return to Cowbridge, was given a complimentary dinner and presented with a gold watch by Colonel Homfray of Penllyn. 'Royal Mail' was not the only famous horse with Cowbridge connections. 'Jingle Geordie' when he arrived at a local stable outside Cowbridge in 1917 aroused considerable local interest, especially among the women folk. Not only had he just been awarded the King's Premium but had previously been among the bunch of horses which trampled the unfortunate suffragette Emily Davison to her death in the Derby of 1912.

For many years now the Point-to-Point races held at Penllyn have been a red letter day in the local racegoers' calendar. There are some racing stories which gain rather than lose credence by repetition. The tale of the ill-fated race that took place at Penllyn on 23 May, 1919 is one of them. At this time,

Dillwyn Morgan of the Bridge Brewery, Cowbridge, owned a fine trotting pony called Daisy, whose coat gleamed like satin and whose speed was a by-word in the borough. She was a dray horse who delivered barrels of ale from the brewery to every corner of the Vale. Mr. Morgan was very proud of Daisy and boasted that his pony could outrace any horse in the locality. He was challenged, however, by a Llysworney farmer who owned a fast hunter. A private race was arranged at Penllyn, wagers were laid and an enthusiastic crowd of supporters turned up at the racecourse to cheer Daisy on. After a thrilling race she flew past the tapes ahead of her rival. Such a voltage of triumph surged through the jockey's body that he hadn't noticed that Daisy had begun to tremble like an aspen. Within seconds, she collapsed on the racecourse and died. The remorse of her owner was so profound that he ordered an inscribed tombstone to be placed over her in the Brewery yard—a lasting testimony to her gallant twenty eight years.

The Cowbridge district has always been a favourite haunt for fox hunting. In the eighteenth century, that doyen of blood-sports in Glamorgan, Squire Richard Jenkins of Pantyrawel and Llanharan, acquired his life-long addiction to hunting at an early age when still a pupil at Cowbridge Grammar School. We learn that 'he together with another young gentleman Mr. Price of Pentyrch managed to get a few harriers together behind the *Duke of Wellington*'. Throughout the nineteenth century, hunting in the district was continued by the Cowbridge Harriers, and in 1873 the Glamorgan Hunt was established by Theodore Mansel Talbot, the son of C. R. M. Talbot of Margam. He built kennels on the Talbot estate at Llandough after being given permission to hunt the whole countryside south of the main railway line from Cardiff to Bridgend. One of the earliest masters of the Glamorgan Hunt was a Cowbridge squire, Richard Thurston Bassett of Crossways (1886-1896). Bassett's huntsman George Cox and his chief whip Harry Lush were held in high repute in hunting circles well into the present century because of their long and faithful service, whilst John John of Church Street known everywhere as 'Old John of the Vale' had begun his apprenticeship as a kennel boy with the Cowbridge Harriers in 1854 and continued to hunt well into the late 1920s, becoming a legend in his own time. Another devotee worthy of mention was Mr. L. G. Williams of Bonvilston Cottage who served as Secretary and Treasurer for thirty-six years. Richard Thurston Bassett was succeeded as master by The Mackintosh of Mackintosh, who in 1906 was followed by Colonel H. R. Homfray of Penllyn Castle. He truly belonged to the genus *homo rusticus*: he was a warm-hearted squire to whom hound and horn were almost as important as public life. His huntsman Frank Grant of Penllyn village, once recalled in the local press an exciting day's sport which took place in 1909 when a large pack mustered along the banks of the Ewenny. The hounds followed the scent straight into Bridgend and the fox was soon seen scurrying across the chimney pots in Nolton Street. The yelping and baying of the hounds and the vociferous encouragement of the huntsmen, naturally brought the whole town to a standstill. A similar incident had occurred about this time at the home of Mrs. Mary John of West End, Cowbridge, during the much patronised Boxing Day meet on Stallingdown. The fox ran straight through her house followed by the pack of hounds, hot on the trail. Under the mastership of Mr. R. H. Williams of Bonvilston, the Glamorgan Hunt had to face difficulties more hazardous than the wily ways of Reynard. The shadows of the World War had closed in and severely restricted fox hunting, but a worse disaster was impending. In 1920 an outbreak of rabies occurred in the district and by government order all the hounds had to be destroyed. The mastership of his successor, the late Captain Homfray of Penllyn, is for-tunately still fresh in the memory of many of the local followers of the chase, as are the names of those genial fox hunting fanatics of the thirties, Bill Dingle of Llansannor and Idris Adams of Llanharan. The Second World War brought fresh troubles to the Hunt, not the least of which was the feeding of the hounds and the horses. Under the circumstances it was felt necessary to destroy the hounds, but in an act of supreme unselfishness, Captain Homfray moved many of them to Penllyn Castle where he, Mrs. Homfray and Miss Serena Boothby cared for them throughout the war com-pletely unaided by staff. In 1961 the hounds were moved into completely new kennels at Llandough and under their present master Mr. A. S. Martyn, continue to flourish. The coming of the M.4 motorway has greatly restricted hunting north of Cowbridge and about a year ago the Glamorgan Hunt met for the last time north of the new road at the *Fox and Hounds*, Llanhari, where they were regaled with the stirrup cup by mine host Geoff. Roscoe. Finally mention should be made of the excellent history of the Glamorgan Hunt recently written by Mr. Lawrence Williams.

The narrowness of the River Thaw at Cowbridge prohibits any serious fishing or boating. However, this was not always so; in John Richards' *The Cowbridge Story* we read that a twelve pound salmon was caught near the bridge during the First World War and it was the only one ever seen in the river. In E. W. Miles' memoirs we are told that in the 1860s, the grammar school boys had rowing boats on the river between the Poplars and the Mill. Miles says the river was wider and deeper at that time, which was probably because of the mill. In more recent times, Miss Freda Evans' father, a keen fly-fisherman, regularly fished the Thaw south of the town. Before the river was altered on the Llandough Meadows each farmer used to keep his own stretch free from reeds so effectively that S. D. Evans, the Cowbridge solicitor, could paddle his boat downstream from Cowbridge to the river mouth at Aberthaw.

How many of the present inhabitants of the borough are aware of the existence of open air swimming baths in the town only a decade or two ago? The pool, which was located in the middle of the Thaw (the New Cut), was built in 1911 and was the brainchild of Alderman David Tilley, then mayor of the borough. He launched a public subscription which raised a hundred pounds to meet the cost. To be 'in the swim' the younger elements had to

63. Official opening of the Cowbridge Swimming Baths in 1911

purchase a season ticket from the Corporation costing half-a-crown and only single sex bathing was allowed. The three schools all used the baths in the pre-war period, and Mrs. Muriel Phillips recalls many a hotly contested swimming contest being held for her High School pupils. Taking the plunge even in midsummer, however, required a doughty spirit. For as well as contending with hordes of horseflies on the surface within seconds of entering the water the swimmer would become as cold as an Arctic seal with a dozen springs discharging icy water from the River Thaw. Perhaps for this reason the baths fell into a sad state of disrepair after the Second World War.

Cowbridge Today

The years since 1950 have seen further building, some public, but chiefly private, as well as the construction of the by-pass. Apart from two small housing estates at Druid's Green and Cae Stumpie, little of this has occurred within the boundaries. In fact the traditional east-west growth along the highway has given place to rapid development along the southern periphery in Llanblethian: so much so, that four medium-sized private housing estates have sprung up at Bowmans Well, Broadshoard, The Verlands, Mill Park, and Brookfield Park. Dotted here and there throughout the parish of

Llanblethian are also the more expensive houses, built for commuters from Cardiff and the industrial complexes of Glamorgan. It is not surprising therefore that although the population of the borough has remained fairly static, that of Llanblethian has increased threefold over the last twenty years or so. This growth has meant that Cowbridge has become, in effect, a pleasant dormitory town, inhabited by many people with no roots in the locality, whose livelihood and prosperity are directly dependent upon good road communications and the motor car.

The recent development in and around Cowbridge has made certain that the High Street businesses have prospered, whilst the inevitable supermarkets, school extensions and other public and sporting amenities have quickly followed. Thanks to the watchfulness of the authorities Cowbridge fortunately has not been turned into a 'developing town' or marred by the worse abuses of modern architecture. Thus the proud Georgian houses with their finely proportioned facades still grace its main thoroughfare, the shop fronts are all suitably styled and the quaint courts, archways and alleyways branching off the High Street help to perpetuate an 'olde worlde' atmosphere. Cowbridge is, of course, situated within a conservation area with over fifty buildings in the town listed as being of architectural or historical interest. It is encouraging therefore to report the existence of an active

64. Town Mill Road, prior to second world war from the Mill towards the South Gate

conservationist committee in the town and that keen interest is taken by many Cowbridge inhabitants in the activities of the Glamorgan Naturalists' Trust. It was this 'spirit of conservation' that was the driving force behind the renovation of Old Hall from a derelict state a few years ago, to provide the town with an excellent new library, clinic and centre for adult education. No place can live entirely on its past history: so it is fortunate indeed that the large influx of newcomers has over the last few years done so much to infuse life into the community in the form of seventy or more organisations and earn once more for Cowbridge the reputation as a cultural centre. Nowhere is the sense of community more in evidence than in the annual 'Cowbridge Week'—a festival of drama, music, sport and fun for all the family.

For such a small town Cowbridge can wear its cultural attire with something of a swagger. In the world of books, several of its authors have earned more than a local reputation for themselves, whilst a poet of lasting fame, Alun Lewis of Aberdare, spent his formative years in its midst as a pupil of the Grammar School. The Rev. L. Hopkin-James was the earliest of the twentieth-century writers: his *Old Cowbridge, Borough, Church and School*, is a valuable source book for any serious student of the town's history.

For the general reader however, *The Cowbridge Story* by John Richards, published in the 1950s is probably more palatable, being a treasure trove of racy anecdotes and colourful characters. The celebration of the 350th anniversary of the founding of the Grammar School at Cowbridge was a milestone that caused a special literary diamond to be cut; the result was Iolo Davies' excellent book *A Certaine Schoole* published in 1967. Of this masterly, full length account of one of the oldest grammar schools in Wales, Professor Glanmor Williams paid the warmest tribute in the *Western Mail*: 'It is a comprehensive and detailed account such as we do not have— probably could not have—for any other school in Wales with the possible exception of Friars' School in Bangor'. The familiar sight of the squat yet cherubic figure of the Rev. Ewart Lewis, shuffling along the High Street with an overloaded shopping bag peeping out beneath his swirling cassock— seemed to many a character straight out of Trollope's *Barchester Towers*. His fourteen years as vicar of Llanblethian with Cowbridge from 1949-1963, 'certainly earned him the reputation of being a character', but as a character in the highest sense of the word. Not least among the qualities that made him one of the best known and most widely respected churchmen in South Wales was the immense breadth of his learning. Throughout his all too short life he devoted his scholarship to the service of the Church and community at large; indeed his *Prayer Book Revision in the Church in Wales*, his essay on the Cowbridge Diocesan Library, as well as numerous learned articles to such journals as *Province, Y Llan* and *Church Times* won him a considerable reputation in the realm of ecclesiastical writings.

65. A Local History Society Meeting

(Photo: Haydn Baynham)

In a town so steeped in history, it is encouraging to report an active Local History Society. Founded in October 1974, its aims are to foster further interest in the history of Cowbridge and district, to preserve a visual, written and sound record of the region's past, and to encourage the preservation of ancient rights, sites, buildings and footpaths.

From its inception until her death on 11 January, 1977 the society was honoured to have as its Life Vice-President Miss Maud Gunter, who in her writings and public lectures was passionately devoted to Cowbridge and its traditions. She is commemorated in the society's annual Maud Gunter Memorial Lecture. The Society has already organised public exhibitions and regularly conducted guided tours of the historic features of Cowbridge and Llanblethian during Cowbridge Week. The Honorary Secretary is John L. S. Miles.

In recent years Cowbridge has earned the reputation of being a music centre, for apart from an excellent choir, the town boasts a first rate Operatic Society and a versatile Folk Group. The Cowbridge Male Voice Choir has probably done more than any organisation to put the town firmly on the cultural map. It appeared before H.R.H. Princess Alexandra at the Royal Albert Hall in 1974, sharing the stage with Dame Vera Lynn and Larry Adler. The choir have also appeared in the T.V. programme 'Corau Meibion' and more recently on the radio show 'Nine Five on Monday', while

66. Cowbridge Male Voice Choir

in April 1979 a successful 17-day tour was made in Saskatchewan, Canada. The choir was formed by a dozen or so enthusiasts meeting in the *Eastgate Hotel* early in 1971 and is now firmly established with audiences throughout south Wales and Southern England. That its short history has been such a successful one has been largely thanks to the high musical standards set by two conductors—David J. Richards, whose baton led the choir through its teething stages, and Iwan Guy, L.R.A.M. a former professional singer who took over early in 1976. A great deal is owed to the high class accompaniment of Miss Carole Vann. A concert at the Town Hall with two visiting Canadian Choirs opened Cowbridge Week in July 1977 and the choir's sixty members have also competed in several Eisteddfodau. The Operatic Society was formed in January 1969 when a group of thirty-five enthusiasts, with a 'modicum of talent but an overriding desire to succeed', met at the Ramoth Baptist Schoolroom. Nine years after the first performance of 'The Pirates of Penzance', the Society has greatly enhanced its reputation aiming at high musical standards in an ever widening repertoire. The Society as well as producing nine operas in a row has given many concerts outside the town, in places as far afield as Bristol. The Cowbridge Folk Group was started in 1969 by Mrs. Elvene Mottershead to sing during Family Services in Holy Cross Church. The group have sung in many churches of the Vale including an unique wedding service at St. Illtyd's Church Llanhari, where all the music for the service was produced by the guitars. The repertoire of the group — known also as Gwerin y Bontfaen — includes religious, folk and modern songs. When they appeared on television a few years ago the group consisted of guitarists Duncan and Christopher Mottershead and singers Carolyn Jones, Gillian Busher, Fiona Cobourne, Diane Dandro, Claire Salmon and Leslie Mottershead. Duncan Mottershead won further musical honours in his early teens by coming second in a 'Young Musicians of Wales' competition run by the B.B.C. The bells of Holy Cross Church with their fine resonant notes have been an integral part of the social history of the town since they were cast in 1722 — having been rung to proclaim good news or bad, including coronations, fires, births, deaths and marriages. The peal of bells is the only complete eight left in the whole of the county that were cast by Evan and William Evans of Chepstow. The present band is made up of male and female ringers, whose ages range from eighteen to sixty-two and as well as ringing the bells, they look after the tower. The tower captain is W. G. Morgan and the steeple keeper is Mr. W. E. Morgan.

67. Cowbridge Operatic Society — 'The Mikado'

68. Cowbridge Folk Group

Amateur Dramatics has always been a popular leisure activity at Cowbridge. Before the Second World War, under the direction of Mr. Owen Phillips of Maendy, major productions were staged every year at the Pavilion Cinema, starting with the one act plays in 1933. Known popularly as 'The Cads', the drama group made their own costumes and scenery and the proceeds of their efforts were always donated to local charities. One of the most successful performances at this time was that of W. Chetham Strodes' three-act play 'The Day is Gone'. The cast was as follows:

'Ernest Webb'—A. C. Burgess	'Rosie Spiller'—Miss Jean Dunn
'Mabel Thatcher'—Miss Gwyneth Thomas	'Mayor Warminside'—
'Stanley Thatcher'—A. B. Codling	A. G. Reed
'George Softly'—T. H. C. Walker	'Miss Tuttle'—Mrs. May Brown
	'Florrie'—Miss Molly Roper
	'Wireless Commentator'—
	D. Glyn Williams

Tragically all the theatrical scenery was destroyed in the Pavilion Cinema fire during the War and the Society was disbanded. The present Cowbridge Amateur Dramatic Society was started in 1946 by a small group of enthusiasts. With a continual influx of new members, it has grown from strength to strength; two full-length plays are now performed each year in the Town Hall in addition to regular one-act plays in the Society's own club rooms at Market Place.

69. Cowbridge Women's Institute Committee 1948
Standing left to right: Mrs. D. C. Watts, Mrs. Philp, Mrs. Morris, Mrs. Rhoderick,
Mrs. P. Thomas, Mrs. Jeremiah
Seated: Mrs. Powell, Mrs. M. Jones, Mrs. Owen Phillips, Mrs. R. N. Bird and
Mrs. J. M. Roberts

At the suggestion of Mrs. Olwen Muir and Denis Ward that Art classes be started in the town, a flourishing Arts Society came into being in 1961. The founder chairman was Major David Muir and Christopher Cory of Penllyn Castle was invited to become President, an office he still holds. The activities of the society have been a highlight in the cultural calendar ever since, especially their annual Art Exhibition, the painting excursions into the countryside in the summer months and the classes, demonstrations and lectures at other times of the year. The society owes a great debt of gratitude to the initial guidance of such artists as Charles White, Morgan Hall and Clodagh Cravos, so much so that membership of beginners and experts alike approximates a hundred.

In a town where the Welsh language has been so neglected until recently, the Cowbridge Welsh Society has striven valiantly to provide a varied programme of lectures and entertainments for all those interested in the wellbeing of the language as well as the culture, history and literary heritage of Wales. Founded in 1946 with Mrs. N. G. Brown, Mrs. J. M. Roberts and D. J. Morris among its leading spirits, the immediate aim of the society was to provide a forum for the comparatively few Welsh speakers left in the locality. Bi-lingual in its approach from the start, it is remarkable how year after year the most prominent men and women in the nation have accepted invitations to speak at the annual St. David's Day Dinner. Merched y Wawr is a more recently formed society which exists to arrange educational, cultural and recreational meetings locally through the medium of Welsh for ladies of the district. It was formed in the house of Mrs. Llio Loveluck in the autumn of 1971 and later meetings were held in Llanblethian Church Hall. To its credit it has introduced an annual Gymanfa Ganu to the area and a Welsh flavour to 'Cowbridge Week' with its Noson Lawen compèred by Hywel Gwynfryn in 1973.

In the realm of Contact and Community Welfare the needs of the inhabitants of Cowbridge are well catered for. The Women's Institute is perhaps the premier organisation of this kind since it was founded as long ago as 1934. Brought into being by Miss Olive Bruce, the Volunteer County Organiser, the first meeting was held in the Council chamber; but later the organisation was fortunate to be granted the South Wales Electricity Board's demonstration room. The W.I. continued to meet here until 1970 when they obtained the Lesser Hall. The original officers of the W.I. were Mrs. Gilbert Williams, chairman; Mrs. David Watts, secretary, and Mrs. Morgan Jones, treasurer. Two Cowbridge ladies have achieved high office in the W.I. in recent years: Mrs. Muriel Phillips becoming a County Chairman and Mrs. D. Watts a County Treasurer. Cowbridge and District Community Concern, since its formation in 1956, has done much to promote charitable causes for the benefit of the community. To date it has been responsible for organising a Mother and Toddler Club, and an Indoor Bowls Club, was instrumental in obtaining the Youth Centre in the old Boarding House of the Grammar School and regularly assists Social Services with local problems. Community Concern together with other local organisations were involved in a major emergency operation in February 1978 when a freak snow blizzard cut Cowbridge off from the world. About three hundred people were stranded, including a bus load of young athletes from Cardiff. With a local hotel cooking up to three hundred breakfasts, and the townsfolk providing everything from blankets to baked beans it was evident that the community spirit was very much alive.

The Cowbridge Division of the British Red Cross Society, Detachment 12 Glamorgan County Branch, has a record of service to the community which stretches back to 1914. The earliest meetings were held in the Institute, where Dr. Torney gave lectures on First Aid. In February 1926, Detachment 12 was re-registered and Mrs. D. C. Edmondes of St. Hilary appointed as Commandant, a post she held until the outbreak of the Second World War. She subsequently received an O.B.E. for her services to the Red Cross. Training in First Aid, Nursing and Hygiene continued with a special emphasis on anti-gas warfare. Mrs. R. H. Williams, who succeeded Mrs. Edmondes as Commandant, was awarded the Order of Merit for Distinguished War Service, which was presented to her by Queen Elizabeth

70. Coronation Year 1953—'Roasting the Ox'

at Buckingham Palace in 1946. Mrs. Williams had organised a First Aid post at the Town Hall which was manned on a rota system for twenty four hours daily. Prisoners-of-war from Cowbridge received Red Cross parcels regularly, whilst refreshments were provided for the Welch Regiment stationed at the Cinema and for other members of the Forces stationed at Penlline Court, Llandough Castle, St. Athan and Llandow from a marquee erected behind the Town Hall. Training continued at the Institute until a new headquarters was opened in Broadshoard in October 1966, on a memorable night when torrential rain caused such flooding in the town that those present had to wade through the waters. The following Friday, members were called out to assist at the Aberfan disaster for which the Cowbridge Division was later awarded a Certificate of Commendation for meritorious service. Other local duties over the years have included nursing at the Jane Hodge Home, treating those engaged in the Oxfam walks from Cardiff to Porthcawl, and rendering First Aid during Cowbridge Week and other important social functions.

The British Legion was formed in Cowbridge on 1st March, 1927 at The Duke of Wellington Hotel. A. W. Gwyn proposed the formation of the Society, together with Dr. David Evans, Capt. T. J. Yorwerth, G. Millman, David Harris, E. D. Lewis and many other prominent people of that time. In the early thirties Len Rowsell took over the Secretaryship and maintained

71. The British Legion Parade on a civic occasion

the branch as a successful feature in the life of the Town. After World War II the old railway station became its headquarters. The present H.Q. is at the rear of Cowbridge Town Hall where monthly meetings are held for both branch and club. One of its greatest stalwarts since World War II was R. C. Wiseman, a greatly respected character, who was treasurer/secretary until well after his 80th birthday. The finances of the branch and club are now looked after by Mrs. Fiona Farrelly. June 1979 saw the 50th Anniversary of the standard. A service was held at Holy Cross Church to lay up this standard and a new one dedicated. The first standard bearer was Sgt. W. Brown followed by W. Batchelor. Its present standard bearer is Gerald Rosser with A. E. Davies as his deputy.

Thus our account of twentieth century Cowbridge draws to a close. In every community the past, present and future are all stages in an unbroken history, and we have tried to show in this section that many aspects of present day life in the town are a direct product of its former days of prestige and affluence. The future lies hidden from us but we can safely predict that certain values will remain. With its ever expanding market, the facility to provide professional and educational services of a high standard to a wide rural area, and a busy well stocked thoroughfare that caters for every modern taste and fashion, Cowbridge will in the years ahead continue to be the commercial and cultural centre of the Vale of Glamorgan and in so doing maintain many important links with its proud past.

72. A general view of the High Street, Cowbridge

(Photo: Haydn Baynham)

73. A view from Town Hall Square, looking into the High Street. One of the town pumps remaining is seen on the right at the side of Taynton House

(Photo: Haydn Baynham)

'. . . But of Llanblethian, the village where I afterwards lived, I persuade myself that every line and hue is more deeply and accurately fixed than those of any spot I have since beheld, even though borne in upon the heart by the association of the strongest feelings.

My home was built upon the slope of a hill, with a little orchard stretching down before it, and a garden rising behind. At a considerable distance beyond and beneath the orchard, a rivulet flowed through meadows and turned a mill; while, above the garden, the summit of the hill was crowned by a few grey rocks, from which a yew-tree grew, solitary and bare. Extending at each side of the orchard, toward the brook, two scattered patches of cottages lay nestled among their gardens; and beyond this streamlet and the little mill and bridge, another slight eminence arose, divided into green fields, tufted and bordered with copsewood, and crested by a ruined castle, contemporary, as was said, with the Conquest. I know not whether these things in truth made up a prospect of much beauty. But I well know that no landscape I have since beheld, no picture of Claude or Salvator, gave me half the impression of living, heartfelt, perfect beauty which fills my mind when I think of that green valley, that sparkling rivulet, that broken fortress of dark antiquity, and that hill with its aged yew and breezy summit, from which I have so often looked over the broad stretch of verdure beneath it, and the country-town, and church-tower, silent and white beyond.'

Extract from *The Life of John Sterling* (Thomas Carlyle, 1851)

Bibliography

Archer, M. S., *The Welsh post towns before 1840* (London, 1970).

Beresford, M. W., *New towns of the Middle Ages* (London, 1967).

Boon, G. C., *Welsh tokens of the seventeenth century* (Cardiff, 1973).

Carlyle, Thomas, *The life of John Sterling* (London, 1851).

Carter, Harold, *The towns of Wales* (Cardiff, 1965).

Clark, G. T., *Cartae et alia munimenta quae ad dominium de Glamorgancia pertinent* (Talygarn, 1910). 6 vols.

Clark, G. T., 'The tower of Llanquian', *Arch. Camb.*, fourth series vol. III (1872), pp. 144-6.

Corbett, J. A., 'The manor of Llanblethian', *Arch. Camb.*, fifth series vol. VI (1889), pp. 68-78.

Corbett, J. S., *Glamorgan: papers & notes on the lordship & its members (Cardiff, 1925).*

Cowbridge Girls' High School, Cowbridge: aspects of an ancient borough (Cowbridge, 1964).

Davies, Iolo, *A certaine school: a history of the grammar school at Cowbridge* (Cowbridge, 1967).

Donovan, Edward, *Descriptive excursions through South Wales* (London, 1805). 2 vols.

Fowler, C. B., 'Discoveries at Llanblethian Church, Glamorganshire', *Arch. Camb.*, fifth series vol. XV (1898), pp. 121-131.

Fox, Sir Cyril, *Life and death in the Bronze Age* (London, 1959).

Fox, Sir Cyril, 'Caer Dynnaf, Llanblethian', *Arch. Camb.*, vol. XVI (1936), pp. 20-24.

Garsed, John, *Records of the Glamorganshire Agricultural Society, 1772-1869* (Cardiff, 1890).

Glamorgan county history. Vol. III, *The Middle Ages*, edited by T. B. Pugh (Cardiff, 1971).

Glamorgan county history. Vol. IV, *Early Modern Glamorgan*, edited by Glanmor Williams (Cardiff, 1974).

Glamorgan Record Office, *The Carne family of Nash Manor* (Cardiff, 1952).

Glamorgan Record Office, *Two ancient boroughs: Cowbridge and Llantrisant* (Cardiff, n.d.).

Gray, Thomas, *The buried city of Kenfig* (London, 1909).

Greaves, Ralph, *A short history of the Glamorgan Hunt* (London, *circa* 1950).

Green, C. A. H., *Notes on churches in the diocese of Llandaff* (Aberdare, 1906-7).

Griffiths, R. A., 'The Norman Conquest and the twelve knights of Glamorgan', *Glamorgan Historian*, vol. 3 (1966), pp. 153-169.

Grimes, W. F., *The prehistory of Wales* (Cardiff, 1951).

Gunter, Maud, 'An ancient borough' in Stewart Williams (ed.), *Vale of history* (Cowbridge, 1960), pp. 38-44.

Gunter, Maud, 'The manor of Llanblethian', in Stewart Williams (ed.), *The garden of Wales* (Cowbridge, 1961), pp. 84-93.

Harries, B. D., *Enwau lleoedd hen arglwyddiaeth Tal-y-fan.* Unpublished M.A. thesis, University of Wales (Cardiff), 1956.

Hopkin-James, L. J., *Old Cowbridge* (Cardiff, 1922).

Hopkins, T. J., 'C.C.'s tour in Glamorgan, 1789', *Glamorgan Historian*, vol. 2 (1965), pp. 121-133.

Hopkins, T. J., 'David Jones of Wallington', *Glamorgan Historian*, vol. 4 (1967), pp. 51-58.

Hopkins, T. J., 'Francis Grose's tour in Glamorgan, 1775', *Glamorgan Historian*, vol. 1 (1964), pp. 158-170.

Hopkins, T. J., 'Two hundred years of agriculture in Glamorgan', *Glamorgan Historian*, vol. 8 (1972), pp. 70-74.

James, B. Ll., 'The Cowbridge printers', *Glamorgan Historian*, vol. 4 (1967), pp. 231-244.

James, B. Ll., 'A Cowbridge society of 1831', *Glamorgan Historian*, vol. 10 (1974), pp. 27-34.

Jones, David, 'Glimpses of the social condition of Glamorgan in the Tudor period', *Arch. Camb.*, fifth series of vol. VII (1890), pp. 81-104.

Jones, Ieuan Gwynedd & Williams, David (eds.), *The religious census of 1851* (Cardiff, 1976).

Kelly's *Directory of South Wales* (various editions).

Lewis, E. O. T., 'The Cowbridge diocesan library, 1711-1848', *Journal of the Historical Society of the Church in Wales*, vol. IV (1954), pp. 36-44; vol. VII (1957), pp. 80-91.

Lewis, E. O. T., 'John Williams: some glimpses of life in Cowbridge, 1700-1850', *Province*, vol. IV (1953), pp. 230-3.

Lewis, E. O. T., 'Two Vale churches: Llanblethian and Cowbridge', in Stewart Williams (ed.), *History on my doorstep* (Cowbridge, 1959), pp. 65-70.

Lewis, T. H., 'Documents illustrating the county gaol and house of correction in Wales', *Transactions of the Hon. Society of Cymmrodorion*, sessions 1946-47, pp. 232-249.

Morgan, Prys, *Iolo Morganwg* (Cardiff, 1975).

Municipal Corporations Commission, *Report of the Commissioners* (London, 1880).

Owen, T. M., *Welsh folk customs* (Cardiff, 1959; 1968; 1974).

Pigot & Co.'s *National commercial directory* (London, 1835).

Price, E. W., *Horn and hound in Wales* (Cardiff, 1891).

Randall, H. J., *Bridgend: the story of a market town* (Newport, 1955).

Rees, William, *South Wales and the March, 1284-1415* (Oxford, 1924).

Richards, John, *The Cowbridge story* (Bridgend, 1956).

Royal Commission on Ancient and Historical Monuments in Wales, *An inventory of the ancient monuments in Glamorgan*, vol I (Cardiff, 1976).

Savory, H. N., 'The excavation of the Marlborough Grange barrow', *Arch. Camb.*, vol. CXVIII (1969), pp. 49-72.

Scammell & Co.'s *City of Bristol and South Wales directory* (Bristol, 1852).

Slater's *Royal, national and commercial directory . . . of South Wales* (Manchester, 1858-9).

Soulsby, I. N. & Jones, D., *The archaeological implications of redevelopment in the historic towns of the Vale of Glamorgan district* (Cardiff, 1976).

Smith, Peter, *Houses of the Welsh countryside* (London, 1975).

Spencer, M. R., *Annals of South Glamorgan* (Carmarthen, 1913; Barry, 1970).

Spurgeon, C. J. & Thomas, H. J., 'Llanquian', *Archaeology in Wales*, no. 14 (1974), pp. 34-5.

Thomas, H. J. & Brooksby, H., 'Archaeological notes: Cowbridge', *Morgannwg,* vol. XVII (1973), pp. 59-60.

Thomas, H. J. & Dowdell, G., 'Cowbridge, Old Brewery', *Morgannwg,* vol. XXI (1977), pp. 98-9.

Thomas, J. D. H., 'Judge David Jenkins, 1582-1663', *Morgannwg,* vol. VIII (1964), pp. 14-34.

Thomas, Lawrence, *The Reformation in the old diocese of Llandaff* (Cardiff, 1930).

Trott, B., 'A missing stage in Iter XII?', *Arch. Camb.,* vol. CXXIV (1975), pp. 113-4.

Turner, H. L., *Town defences in England and Wales* (London, 1970).

Wade-Evans, A. W., *Welsh Christian origins* (Oxford, 1934).

Webster & Co.'s *Postal and commercial directory of the city of Bristol, and* (London, 1865).

William, A. H., *John Wesley in Wales, 1739-1790* (Cardiff, 1971).

Williams, Edward (Iolo Fardd Glas), *Perllan Gwent* (Cowbridge, 1839).

Williams, G. J., *Iolo Morganwg,* cyf. I. (Caerdydd, 1956).

Williams, G. J., 'Daniel Walters: a poet of the Vale', *Glamorgan Historian,* vol. 3 (1966), pp. 238-243.

Williams, Glanmor, *The Welsh Church from Conquest to Reformation* (Cardiff, 1962).

Williams, Herbert, *Stage coaches in Wales* (Barry, 1977).

Williams, Stewart (ed.), *South Glamorgan: a county history* (Barry, 1975).

Williams, Stewart, 'David Jones of Wallington: historian of the Vale', in *The garden of Wales* (Cowbridge, 1961), pp. 70-76.

Williams, William, 'William Howels, o Longacre, Llundain', *Y Traethodydd,* vol. V (1849), pp. 156-165.

Worrall's *Directory of South Wales* (Oldham, 1875).

Wrenche, W. G., *Wrenche (Pransiaid) and Radcliffe: notes on two families of Glamorgan* (Cardiff, 1956).

Mr Francis has also consulted the following material:

Evans, John, 'Silurian's notes and paragraphs', *Glamorgan Gazette.*

Loudon, J. B., 'Ewart Owen Thomas Lewis: an obituary', abstracted from *Morgannwg,* vol. VII (1963).

Yorath, Chris, article on Cowbridge published in *Western Mail.*

Williams, A. J., 'Cowbridge Conservation Area . . . an appraisal', *Province* (Church in Wales publication)

Bovian and Cowbridge Girls' High School Magazine.

Llanblethian and Cowbridge Church Magazines.

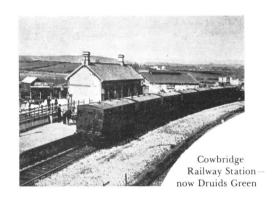

Cowbridge
Railway Station —
now Druids Green